The Texas Calaboose
and Other Forgotten Jails

Number Twenty-Nine

Tarleton State University Southwestern
Studies in the Humanities
T. Lindsay Baker, General Editor

THE TEXAS CALABOOSE

AND OTHER FORGOTTEN JAILS

William E. Moore

Foreword by T. Lindsay Baker

TEXAS A&M UNIVERSITY PRESS
COLLEGE STATION

First edition

This paper meets the requirements of ANSI/NISO Z39.48-1992 (Permanence of Paper).
Binding materials have been chosen for durability.
Manufactured in the United States of America

Library of Congress Cataloging-in-Publication Data

Names: Moore, William E., 1943- author.
Title: The Texas calaboose and other forgotten jails / William E. Moore; foreword by T. Lindsay Baker.
Description: First edition. | College Station: Texas A&M University Press, [2019] | Series: Tarleton State University southwestern studies in the humanities; number twenty nine | Includes bibliographical references and index. |
Identifiers: LCCN 2018035635 (print) | LCCN 2018036834 (ebook) | ISBN 9781623497163 (ebook) | ISBN 9781623497156 | ISBN 9781623497156 (cloth: alk. paper)
Subjects: LCSH: Jails—Texas—Guidebooks. | Prisons—Texas—Design and Construction—History—19th century—Guidebooks. | Historic buildings—Texas—Guidebooks. | Imprisonment—Texas—History—19th century—Guidebooks. | Texas—Social life and customs—19th century—Guidebooks.
Classification: LCC HV9475.T4 (ebook) | LCC HV9475.T4 M66 2019 (print) | DDC 365/.9764—dc23
LC record available at https://lccn.loc.gov/2018035635

A list of titles in this series is available at the end of the book.

Title page and chapter illustrations © istockphoto.com

This book is dedicated to those constables and night watchmen who were charged with maintaining law and order during turbulent times when there was little protocol except to arrest and lock up prisoners in tiny calabooses until they could be released or transported to the county jail. They often carried out their duties for little or no pay and had to be available in all kinds of weather twenty-four hours a day.

Song of the Marshal

Come, Oh! Come with me,
To the Old Calaboose.
Come, Oh! come with me,
You'll no longer be loose.

All around and above,
Both strong and substantial,
'Twas built for your sort
By the Committee Financial.

Then walk off quite nimble—
We'll go to the place,
I think from your looks
You are a hard case.

And as we glide along,
My song shall be:
"Old Loafter, Old Loafter,
Here's a home for thee!"

—San Francisco, 1854. Old Bach.

**Alamo Star* (San Antonio, TX),
July 15, 1854.

Contents

Foreword

William E. Moore is an archaeologist and I am a historian. We share an inclination, no, a passion for prowling around places that other people take for granted. As an archaeologist, he looks for the physical evidence that past humans left behind, and as a historian, I try to learn the stories that tell us about these Texans from times gone by. Often, our evidence takes the form of the buildings and assorted objects they left for us to discover.

Moore discovered the existence of calabooses by accident. He was prowling around in Gause, a little town in eastern Milam County. Behind Coats Grocery Store, he and a colleague found a two-room concrete structure that had bars on its windows. These were bars to keep someone in, not to keep burglars out. On making inquiries, he learned that this was the Gause calaboose. He knew the term from Western movies, but little did he expect to fine one in the old cotton country of the Brazos valley.

Like William E. Moore, I stumbled onto my "first calaboose." In the 1970s, I time and again drove back and forth between my home town of Cleburne and college in West Texas. To see "new country," I sought out multiple routes that would take me places I had not before visited. One of these cross country journeys took me through Stephenville westward to Desdemona, where an oil boom had taken place in 1918–22. The little town swelled in population, and some of the new arrivals became disorderly. Locals consequently erected a brick calaboose as a place for rowdies to sleep off their drunken states or to hold them until officers could convey them to the county jail in Eastland. The boom passed quickly, but the little one-room holding pen remained to attract my attention, its iron door standing open. Immediately, I realized it was some type of jail, but it took me a while to figure out how this structure and other calabooses fit into the history of their communities.

In time I came to realize the social significance of calabooses in small-town Texas. Combined with the efforts of law enforcement officers, these structures enabled people living in small communities to enforce what they considered to be the norms of civilized behavior. Because they were designed and built to keep ingenious prisoners inside, they often were among the most substantially built structures in towns. In some instances, entire towns have been abandoned and buildings razed, leaving only the durable calaboose alongside foundations from other now-lost buildings. These places designed for holding either criminals or the unruly sometimes mark ghost town sites as the last intact structures from communities. William E. Moore has done all of us a genuine service in locating, researching, and documenting these sometimes threatened structures across the state.

After I recognized the significance of calabooses, like Moore I started going out of my way to document them in photographs. Eventually I wrote two books on abandoned towns in Texas, finding multiple calabooses scattered over the Texas landscape. I was so taken by the one-room, flat-roofed concrete cell at the site of the 1920s Best boomtown in Reagan County that the designer of my second ghost town book used a prisoner's eye view outward through its barred window as cover artwork. Moore seems to have found this same little jailhouse to be as intriguing as it was for me.

Thanks go to William E. Moore for his efforts to enrich our understanding of law enforcement in small-town Texas. His lone star calabooses give us important insights into how social control functioned in rural and village settings. This volume takes its place in the Tarleton State University Southwestern Humanities series by encouraging us to go into the field ourselves to view these miniature jailhouses and to assess and better understand how maintenance of social order played out during the Texas past.

—T. Lindsay Baker
Tarleton State University

Preface

I have been to all 254 Texas counties and seen many interesting sights. However, I was not prepared for a new and exciting adventure when Rhonda Holley and I were in Gause, Texas, in April 2013 to visit an old house that was destined to be demolished. I had seen this house many times on my way to Fort Hood while working on a large archaeological project for Texas A&M University. I was always struck by the fact that only the porch had been recently painted, and it was obvious that the rest of the house had not seen a new coat of paint in a very long time. The lady who lived there at the time of our visit had passed away, and the entire house was in very poor condition. We had visited this house once before, and Rhonda was curious to see if it was still standing. It was, and there was some discussion about it being haunted and what it would be like to spend a night there. After leaving the house, we decided to visit the Gause City Cemetery, which was established in 1887, and the Peaceful Rest Cemetery, an African American resting place that has been designated as a Historic Texas Cemetery.

Behind Coats Grocery Store on the highway, we noticed a tiny concrete structure that aroused our curiosity. We were very surprised to see metal bars in the windows, and when we asked about it we were told that it was the town calaboose, built in 1921. It had a dirt floor and no electricity or plumbing. We thought a lot about what it must have been like to be locked up in such a place in times of extreme heat and cold.

I had heard the term *calaboose* before in western movies, but I had never given any thought to what it meant. But here in Gause, Texas, was the real thing. A small, almost whimsical structure made of concrete that seemed totally out of place in the twenty-first century. It's once important role in an emerging community had been downgraded as a place to burn trash and a palette for vandals' graffiti.

Webster's unabridged dictionary defines a calaboose as simply a prison or jail. But a calaboose is more than that. It represents a time capsule in small vernacular jail architecture that was present in many forms throughout the country until the middle of the twentieth century, and it was a common feature on the Texas landscape for many years. I hope my readers will appreciate these unique structures as I do.

Acknowledgments

I am grateful to those who took time from their busy schedules to help me with this project by providing historical information, photographs, and taking measurements. Rhonda K. Holley was with me when the calaboose in Gause was discovered, and she has accompanied me on numerous trips since. Others who traveled with me include Max Brown, Victoria Hoffman, Floyd Kent, Michael Kraft, Darryl Pearson, Nora Rogers, Donna Smith, Roger Moore, Rolland C. Reynolds Jr., Shari Watson, and Joe Weaver. Architectural historians Adam Alsobrook, Gregory Smith, and James Malanaphy at the Texas Historical Commission in Austin and Anna Mod in Houston helped describe some of the buildings using the proper architectural terminology. One of the more useful references was the fire insurance maps created by the Sanborn Map Company of New York. The staff at the Perry-Castañeda Library on the campus of the University of Texas at Austin and the Dolph Briscoe Center for American History, also on the campus of the University of Texas, are acknowledged for their assistance. The GIS/Data Center at Rice University has a subscription to the Digital Sanborn Maps (Texas 1867–1970) collection through ProQuest. Staff members at the Rice GIS/Data center who made it possible for me to obtain copies of maps include Kim Ricker, head of the GIS/Data center; Jean Aroom, GIS support specialist; and Hannah Krusleski, a student worker who made the copies for me. Lili G. Lyddon is a professional draftsperson who has worked for me for over thirty years, and she is responsible for the excellent drawings of floorplans and the map depicting the distribution of known calabooses in Texas. The manuscript was read and/or edited by Sallie

Cotter Andrews, Ashley Blankenship, Rhonda Holley, Roger Moore, Pam Price, and Joe Ann Standlee. Stephen Bales is a humanities and social sciences librarian in the Texas A&M University Libraries System who made it possible for me to obtain reference materials from the Evans Library on the campus of Texas A&M University and other universities. Bob Skiles is a professional archaeologist in Austin, Texas, who researched newspaper articles dealing with calabooses in Texas and shared his findings with me. Jonathan Jarvis is the associate director at the Texas Archeological Research Laboratory that is part of the University of Texas at Austin system. I am grateful to him for his role in recording these calabooses and jails as historic structures. Michele Amason was instrumental in putting together a final manuscript. She assisted with organizing and formatting using the latest computer software. Finally, it would not have been possible to collect much of the information presented in this book without the help of city workers, local informants, historical societies, chambers of commerce, and the owners of these calabooses and jails. I owe them a huge debt of gratitude but, unfortunately, they are too numerous to mention here.

The Texas Calaboose
and Other Forgotten Jails

Introduction

Texas occupies an area of 266,807 square miles and is the second largest of the fifty states. Its 254 counties represent the most in the country. In 1836, Texas gained its independence from Mexico and became a sovereign country. At that time, the state was divided into twenty-three municipal districts, most of which had already been established by the previous governments of Spain and Mexico. These districts later became the original counties, and some covered vast areas. Bexar County, for example, extended west to El Paso, south to the Rio Grande, and north to the Panhandle. The enormity of the land called Texas can be visualized in part by the fact that over one hundred counties came into existence solely from this one county. These vast areas were difficult to administer in terms of an effective judicial system and law enforcement. Texas lawmakers recognized this problem, and in 1845 the Congress of the Republic created the county court system, which authorized the appointment of a chief justice, a place to hold court, and provided funds for the construction of jails. The Congress also empowered itself to create new counties from the twenty-three existing districts. Except for a few of the larger counties west of the Pecos River, the size of a county was often determined by the distance a person could travel to and from the county seat in one day. In the Panhandle, most counties were laid out in squares of thirty miles, and the county seat was located within three miles of the center of the county. Although there was to be a jail and courthouse at each county seat, it was not always easy to transport prisoners that distance immediately after an arrest was made. This was especially true in bad weather. Many small towns were unincorporated and had no formal law enforcement. They also lacked the money to build and maintain elaborate jails. Communities that could finance the construction of a calaboose often used materials that were readily available or could be obtained at the lowest price. Many calabooses had dirt floors and few had sanitary facilities or electricity. Some towns could afford elaborate metal cells fabricated by companies that specialized in jail and prison hardware. These were placed inside buildings and were touted by some companies as "escape proof." One of the problems inherent in this project is the creation of a formal definition of a calaboose. As mentioned earlier, *calaboose* is simply a word that is synonymous with *jail*, and applying the label of calaboose to a structure was a decision I had to make using various criteria, with size being paramount. Those structures that I place in the category of the classic calaboose are one story, typically have one or two cells, and rarely exceed 300 square feet in size. The jails in Bartlett and Granger are exceptions. They have three cells and are referred to here as calabooses even though their footprints are greater than 300 square feet.

Calabooses were constructed, owned, and managed by city or county officials. There is no time frame during which these buildings were the sole place for incarcerating lawbreakers, but it has been documented that they became less common as roads and other methods of transportation improved during the middle of the twentieth century. Exact dates of construction are rare and usually obtained through courthouse records, minutes taken during city council meetings, and newspaper articles. Many of the dates provided in this book are based on the memories of residents and are very general, such as "circa 1910" or "sometime during the 1920s." Even though the primary focus of this book is the Texas calaboose, it would be remiss of me to overlook some of the tiny jails that do not readily conform to an existing set of rules. Those that fall in the so-called gray area are open to interpretation as being a calaboose or jail. The only parameter for inclusion in this book is a building that does not exceed 1,000 square feet in size. Some of these edifices are very interesting in terms of their architecture and/or history. If they were not included in this book, it is possible that they would not find a home in a future monograph. Although the exact number of calabooses and other tiny Texas jails that once existed will never be known, it is plausible that at least one was present in every county of the state at one time.

Transportation of prisoners was performed by a variety of conveyances such as horseback, wagon, train, and motorized vehicles as they became available. They were moved from local jails to county jails and from county jails to state and federal prisons. Vagrants, able-bodied men with no visible means of support, often referred to as tramps and hobos, and those who were unable to pay their debts were sent to places known euphemistically as the "Poor Farm" or "Convict Farm." Once incarcerated, some prisoners were forced to work on road gangs, construction projects, and in fields. An article in the *Cameron Herald* dated December 24, 1914, announces the arrival of a portable convict jail ordered by the commissioners' court "for the purpose of housing the county convicts, since they have put them on the public roads."[1] The new acquisition had berths for eighteen prisoners, but it could accommodate as many as twenty-five inmates if necessary. It had a "heating device" that was supposed to make it comfortable during cold weather. The first group of convicts to take advantage of the new jail "were placed on roads in Commissioners Precinct No. 2, where they will be kept for the first quarter." During the course of this study, examples of two portable jails were discovered. One made of wood is on display at the Heritage Village in Seguin, and a metal cage can be viewed at the Grayson County Frontier Village in Denison.

Mobile jail in Seguin (photo courtesy of Darryl Pearson).

Mobile jail in Denison (photo courtesy of Brayden Southerlend).

Guard house at Fort Phantom Hill (photo courtesy of Rolland C. Reynolds Jr.).

Early Texas forts often had nanoscale structures for the sole purpose of incarcerating soldiers guilty of violating military protocol. These buildings were typically referred to as guardhouses and stockades. Many are virtually indistinguishable from their calaboose counterparts in towns and cities. The guardhouse at Fort Phantom Hill in Taylor County is a superb example. Texas embraces some of the more architecturally significant county jails in the country; these were designed in the latter part of the nineteenth century by notable architects of the day, such as Frederick Ernst Ruffini. These buildings were intended to be a testimony to the skill of the architects, and the use of expensive materials such as granite and marble was commonplace. These magnificent jails are not included in this book as they conform to a totally different genre of jail construction. I recommend *Texas Public Buildings of the Nineteenth Century* by Todd Webb and Willard B. Robinson,[2] and *Wanted: Historic County Jails of Texas* by Edward Blackburn Jr.,[3] for those interested in this era of county jail construction that will probably never be repeated and certainly not surpassed.

The Lone Star State has had its share of infamous outlaws who spent time in the local calaboose. Other unfortunate occupants included regular folks who drank too much on a Saturday night or participated in barroom brawls. Incarceration in a calaboose or jail through the early years of the twentieth century was not a pleasant experience, even in the best of conditions available at the time. Those that were treated well were fortunate to have been under the control of more humane law enforcement. Crimes were considered events that had to be dealt with harshly, and a night in a sweltering or freezing calaboose with no plumbing or other amenities was often considered normal. After all, those locked up were criminals. Conditions improved when city and county jails became the main source of detaining prisoners, but those that were unfortunate to be there did not even view these places kindly.

The discovery of oil in Texas created jobs. The work was hard, and the workers were often referred to as "roughnecks." During their off hours, many oil field workers were well acquainted with the drinking establishments that sprang up near the oil fields. Overindulgence was a common problem that landed them in the town calaboose or one built and owned by the company they worked for. One rare survivor of a company-owned calaboose can be viewed at the Pioneer Village Museum in Corsicana (see chapter 5). While it is best described as a calaboose and was probably known by that name at the time, it was associated with the oil field town of Powell that was built and managed by private interests. Other towns were built and governed by sawmill companies that also erected calabooses for their private use.[4]

A common misconception, and one that I embraced at the beginning of this endeavor, was that the calaboose was strictly a small-town fixture. Why would a county seat with an imposing two-story county jail want or have a need for a calaboose? This question has several answers. Newly created county seats did not always have the funds for the more expensive county jails that today attract the attention of historians, photographers, and tourists. A modest alternative was often the only sensible and affordable solu-

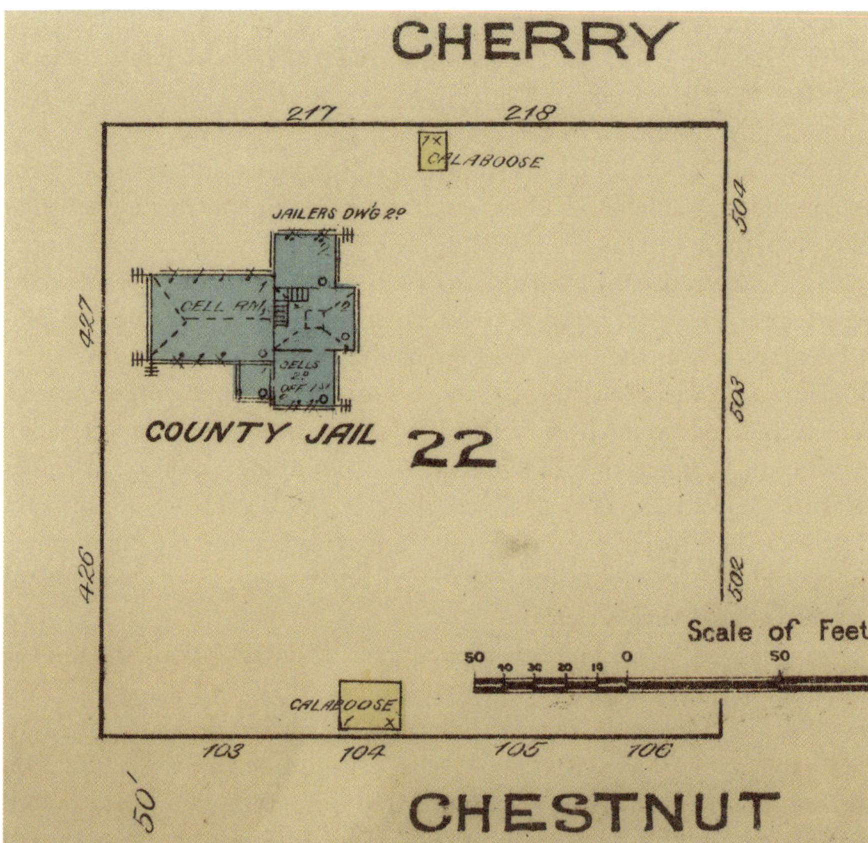

***Kaufman, Texas, April 1885.* Sanborn Map and Publishing Company, 117 and 119 Broadway, New York City, sheet 1 (map courtesy of Briscoe Center for American History).**

tion until a more "respectable" building could be financed and built, and some of these buildings were used contemporaneously with county jails until no longer needed. In 1884, for example, Kaufman County financed the building of a two-story stone jail on city block 22.[5] The first Sanborn map for the town of Kaufman was published in 1885, and it depicts two small one-story wooden calabooses on the same city block as the county jail.[6] The length of time they served the town was not determined but it is known that they were no longer present when the Sanborn map for 1889 was published.

The calaboose occupied a special niche in the early history of Texas, and it is the purpose of this book to discuss them in terms of their importance to local communities with emphasis on span of use, distribution across the state, and methods of construction. As stated earlier, there are tiny jails in

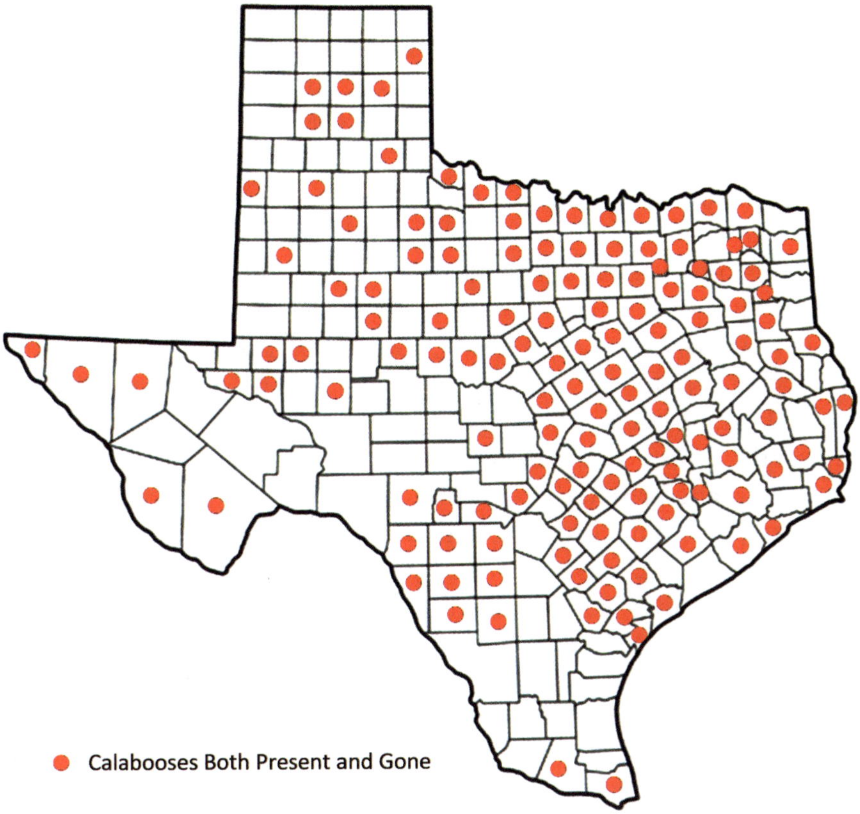

Distribution of known calabooses in Texas (drafted by Lili G. Lyddon).

Texas whose size places them somewhere between my definition of a calaboose and the larger city and county jails. The title of this book, *The Texas Calaboose and Other Forgotten Jails*, was chosen to be inclusive of some of the little known one-story jails of less than 1,000 square feet. The purpose of this study is not only to photograph and describe the standing calabooses but also to document those that have long since been taken from us.

My research has identified more than one hundred surviving structures in seventy-three counties that I have classified as calabooses. Eighty-seven were selected for inclusion in this book. Additional buildings are believed to be calabooses based on the testimony of local informants and the physical appearance of the buildings. However, until they can be confirmed as calabooses, they are classified as "suspicious structures." Many calabooses are the property of the city or county and remain locked for security and protection from vandals. Others are privately owned, and permission is needed to visit them. A secondary result of my search for extant calabooses is the documentation of a greater number of similar buildings, most of which no longer exist. The majority of these were found depicted on Sanborn maps, while the remainder were brought to my attention through other sources such as newspaper articles, personal interviews, and photographs on various internet sites. Those on the Sanborn maps that appear to conform to the size of a calaboose, per my definition, are usually referred to by the mappers as calabooses, jails, and lockups. The alikeness of these words is epitomized by their arbitrary usage. Two examples are present on the Sanborn maps for Forney, Texas, dated 1901 and 1919. In 1901,[7] a wood lockup is depicted, and the same building is labeled calaboose in 1919.[8] The term *calaboose* appears to be the word of choice as it far outnumbers those with other names. The distribution of all known Texas calabooses, past and present, is depicted on a county map of the state. Those calabooses and jails not discussed and illustrated in this book can be found on my personal website—www.tinytexasjails.com. The Texas calaboose represents more than just a place to lock up prisoners. It is an excellent example of vernacular architecture that has not been described previously.

Structures described here as too large to conform to the definition of calaboose but smaller than the bigger county jails are included under the label "Tiny Texas Jails." The criteria for these buildings are one story and between 300 and 1,000 square feet. Fourteen examples are included in this book.

Metal cages and cells were generally manufactured by companies that specialized in jail and prison equipment and were shipped to the buyers by train. No evidence of these cages having been used outdoors on a regular basis has been uncovered. They were housed in calabooses and jails of all sizes. Only in a few cases was it possible to determine that a particular cage was associated with a calaboose. Nineteen examples are included to demonstrate the variety that was available.

I

History of the Calaboose

The need for places of incarceration has been an issue for millenia. During the time when Texas was a Republic and in the early difficult years of statehood, housing for criminals was often regarded as a necessary evil, and many such structures were primitive at best. It was not uncommon for prisoners to be held in private homes or shackeled to stationary objects such as hitching posts, trees, and even windmills. Ed Blackburn Jr. writes that the first jail in Marathon was the "leg of a windmill to which prisoners were chained."[1] A similar story involves the proposed construction of the first jail in Coryell County. When the county's Judge Mayberry talked about the building of the Gatesville calaboose in 1855, he said, "Coryell County can come into the modern age and stop chaining its prisoners to trees around the courthouse for varmints to chew on at night."[2]

Although *jail* is the word commonly associated with these buildings, they were often referred to colloquially as calabooses, hoosegows, pokeys, bastilles, and lockups. An article in the *Muskogee Times-Democrat* refers to the local calaboose as the "holdover."[3] Because these terms all had the same meaning, the decision about which descriptor to use probably varied from town to town as well as among different social classes. The origin of words such as *hoosegow* was probably rooted in the local venacular of the day. The word *calaboose*, however, came to the English language with a definite predecessor. In Spanish Texas and elsewhere along the border of Mexico and the United States, this word represents a logical derivation by the later Anglo populations of the Spanish word *calabozo*, whose meaning was literally jail or dungeon. These names used to describe early jails in Texas were usually associated with tiny structures, sometimes not more than 75 square feet in size.

Liberties with the English language were often taken by locals when referring to the community calaboose. One interesting example is the use of the word "Bastille" as a verb, as used in an article in the *Daily Banner*, published in Brenham on June 22, 1879. "Mary Brewer, the colored woman, 'bastiled' on Saturday, had fits in the calaboose and was let loose to save the expense of a coffin."[4] Although the majority of prisoners who spent time in the local calaboose were the Saturday night drunks and ruffians, others were locked up for theft, counterfeiting, owning or discharging illegal firearms, prostitution, and telling fortunes without a license. The temporary nature of the calaboose is mentioned in the following quote: "The calaboose was a place in which drunks and fistfighters were placed to sober up and cool off. These were interim holding areas, only; lawmen transported serious lawbreakers to courthouse town jails the next day."[5] Many towns were the seasonal homes of migrant workers hired to pick cotton and perform other similar tasks. Since they were often paid weekly, Saturday night was an especially busy time for the local calaboose. This happening is aptly described in the following excerpt from an article in the *Orange Daily Leader* dated September 9, 1921: "The smaller towns were filled with cotton pickers, mostly negroes, and it seemed that their only purpose in coming to town was that they might indulge to their heart's content in liquid fire. The 'chief' always put on 'extras' when Saturday rolled around. He knew that it would take the combined effort of a half dozen or more men to handle the situation. Until noon things were pretty quiet, but after that came the rush. By 5 o'clock everybody was in a weaving way and the 'braver ones' began to take it out on their weaker brothers. One by one they were carried to the calaboose. By night the old reliable 'boose' was filled to overflowing."[6]

The preponderance of those who spent time in the local calaboose was so widely skewed toward alcohol-related incidents that there were days or months when there was not a single soul in many of these buildings. A column in the *Hubbard City News* dated September 21, 1907, reported that the city of Longview offered its local calaboose for sale because it "has been used but a few times since prohibition went into effect."[7]

Those who spent time in a Texas calaboose were mostly men. However, large numbers of women were locked up for prostitution. The *Galveston Daily News* reported on the plight of such women in the Houston calaboose in 1876: "In the calaboose this evening, about fifteen or twenty soiled doves [prostitutes] were imprisoned, in default of payment of $15 fines, for infraction of the bagnio ordinance."[8] *Bagnio* is a synonym for bordello. This word was used in the past to describe an Italian or Turkish bathhouse.[9]

A night in the local calaboose was not a pleasant experience even when electricity and other amenities were available. Most calabooses did not have that luxury, and sanitary facilities were often absent. Conditions ranged from tolerable to unbearable. Time spent in the McKinney calaboose in 1884 is graphically described in the *Democrat* published in McKinney, Texas: "A more loathsome, nauseous place cannot be imagined than this city calaboose. It is a stench from top to bottom; it is lined from cellar to garret with vermin and is reeking all over with filth."[10]

Other descriptions of a calaboose include "bat cave" and "sweat box," and one was described as needing to be fumigated. An article in the *Sherman Daily Register* in 1887 published the following description of its calaboose: "A new calaboose is very badly needed in this city, the present one being little better than a hog pen."[11]

The temperature inside a calaboose could vary from freezing to stifling heat. The only relief from those hot summer days was air flow through windows or doors. Unfortunately, doors did not always have an opening for ventilation, and the size of windows varied from adequate to nonexistent. The windows in many calabooses were too high up to allow sufficient ventilation, and there were no windows in those "hellholes" in Carbon and Desdemona. The suffering caused by extreme heat was mentioned in a Houston newspaper on July 4, 1870: "The City Marshal had three or four luckless wights in the lockup this morning. Couldn't wish a fellow in a worse place than that calaboose, with the mercury close to one hundred."[12] The inclusion of the word *wights* reflects the practice of using archaic dialect by some writers in the latter part of the nineteenth century. Wight is a word of Germanic origin that was used to describe someone considered to be unfortunate.[13]

Not one of the calabooses in this sample had a direct source of heat for prisoners who suffered while being locked up in cold weather. Openings in windows and doors were usually the only source of light. The interiors of many calabooses were dark, even in the daytime. Confinement in a small space in virtual darkness might be viewed as another form of punishment, even bordering on cruelty. Although the presence of large windows would have been welcome in hot weather, they would have had a negative effect during heavy downpours, especially when the floor was dirt. The accomodations in most jails were sparse at best. Stand-alone beds were present in some, but sleeping on the floor was more the norm, especially when the calaboose was full. A crowded calaboose allowed little room for moving around, and personal space was nonexistent.

Large numbers of people in a small area posed even more of a problem when sexes and races were mixed. The need for segregation by race, sex, or type of offense is rarely mentioned in the sources I was able to review. At times, this must have been an issue, but apparently it was commonplace to mix prisoners. This would have been the case in those calabooses with only one room. An article in the *Honey Grove Signal* in 1895 illustrates how crowded conditions often prevented any type of separation of prisoners when large numbers of people were locked up at the same time. "About 30 negro males and females and one white man were put in the calaboose for every known crime."[14] Two structures designed specifically for segregation were identified. In Comanche, a jail with three cells was built in the 1940s and placed next to the two-story county jail. Two cells were furnished with sinks, showers, and toilets for the comfort of female prisoners, perhaps with children. The third cell was an open room and was used for male prisoners.[15] The county jail in Trinity has an interior room that was designed for women only, and it had a toilet.[16] No such amenity was observed in the larger room for the male prisoners.

Time spent in the calaboose was considered by some as a just punishment no matter how harsh the conditions. Others, however, felt sorry for those who were forced into a man-made hell. The calaboose in Holliday had two very small windows on the back wall centered on each cell, and the doors were solid metal. Fred Maier is a resident of Holliday, and he related a story about how a local citizen cut round holes in the doors to allow some measure of air flow because of "oven-like" conditions.[17]

Ross Estes related a story to Robert J. Duncan, who compiled the information into a book titled *I Remember Things: An Informal History of*

Tioga, Texas. "Ol Doc got drunk one time and they put him in this little old calaboose out here. Had an iron door to it, and they Locked him up in there. He'd got drunk, cussin'; the law took him down there and put him in that calaboose. It 'us hot in there. He 'us big and fat anyhow, and it 'us summertime. They was some little boys around there, and Doc, he looked out them little windows. He hired them boys to carry him water up there. They carried him water 'til 12 o'clock. They 'us just kids and they got sleepy and wanted to go home. He got them to go up to the house, then, and wake his wife up, and tell her to give him water 'til after daylight."[18]

Iron rings and chains were sometimes used to secure unruly prisoners. Spending time in that manner would have added another level of discomfort. The state of being confined was not the only form of torture. Those men in charge of maintaining law and order were not always nice to prisoners of either race or sex. Inappropriate treatment sometimes took place in the form of physical abuse or public humiliation. The city marshal in Arlington, for example, allowed young boys to turn hoses on prisoners and verbally humilate them.[19]

Transporting the prisoner to the lockup was usually a humane event, but an intoxicated prisoner in Orange who was unable to walk on his own was dragged through the streets. "Late yesterday afternoon, John Riley who is employed as gardener about town was arrested by the police for drunkeness and locked up in the calaboose. Riley was picked up on Green avenue and his condition was such that he refused to walk, hence he was dragged through the streets by the police. The sight was disgusting to say the least, that such shame should be flaunted in the very face of decency. Evidently the city authorities are not fully cognizant with the condition of a beastly drunken mortal, a half mile from jail. If they were, we feel confident a conveyance of some sort would be ordered into requisition in circumstances of this character."[20]

Because of the harsh conditions in many calabooses, it is understandable that prisoners would attempt to escape even when it meant risking their lives. In the vernacular of the time, the term "French leave" was a frequently used synonym for escaping from jail. The tactic of using fire as a means to escape was dangerous, but it was apparently used as a recurring event based on the number of incidents reported in local newspapers. Sadly, too many such attempts ended in tragedy, such as the one described here that occurred in Honey Grove in 1905: "Last Friday night Estes Smith, a well known young man about town, met a horrible death by burning in the city calaboose."[21]

Other methods included digging out from beneath the walls, cutting holes in the floor, and cutting or prying the bars on windows until an opening large enough to crawl through was created. Some calabooses were very sturdy and appear to have been virtually impossible to break out of. However, one of the major flaws in the design and construction of many calabooses was the lack of a door or shutter to cover the windows. This allowed outsiders to pass all forms of contrabrand to the hapless individuals inside. Several escapes were blamed on outside help, as exemplified by a prisoner in the Orange calaboose who broke out with help from a friend. "The Negro who was arrested in the Williams saloon several nights ago while attempting to conceal himself, as it was thought, for the purpose of robbing the house, escaped from the city lockup night before last and got away. The bars on the window next to the river were pried out with a piece of plank that some one had given in to the prisoner. Marshall [*sic*] Crane says that the calaboose is becoming very much in need of repairs."[22]

The citizens of Waco attempted to stop this practice by erecting a fence around their calaboose. "The council has ordered a heavy and high iron fence built outside of the windows, thus preventing persons from putting things in the calaboose."[23]

For those who found life in the calaboose unbearable, suicide was sometimes the solution. It is most unfortunate that someone would resort to such extreme measures, but suicide was not an isolated ocurrence. The two most usual types of reported suicides were hanging and death by fire. It was not always possible to determine if a prisoner who died in a fire was actually trying to burn his way out or if the fire was started by accident. "William L. Lacy was the son of Ewing Lacy, one of the wealthiest citizens in Marble Falls. He was put in the calaboose for being intoxicated. He died in a fire that locals believed he started.[24]

The story of one of the more gruesome cases of suicide was published in the *Brenham Daily Banner*: "On the 13th of September, 1892 Andrew J. Jennings checked in at the Wood Hotel. He experienced an apparent case of delerium and asked to be taken to the jail. He was hallucinating that he was being pursued to be killed so he cut his throat with a razor."[25]

The expense of building even the smallest calaboose could be a huge drain on the financial resources of small towns and unincorporated communities. Coupled with the outlay of funds for construction was the salary of those charged with upholding the law. Therefore, local citizens with titles of constable, marshal, or night watchman often represented the only deterrent to the crime that could become rampant on Saturday night when the local saloons discharged their customers. Some of the night watchmen worked as volunteers. Other ways to reduce the cost of construction was the practice of recycling materials from other buildings and use of the most available and affordable materials. One documented incident involving the use of salvaged materials is described in an article in the *Caldwell News and Burleson County Ledger* dated 1935: "The jail will cost approximately $200. Old lumber from the old Fire station is being used to construct the forms for the concrete."[26]

The rock structures in Fort Griffin, Mason, and Ringgold were built of native stone, and the decision to use that material may have been based on availability. Those in Desdemona and D'Hanis appear to be good examples of using the best available resource. The Thurber Brick Company was only twenty-one miles northeast of Desdemona, and the D'Hanis brick company was in that town. The very small jail in Snook is a possible example of repurposed brick. Charles Sebesta, a longtime resident of that town, said that the local grocery store was the only brick building in town at the time that the calaboose was built.[27] It may be that there was enough brick left over from the store to allow the town to build the small calaboose. This theory seems to be validated by the fact that it is only 72 square feet in size, and the door is less than 5 feet high. Possibly, there was not enough leftover brick to create a larger structure. Wood was often used in the construction of buildings in the town, including residences and calabooses. The railroad made it possible to transport this commodity long distances and for it to be affordable as well. In towns where sawmills were operating, wood was probably the most efficient and cost effective building material. Given the skill of framers, today as well as in the past, many of the small wooden calabooses constructed with milled boards on a wooden frame could have been completed in one or two days. The cost differential between quarrying and transporting stone by wagon versus milled lumber arriving on a train was probably significant. Also, the process of quarrying and shaping stone was very labor intensive. The metal doors and bars for the windows probably would have been made in advance. Numerous stone buildings in Texas were constructed at the same time as wooden ones, but they were built by people with the resources to finance such a project. Those buildings typically consist of courthouses and other public buildings, commercial buildings, and residences for the wealthy. During the early to middle part of the twentieth century, concrete was a common building material and was often used even when other resources such as stone and wood were available. The use of concrete in East Texas may seem to be an anomoly in an area known for its forests and lumber industry, but the cost and ease of construction apparently overrode other choices.

It is often impossible to determine when some of the early jails were built. Local informants typically repeat what they have been told, but they cannot always be relied on without some form of empirical data such as a newspaper article or city and county records. A jail may appear on a map dated 1910, but if there are no earlier maps, all that can be said is that it was present at that time. The oldest Texas jail that is still standing is believed to be the one in Gatesville. It is reported to have been constructed in 1855. Blackburn describes it as Coryell County's first jail below ground and refers to it as the sole-surving dungeon jail in Texas. "Coryell County's first jail was a typical, although small dungeon with double-log oak walls. The cell was a subterranean excavation 4 1/2 feet deep, accessed only by a

Metal cage in the basement of the police department in Ennis, Texas (photo by the author).

trapdoor.[28] This historic structure is housed at the Coryell Museum and Historical Center and is available for viewing. The oldest documented aboveground jail or calaboose is located in Mason. The date associated with the construction of this building is 1857. The most recently constructed calaboose that has documentation is the one in Van Alstyne. Per an inscription on one of the bricks, it was built in 1947 by Fielder Tile. Some calabooses were still being used into the middle of the twentieth century, but they were no longer the major form of incarceration in rural Texas after the introduction of the popular Farm-to-Market road system. These new paved roads made it easier for prisoners to be transported to county jails. At that time, counties had more reliable transportation than in the days of the wagon and Model T automobile. Before the construction of paved roads, muddy roads were sometimes impassable in bad weather. The first Farm-to-Market road in Texas was completed in January 1937. There was a three-year pilot program to test the efficiency of these new roads, and the program was so popular that the Farm-to-Market Act was created in 1949 to provide access to as many rural areas as possible.

One very interesting jail in Ennis is still used as a temporary lockup. It is in the basement of the police department that was built in 1916. Except for certain modern conveniences such as central air and heating and better lighting, this jail has experienced very little change since it first received prisoners over one hundred years ago. Later, as larger jails became more commonplace, the tiny calabooses and hoosegows diminished in number and gradually disappeared from the landscape. An empty calaboose was sometimes a convenient place for occupants other than prisoners. In Orange, the city marshal reported that "he had considerable trouble in keeping the dogs in the calaboose that had been taken up in violation of the city ordinance."[29] Sometimes abandoned jails were transformed so drastically that they were no longer recognizable as a place where criminals had been the primary occupants. Evelyn Stowers is the president of the Eagle Lake Preservation Alliance, and she stated that the second calaboose in Eagle Lake was built in 1904 to replace a wooden structure that had burned.[30] This event was recounted in the *Palestine Daily Herald* in 1903: "Charles Cabniniss and Manuel Allen, two negro prisoners, were burned to death in the calaboose at Eagle Lake, where they were being held awaiting transfer to Columbus.[31] In the 1940s, the replacement was altered to be used as a building for the local Girl Scout troop. The door and windows were fitted with modern equivalents, and a bathroom was added. Today it bears no resemblance to its former self. Even though there is a sign in front that proclaims it as a historic calaboose, some residents of the town still refer to it as the Girl Scout building.[32] The brick calaboose in Petrolia experienced a different reincarnation. Cathy Touvell is the property manager for this building, and she said that Petrolia is a very small town. When the need arose for extra office space, the door and windows were replaced and it became an office for one of the city workers.[33] Today, the door and windows are covered with plywood, and it appears to most onlookers to be just a small abandoned building. One of the more common uses for an abandoned jail is storage. Virtually all of those still owned by the city or county, as well as some that are privately owned, serve as convenient buildings for storing various items such as old tires and street signs. The calaboose in Comfort contains hazardous materials, as did the one in Castroville in the past. The calaboose in Grapeland was saved from destruction by a lady who purchased it for use as a chicken coop.[34] Perhaps the most unusual use for an abandoned jail occurred in the tiny Panhandle town of Hale Center where it was being used as a backstop for youth baseball games.[35]

The word *calaboose* has a definite association with the Old West, and it sometimes evokes thoughts of romance. Jails were often a major part of western novels and movies. One of the most obvious examples is a movie made in 1943 that was simply titled *Calaboose*. It starred Jimmy Rogers and was directed by Hal Roach Jr. Many people are intrigued by places that have involved famous people. In the western genre, these people were usually outlaws. In a 2012 article about the arrest of the Apache Kid in Arizona, R. K. DeArment states that the sheriff moved quickly "to relieve the pressure of his overloaded calaboose . . . by arranging transportation to take the Apache Kid to Yuma prison."[36] William "Bill" Preston Longley was a notorious Texas outlaw who was eagerly sought by the law. In 1875, he spent time in the calaboose in Van Alstyne.[37] Longley was arrested for murder in 1877 and placed in a metal cell in Giddings while awaiting trial. The cell is now located on the grounds of the Lexington Log Cabins and Historical Society. The following brief history of this cell is written on the front wall. "A portion of the cell was built for custodial security of Bill Longley while awaiting trial in Giddings. Born October 6, 1851; Died October 11, 1878."[38]

The word *calaboose* sometimes found its way into popular fiction. In a story by the famous author O. Henry titled "The Fourth in Salvador," one of the main characters says, “We don’t want to get in the calaboose.”[39] In his story, the local calaboose is also referred to as the “Calaboosum.” Gangsters were also seen by some as heroes. As a result, any mention of them is of great interest to the public. Bonnie Parker, of the infamous Barrow gang, and Ralph Fults, another member, endured a brief stay in the calaboose in Kemp in 1932 after being arrested in Cedar Creek.[40] “Later the Sheriff transferred the prisoners to Kemp and locked them in the tiny, one room jail a block south of town. The whole town of Kemp turned out for a look at the desperados. Bonnie examined the many pairs of eyes that peered through each of the cell’s two small windows.”[41] As a sidebar, Clyde Barrow was incarcerated in the prison at the Eastham Unit twenty-one miles south of Crockett in the southeastern corner of Houston County, and that building is still standing.

Tiny Texas jails can be placed in several categories. Those built and operated by towns and communities for the purpose of housing local citizens and transients are the most common; they vary in size from as little as a metal cell for two people that is only 42 square feet to others whose

Suspicious structure near Weatherford (photo courtesy of Roger G. Moore).

footprints are as large as 448 square feet. Jails built for other purposes include stockades and guardhouses on US Army forts designed to protect settlers on the frontier from hostile Indians and housing for state and federal prisoners who worked on road gangs and in the fields. An exellent example of housing for state and federal prisoners is the small concrete jail in Memphis. It has two cells and occupies a footprint of 350 square feet.

Sometimes, buildings are observed that quietly advertise themselves as being a calaboose. Often, there are no definitive data, such as a door or windows with metal bars, and much of the local populace has no idea about its original function. Further research may also prove inconclusive. These buildings are categorized in this study as "suspicious structures" until their actual purpose can be determined. In some cases, it can be difficult to imagine why some of these structures exist unless they were intended to be used as a calaboose. One very good example is a small building standing alone on a hill overlooking the floodplain of a creek in Parker County near Weatherford. Banks present a different problem. They are usually small like a calaboose and very well made. One of the telltale signs of a bank vault are the remnants of a concrete foundation around it on which the rest of the structure rested. When some of the older banks were built, the slab for the floor was the first phase of construction and the vault was built around it. Banks were meant to convey security since they housed real money. The perception of security was easier to promote when the bank was made of a durable material such as stone or concrete. Vaults with massive metal doors inside a sturdy structure were commonplace and many remain today, long after the banks were demolished. These and other suspicious structures observed during research for this project can be found on my website at www.tinytexasjails.com.

There is a humorous side to some of these Texas calabooses, such as the event in Trenton by local pranksters. The first calaboose was erected adjacent to the railroad and destroyed when several youths attached it to the train as a prank. When the train pulled out, the calaboose was dragged until it fell apart. A replacement jail was constructed in a different location so that a similar prank could not be repeated.[42] Later, it was returned to its original location where it remains today. In Tioga, a portion of one of the brick walls had deteriorated to the point where one of the regulars placed there to sober up could crawl out the next morning and go about his business with no threat of reprisal from the law.[43]

Some towns have borne the expense of restoring or relocating their calabooses to use as an example of how criminals were dealt with in the early days. Two towns merit attention here. The city of Grapevine moved their old calaboose to a prominent spot downtown next to a bus stop. A plaque informs the curious onlookers about what they are seeing. This action by the city has created enormous interest by those waiting for the bus and during special events such as the annual Christmas parade and field trips by schoolchildren.

Frisco had a calaboose made of concrete that had been so poorly constructed that it was in imminent danger of collapse. The old structure was demolished and a replica built on the grounds of the Frisco Heritage Museum using as much of the original materials as possible and keeping true to the size and floor plan of the original.

One of the more pleasant and exciting ways to discover a tiny Texas jail for the first time is to take a leisurely drive through the alleys and side streets of small towns. Not only are there local cafés, antique stores, and museums that serve as respites from the often monotonous hours of driving, there is always the possibility of a most unusual discovery that makes the trip worthwhile in spite of not finding a sometimes elusive calaboose. An example of one of the more interesting sights in small town Texas is a hygieostatic bat roost that was built in 1918 near Comfort to colonize bats. This Victorian-style structure is listed in the National Register of Historic Places as the last survivor of seven roosts built in Texas and the oldest of the three known existing roosts in the United States. The purpose of constructing the bat colonies was to control malaria by natural means. Texas leads the nation in the number of historical markers that have been verified by the state.

Any trip, regardless of its purpose, can provide a lesson in Texas history and is highly recommended. In addition to the curiosity factor that these calabooses possess, they are truly significant historic structures that represent a way of life in Texas that is not likely to be repeated.

2

Cages and Cells

My early perception of what a jail would have been like during the early days of this country was largely based on western movies. Hollywood usually depicted a wooden building on the main street with a large room for the sheriff and one or more cells with a window or two on the back wall. Escapes accomplished by using a horse and rope to remove the bars were a common event in these celluloid thrillers. Perhaps the tiny one-room calaboose did not portray the image that filmmakers in Hollywood wanted to be associated with their interpretation of the "Old West." Plus, it would have been virtually impossible to film interior scenes in such a small space. Many early Texas calabooses and jails consisted of metal cages with one or more cells enclosed in a structure that was often only a few feet larger than the cage itself. The open space between the cell walls and the walls of the exterior building was referred to as a "walk around"; it allowed law enforcement officers to view the cells from different sides. In some calabooses and many of the larger jails, prisoners were often allowed outside the cells to use the walk around for exericise or to look out the windows. Even though stories of cages having been used as lockups in the outdoors are common, most were housed in a building. I recall seeing prisoners on the second floor of the Bastrop County jail looking

Manufacturer's plate for Pauly Jail Building Company (photo by the author).

out the windows in 1971. Later, when I visited the jail as a tourist I realized that they had been allowed to leave the cells to get exercise. One account of metal cages being used outdoors occurred circa 1937 in Carrizo Springs. The old stone jail had been demolished and the metal cages therein were used outside while a new jail was being constructed.

Despite the fact that some cages could have been fabricated locally, the majority were probably purchased from firms that specialized in the manufacture of jail cells and related hardware. The company most often associated with the construction of metal cages and cells found in Texas jails is the J. Pauly Manufacturing Company in Saint Louis, Missouri. Cells made by Pauly are often identified by metal plates on the cages they built.

Manufacturers like the E. T. Barnum Iron and Wire Works in Detroit, Michigan, provided catalogs for customers to peruse and order from. The Barnum company supported their case for steel jails and cages with the following statement in their catalog: "A secure lockup or jail will conserve morals and lessen crime in your community."[1] The walls or panels were made of solid steel plate with no openings, or in the "lattice" pattern that was created by crisscrossing flat steel bars that were riveted in place at each juncture. The Barnum catalog states that these lattice-type panels were made of steel that they advertised as the Barnum Bessemer Prison or the Barnum Laminated Tool-Proof Steel.[2] They were used mainly as walls but some were also placed on the tops of cages. The individual panels were then rivited to a heavy steel angle frame making the end product "the safest and strongest cage made."[3] The resulting square openings are the reason for the term "lattice," and the size of these openings varied but squares of 3 or 4 inches appear to have been most common. Many cages had a food opening that, according to the catalog, "obviates the necessity of opening the door to pass food to the prisoner."[4] Some cages were fabricated without the steel bottom because they were to be bolted to a cement, stone, or plank floor.

Barnum offered purchasers a variety of models with the option to upgrade by adding amenities such as "bunks hinged to side walls and arranged to swing up against the wall when not in use."[5] This feature was not limited to Barnum products. A very fine metal cage with folding bunks can be viewed in a city park in the East Texas town of Montgomery. This one was made by the Pauly Company. Sanitation was often an issue in the early calabooses. E. T. Barnum offered an "odorless night soil bucket with corner commode and ventilating pipe"[6] that was advertised as providing a "sanitary cell of the most modern construction."[7] A metal bucket similar to the one described here is present in the metal cage in Athens, Texas, and is the only example known at the time of this writing. There was also the option to deviate from the advertised floor plans to accommodate the town's needs.

The method of shipment may have varied depending on the cost, distance to the market, and availability of towns to assemble panels using local labor. Some of the metal cages, when assembled, weighed several thousand pounds; it would have been extremely difficult to offload them from a train and transport them to their final destination in the days when wagons were the only local method of transport. The Barnum catalog describes the common method of shipment from their plant: "Cages are made in sections, set up in factory, fitted together carefully, painted, marked, taken down and shipped. Any mechanic or blacksmith can set them in position and at small expense.[8]

This method of shipment was also the norm for the J. Pauly company in Saint Louis. Research by Ed Blackburn Jr. revealed the following: "Their jail cells were designed, constructed, and assembled at the plant, then disassembled and shipped to the new or remodeled jail, where they were assembled in place."[9]

Mark Greer is a resident of Valley Mills, and he told me that the town's metal cage, also made by Pauly, had been secured to a concrete slab before the brick exterior of the calaboose was laid.[10] The same was true for the jail in Dallam County. In 1911, the county purchased a small cell block from Southern Structural Steel Company. "When a structure measuring 16" x 20" was built around it, the county had its second jail."[11]

The majority of cages documented here are of the "strap iron" variety developed by Peter Joseph Pauly, who immigrated to the United States in 1846 from Koblenz, Germany, and began his career as an apprentice to a blacksmith at three dollars per month. He was known for his skill at working with wrought iron, mainly to repair steamboats. The arrival of the railroad greatly diminished the river business and he changed the focus of his business to the manufacture of small steel cages anchored to wagons that were used as mobile jails. He recognized the benefits of using iron instead of steel and became known as the "Pioneer Iron Jail Builder." As a result, the Pauly Jail Building and Manufacturing Company was created. Pauly worked with his brother, John, and the jails they built became famous throughout the United States and Canada. Peter Joseph Pauly is credited with inventing the lever locking device and key bar lattice. The products they turned out found their way to an estimated fifty-eight county jails in Texas.

The cost of purchasing these cages plus shipping charges must have been substantial. Because of cost and durability, it makes sense that they would have been used for many years and sometimes recycled for use in another town. An article in the *Denison Press* recounts the relocating of iron cells from the old Sherman jail to Denison for the purpose of erecting a calaboose.[12] Two metal cells manufactured by the Stewart Iron Works Company of Cincinnati, Ohio, circa 1898 were moved from the city hall in Uvalde to Sabinal, where they were placed in the town's newly constructed jail. In Weimar, a large metal cell was transported from the old two-story brick calaboose to an improvised facility on the same block. Entire calabooses were sometimes sold to other towns in need of such a facility. In 1907, the city of Longview offered its calaboose for sale and advertised it as a "fine calaboose and a steel structure."[13] This statement implies that a metal cage was the item for sale.

The size of metal cages and cells varied considerably. The cages in Crystal City and Helena were measured at approximately 42 square feet, and they are tied for the smallest cages found during this study. The largest cage documented during this study is in Leakey. It is 107 square feet in size and contains two cells.

There were two ways of manufacturing metal cages and cells. The strap iron method has already been discussed. In some cases, thin sheets of metal were used that were much lighter than their more massive strap iron counterparts. The openings that are analogous to those produced by the crisscross method of strips of iron were created by a machine that punched them out, probably all at the same time. I had not given any thought to this method until it was called to my attention by Dolores Herrington, who was searching for information about the cage in Athens, Texas.[14] There is no plaque that advertises the manufacturer, but the word "Carnegie" is inscribed on the exterior. Andrew Carnegie is often touted as leading the expansion of the American steel industry in the latter part of the nineteenth century. Although I was unable to find documentation that any of the companies Carnegie owned were engaged in the manufacture of jail cells, it seems likely that the cage in Athens was made using Carnegie steel. Other cages described in this book were similarily made, and their manufacturers might have also purchased their steel from one of Carnegie's subsidaries. Examples are in Asherton, Dessau, and Leakey.

There are two metal cages on the grounds of the Old Jail Museum in Palo Pinto. One is a replica that is barely big enough for one person. It is believed that the original version was loaded onto a wagon when transportation was needed to take a prisoner to the county jail or state prison in Huntsville.[15] Larger cages were also used as mobile jails. One example is a metal cage on the grounds of the Grayson County Frontier Village in Denison that was attached to a wagon and used to transport road gangs to and from work.[16] A wooden cage located in Seguin is another example. It has been restored and is available for viewing at the Heritage Village Park in that town.

A most unusual strap iron cage was found in the backyard of Mary and Monty Phillips of Lockhart. It was buried, and the only way prisoners could enter it would have been through the roof. Military artifacts such as bullets and collar insignia as well as hand-forged horseshoes suggest a possible camp for the US Army at this location. Another possibility could have been a lockup for slaves. The Phillipses' property may have been part of a plantation at one time. Mary Phillips has conducted extensive research of Caldwell and surrounding counties. She found a quote written by a slave about an aboveground calaboose on Billy Coats's plantation in Bastrop County near Elgin: "They was a calaboose right on the plantation, what look like a ice-house, and it was sho' bad to git locked up in it. Us got provisions 'lowanced' to us every Saturday night."[17]

These cages present an imposing image capable of conjuring up thoughts of those who were unfortunate enough to spend time in them. Those metal boxes that stood outside became virtual ovens in the summertime. It was obvious that comfort was not a high priority for those towns determined to create a punitive environment for evildoers. Given the high incidence of escapes from the more conventional calabooses made of wood and those with windows that allowed contraband to be passed to the prisoners, these metal cages were virtually escape proof. The tiny holes in the latticework were too small to allow larger objects such as guns to be smuggled to prisoners, and the massive locks were much more difficult to tamper with than some of their more modest counterparts in the more flimsy wooden structures.

Prior to my research for this endeavor, my knowledge of the professionally manufactured cages and cells made of iron and steel was passive. The relationship of these stout enclosures to the need for imprisonment during the early days of Texas is something that I have found to be compelling. They were expensive—yet many towns opted to pay the price for the security they provided. Even though some of the cages and cells embraced in this volume may have been intended for use in some of the larger city or county jails, they are incorporated into this book because they exemplify the various methods of construction that were available. During my travels in Texas and on the internet, I came across many metal cages with one or more individual cells. The greatest number of these daunting enclosures stand alone on the grounds of a city park, courthouse square, or in a local museum. Initially, however, they were usually housed in a structure ostensibly as protection from the elements. The two-cell cage in Spofford is the only one in this group in its original location. It remains well secured to its concrete foundation, but the original framework of the calaboose has deteriorated to the point of virtual oblivion. The two-cell cage in Crawford is in the original building, but the structure was moved to its current location from another part of town. Sabinal and Weimar contain metal cages that were brought to their jails from other locations and used until they were no longer needed. The cages in Emory, Hico, and Sour Lake are inside modern structures where they will be protected, but they were never used in these buildings. Many of the cages are similar in design, and only five different floor plans were identified. No cage with more than two cells was documented. Although it appears that most Texas calabooses were never fitted out with an elaborate cage ordered from a distant manufacturer, they were an integral part of the way some prisoners were confined in these tiny buildings. Those fabrications of iron and steel illustrated and discussed in this book could have been the regrettable abode of many Texas malefactors and forlorn wrongdoers who were the unwilling occupants of a Texas calaboose or jail.

3

Research Methods

The documentation of the standing calabooses and jails discussed in this book is the result of many long days of research and travel. A major source of information was the collection of Sanborn fire insurance maps. The D. A. National Sanborn Insurance Diagram Bureau was founded by Daniel Alfred Sanborn in 1867. His company created a uniform series of large-scale maps that depict towns in minute detail. The company logo and date of the map is usually in the upper right-hand corner of the first sheet. The design varies but sometimes is quite elaborate. The purpose of the maps was to estimate fire insurance risks for companies whose business it was to provide insurance against fire. Structures on the Sanborn maps were color coded by building material and labeled according to their function. Other details included names of streets and businesses, addresses of buildings, city lot and block numbers, and a key to all streets and special buildings such as the courthouse, county jail, city hall, and fire station.

These maps sometimes make it possible to confirm and locate calabooses no longer present. The Sanborn map for the town of Rising Star, dated 1921, provides an excellent example. It depicts a small rock calaboose very close to a wooden structure labeled as city hall. The location and size of

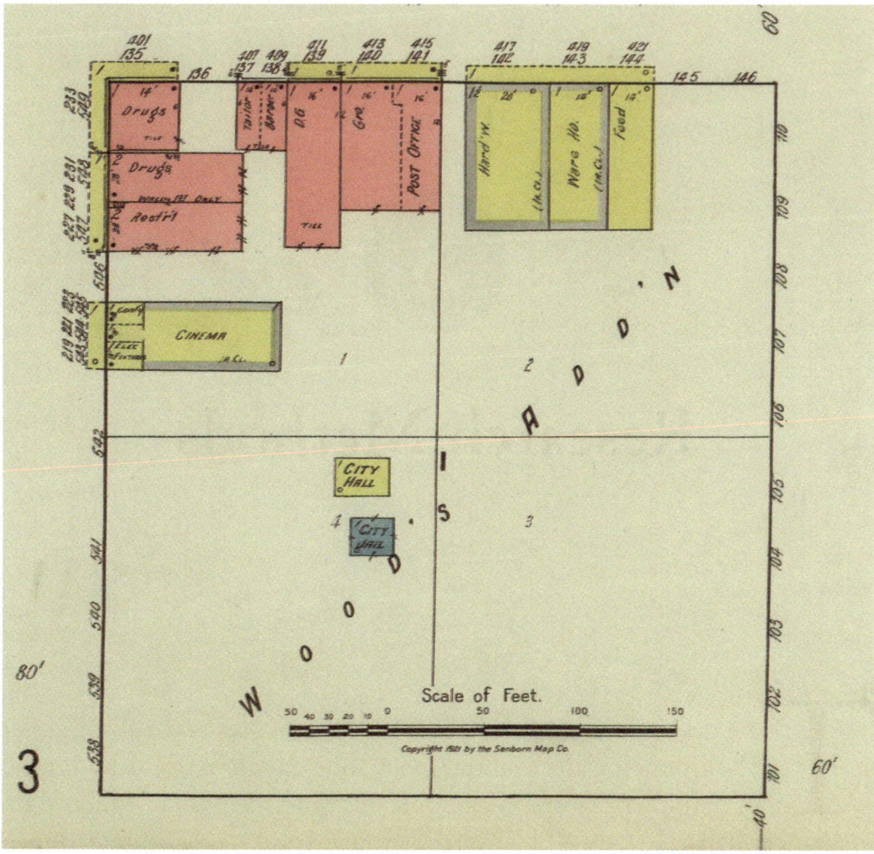

Sanborn map for Rising Star, Texas, dated 1921, sheet 2 (map courtesy of Briscoe Center for American History).

these buildings are comparable to those in an undated photograph on file at the University of Texas at Arlington. This image is also available for viewing on the the Portal to Texas History site managed by the University of North Texas in Denton.

Every Sanborn map available at the Perry-Casteñeda Library in Austin, Texas, and the Fondren Library at Rice University were examined. In some cases, the originals at the Dolph Briscoe Center for American History on the campus of the University of Texas at Austin were also checked. The total number of towns checked is 424.

Google Earth has also proved to be a valuable resource. Using the "Street View" option, the presence of a calaboose can sometimes be spotted or confirmed. Additional research was conducted by regular visits to web-

Courthouse and jail at Rising Star, Texas (photo courtesy of *Fort Worth Star-Telegram* Collection, Special Collections, the University of Texas at Arlington Libraries, Arlington, Texas).

sites such as Red River Historian; Texas Escapes; Special Collections, UTA Library; and Traces of Texas as well as Facebook pages such as "Texas Lawmen, Outlaws & Jails/History." These sites post pictures of current and historic photos of a wide range of subjects including jails. However, there is no substitute for driving the back roads of Texas and visiting small towns with colorful names like Carbon, Happy, and Noodle. Driving slowly and eyeing every suspicious building is all too often unproductive, but persistence sometimes pays off and, "suddenly," there it is—another calaboose waiting to be discovered. The elusive calaboose may be next to the courthouse or county jail, secluded in an alley, or behind a chain link fence at the local water plant. The one in Wellborn was so obscured by brush that it was virtually impossible to recognize it. Only after the owner cleared away the vegetation did another calaboose emerge. Another necessary element of this type of endeavor is to take time to talk with residents and historians as well as staff at local libraries and public agencies. In Hughes Springs, on my way to a known jail, I asked one of the residents if there was a calaboose in town. He replied that there used to be one by the railroad tracks. I saw no signs of a calaboose, and when I asked another person he showed me exactly where it once stood. This venerable old structure lives today through a photograph hanging on a wall in city hall.

Hughes Springs calaboose (photo courtesy of City of Hughes Springs).

Many residents of towns with a calaboose are unaware of its presence. When asked about the local calaboose, the reply may be, "There is no jail in this town," or, "That's the city's storage building." However, the truth is that eighty years ago that storage building once was the town lockup. When possible, all known standing calabooses and miniscule jails were visited. They were documented with high definition photographs, detailed measurements, and size and placement of windows and doors. It was not long into this study that it became apparent that not all calabooses and cages were constructed with the same floor plan. Maps were drawn to scale that depict every floor plan of calabooses (appendix D) as well as the metal cages and cells included in this book (appendix E).

Other information collected, when possible, includes street names, addresses, date of construction, owner, materials used in construction, number of cells, condition, special features such as plumbing and electricity, unusual architectural style, and graffiti. The presence of primitive scribblings on the walls of calabooses provides valuable information about the years it was in service and a genealogical record of the hapless people who wrote these messages, possibly out of boredom or to call attention to their time in a form of purgatory or legalized hell on earth.

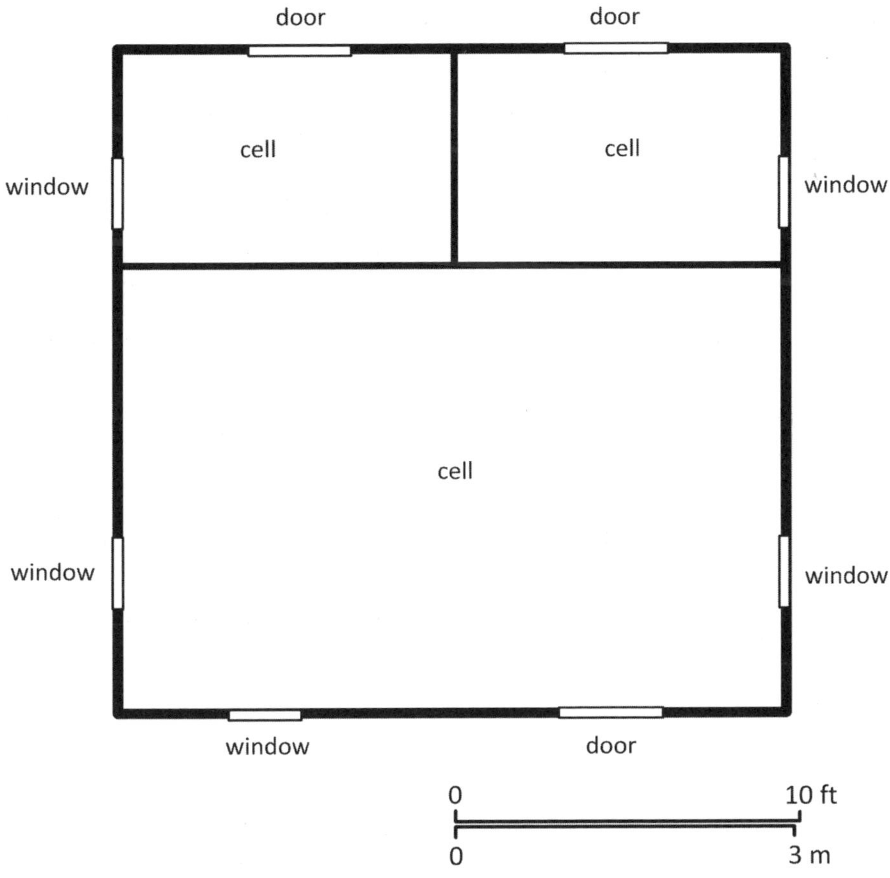

Floor plan of the Bartlett calaboose (drafted by Lili G. Lyddon).

Most calabooses were recorded as historic sites at the Texas Archeological Research Laboratory (TARL) on the campus of the University of Texas at Austin. The numbers assigned to these structures allow professional archaeologists to access the information. These site numbers are listed in appendix A. Site numbers were also issued for some jails (appendix B) as well as cages and cells (appendix C). One of the first steps taken by archaeologists while planning for a job is to review known prehistoric and historic sites in their project area before entering the field. Since very little data exist concerning calabooses, this information can be especially helpful as it may be the catalyst needed to save some of these structures from

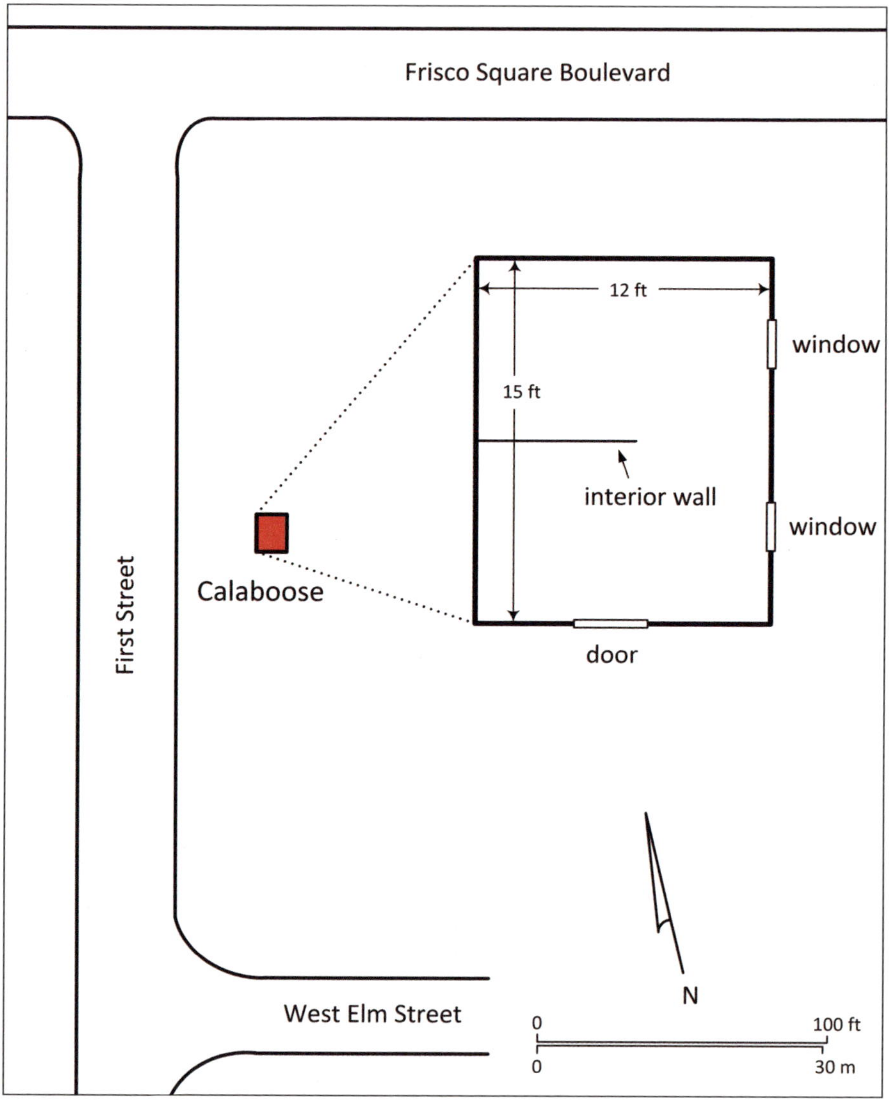

Site map for the Frisco calaboose (drafted by Lili G. Lyddon).

demolition. Archaeologists are expected to document historic structures in detail, and one of the normal tasks is the creation of a site map. This level of work is beyond the scope of this study for every calaboose recorded. However, the calaboose in Frisco was planned for immediate demolition due to safety concerns. In that instance, a site map was created so that its original location would not be forgotten.

Other sources that proved useful include treatises on Texas courthouses and jails, county histories, vertical files in local libraries, and newspaper articles. Books that often traveled with me include *Wanted: Historic County Jails of Texas* by Ed Blackburn Jr.;[1] *Just Visitin': Old Texas Jails* by Joan Upton Hall;[2] *More Ghost Towns of Texas* by T. Lindsay Baker;[3] *The Roads of Texas* by Willa Christopher Muller;[4] and other road atlases. Even with the completion of this book, I continue to document calabooses. Those that I have discovered following publication have been added to my website—www.tinytexasjails.com.

The purpose of this study is not only to photograph and describe the standing calabooses. It is also to document those that have long since been taken from us. The Texas calaboose represents more than just a place to lock up prisoners. It is an excellent example of vernacular architecture that has not been described previously.

4

Construction Methods

Calabooses can be compared to houses in that they share the same structural elements necessary to be functional such as floors, walls, roofs, doors, and windows. The obvious difference is that a calaboose was constructed as a place of punishment with little consideration for comfort. Calabooses are much smaller than most houses and often lack electricity, plumbing, or furniture—and sometimes windows. Since many calabooses were built in small unincorporated towns with limited funds or as interim lockups while the formal county jail was under construction, cost was often a major concern. It was, therefore, common for the most expedient materials to be used. Examples are the calaboose in Marble Falls, where plow parts were used to create the exterior door, and Caldwell, where salvaged wood was repurposed to make the forms for pouring concrete. Construction always began from the ground and proceeded to the installation of the roof. The first step in building a calaboose, as with any structure, is to decide the size and shape of the footprint that it will occupy when completed. This includes height of the walls and the type of roof. Other important issues to be considered during the planning stage are the kinds of materials and availability of experienced labor. All calabooses described in this book fit the description of a rectangle. Some have four sides of equal length and are classified as square. Others are best referred to as an oblong or nonsquare rectangle that can be described as rectilinear.

Doors

The size and placement of doors and windows must be determined during the planning stage. The exterior door was usually centered on the facade of the calaboose or cell in those cases where two or more cells were constructed side by side. There are a few examples of doors offset to the right or left of center. These usually opened into an entry room or vestibule that served as office space for law enforcement or additional space for prisoners in cases of overcrowding. If the door was offset to the right of center, the cell would have been to the left, and the opposite would be true if the door was left of center. Most exterior doors were relatively similar in size: about 3 feet wide and 6 to 7 feet tall. They were made of wood or metal and sometimes consisted of two parts, an outer door and an inner door. One door was usually made of metal bars while the other one was a solid sheet of wood or metal that could be shut to keep out inclement weather or for more security. Some had openings that allowed law enforcement officers to view the prisoners and to pass food and other items without venturing inside. These openings also provided a modicum of light and ventilation. The calaboose in Bedias has a solid wooden door, but there is a very small opening with metal bars next to the door that could have been used for interaction with the prisoners.

Windows

Windows varied greatly in size and shape and always contained bars or other kinds of barriers to deter escape. One anomaly is the window treatment in the calaboose in Holland where truck wheels substituted for the traditional barred window. The disparity in size is illustrated in the tiny windows in the Somerville calaboose that measure just a few square inches to the very large one-of-a-kind window in the calaboose in Wellborn that has a span of 8 feet wide by 2 feet high. Rebar and other forms of circular or flat strips of metal placed vertically or horizontally in the window opening were the norm. One of the more common patterns was a combination of horizontal and vertical bars welded at the joints to form a crisscross pattern. In some cases, shutters were affixed to the exterior wall, which allowed the opening to be sealed for protection from the elements or as an extra level of security and possibly as a form of punishment. Because the comfort level inside a calaboose depended largely on windows, the location was sometimes as important as the size. Some were so high up on the wall that the resulting flow of air would be an indirect benefit at best. Even more extreme is the calaboose in Carbon, which has no windows.

Roofs

Although some of the roofs present in this sample may not conform exactly to a formal architectural definition, six known types were identified. They are barrel roofs, flat roofs, gable roofs, hip roofs, pyramid roofs, and shed roofs. Flat roofs and gable roofs are the most prevalent.

Barrel Roof

A barrel roof (a.k.a. barrel vault roof) is one with a semicircular cross section. The curved surface provides excellent rain runoff and lessens the amount of snow accumulation. They don't leak as readily as a flat roof and absorb less heat. They can also be considered by some to be more aesthetically pleasing, which may not have been a consideration in the construction of a building to house criminals. All the calabooses with this type of roof are made of poured concrete. The original roof on the calaboose at Fort Griffin may be an example of a barrel roof on a stone building, but it is too fragmented to make this determination with confidence. The calaboose in Grapevine is one of the best examples of a barrel vault roof in the current sample.

Flat Roof

The term *flat roof* is a misnomer; most of the so-called flat roofs have a gentle slope or pitch for water runoff, and this is true in the current sample. A roof can have a pitch of approximately 10 degrees and still conform to the definition of being flat. Flat roofs are present on both square and oblong calabooses. Some roofs described here as flat have a parapet on three sides.

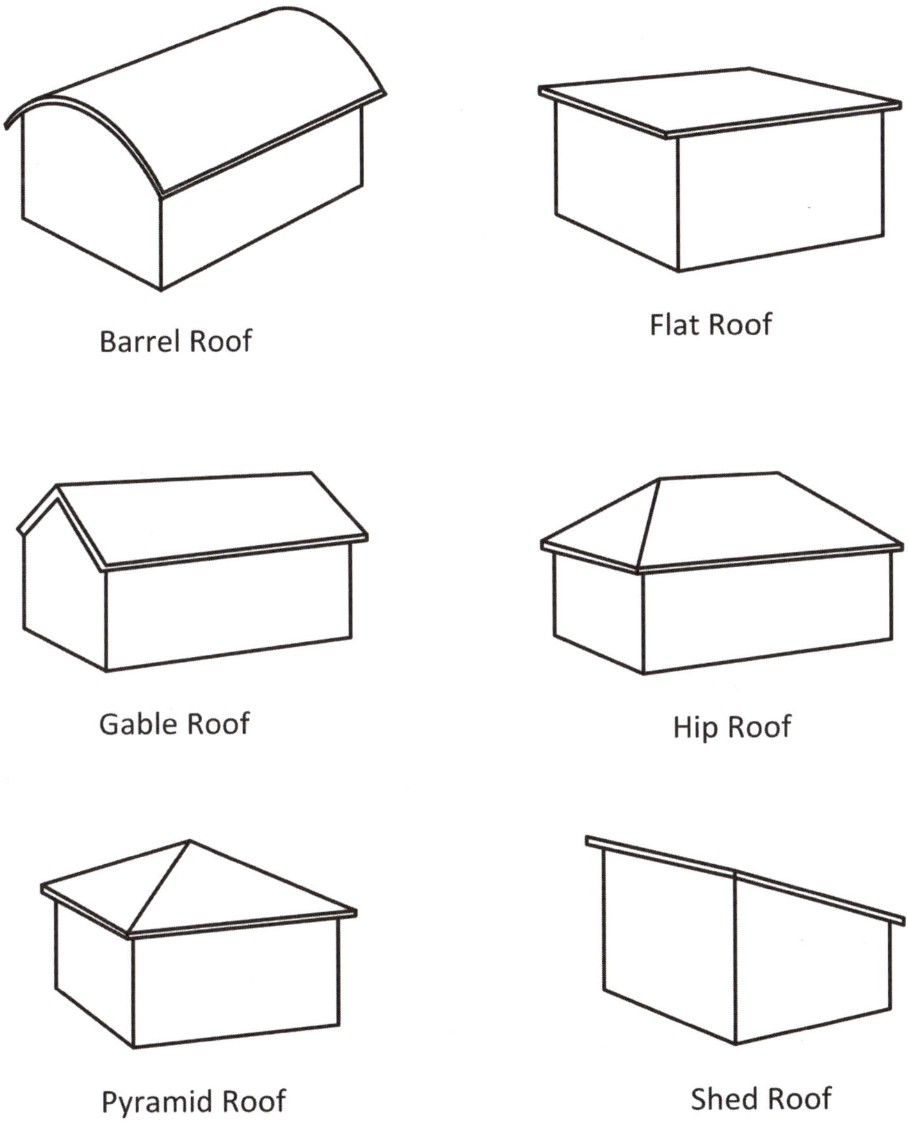

Roof types found on Texas calabooses (drafted by Lili G. Lyddon).

Parapets are a method of controlling the flow of water runoff and, in some cases, also served as a decorative treatment such as those on the calabooses in Boling, Chillicothe, and Marble Falls.[1]

Gable Roof

The term *gable roof* can be confusing because a gable is not an actual roof shape. Gables are the triangular areas created in the upper part of a wall because of the juncture of the sloping ends of a double pitched roof. Another way of describing a gable roof is a simple design shaped like an inverted V. This type of roof is only present on oblong calabooses, and they form a gable at each end.

Hip Roof

A hip roof is one where all four sides slope downward to the walls. The slopes are usually gentle. This type of roof has no gables or other vertical sides. It is only found on structures whose shape is oblong.

Pyramid Roof

Pyramid roofs are another type of hip roof and are only found on structures that are equidistant on all four sides or square in plan. This type of roof is simply defined as a roof with four slopes or faces that meet at a peak. The calabooses in Deport, Jewett, and Trenton fit this definition.

Shed Roof

The shed roof is also referred to as a mono-pitched roof. This is a roof with one slope attached to a taller wall that extends to the ground at an angle of 90 degrees. Another definition is a roof with a pitch greater than 10 degrees. The only calaboose in the current sample that serves as a good example of this roof type is in Monahans where the pitch is approximately 17.4 degrees.

Many of the older calabooses had wood roofs before tin was available and affordable. Every wood calaboose depicted on the Sanborn maps had a wooden roof, but the maps do not make the distinction between shingles and boards. Most of the wooden calabooses in the current sample have roofs covered with shingles or tin. Although some of these tin roofs could be original, it was a common practice to replace rotting wood with tin when it became available. Tin was probably cost effective, easier and faster to install, and longer lasting than wooden shingles. These roofs are usually sloping, a characteristic typical of the single pitch roof.

The most common materials used to build a calaboose consisted of wood, concrete, brick, and stone. A few were created using manufactured blocks, and some were simple wooden frames covered with galvanized steel sheet material or corrugated iron, commonly known as tin. In the more arid areas, jails and other buildings were sometimes made of adobe. The final appearance of a calaboose depended on the type of materials used and the amount of time the builders put into their work. Most are simple structures while some, such as the calaboose in Stockdale, have architectural embellishments that had nothing to do with security or functionality.

Building Materials

Wood

The wooden calaboose was by far the most numerous. This was not unexpected since calabooses were being built and used before concrete and brick were readily available and affordable. Wood was often the easiest and fastest to construct, and carpenters were probably more numerous at the time than bricklayers and people with experience pouring concrete. Some of these small wooden calabooses could have easily been put together in one or two days by experienced framers. The calaboose in Burlington exemplifies the simplicity of design that was sometimes chosen.

Some walls were created by nailing milled boards horizontally to upright boards that measured 2 inches by 4 inches (a.k.a. two-by-four). The resulting double wall created a stronger building and provided an extra degree of security against escape. Other walls were more complicated. Boards of various sizes were placed flat on top of one another and held together with large nails or spikes. Typically, two-by-fours were used, but some calabooses were built with boards that measure 2 inches by 6 inches. This method resulted in walls that were wider and stronger. The boards sometimes overlapped in a pattern like some log cabins. The calaboose in

Hermleigh has corners that are best described as "butt joints." The practice of board and batten construction was commonly used when the exterior siding was placed vertically.

The floors of the wooden calabooses vary from bare ground to wooden planks when the structure was built using the pier and beam method. The floor of the calaboose in Sealy consists of two layers of boards arranged crossways for strength. Very little effort was required for those with dirt floors except for digging holes to support the beams that the siding would be nailed to. In some cases, there is evidence that the ground was leveled or contoured to allow water to run off during heavy rains.

Concrete

Calabooses constructed with concrete were built using the poured-in-place method that was common during the early part of the twentieth century through the end of calaboose production. The slab was poured first using wooden forms to contain the concrete much as it is done today. For the slab to not crack, some form of steel reinforcement (colloquially known as rebar) would have been used. Unfortunately, no rebar was visible in any of the slabs in this sample. All concrete calabooses described in this book were made using this method.

Wall construction also required horizontally placed wooden forms and could take as many as ten pouring episodes to reach the desired height. Although various widths are present, it makes sense that boards of a standard size would be used in lieu of milling boards to a special size, which would incur extra cost. Horizontal lines visible on the outside of the finished building indicate the width of the boards used to create the forms and the number of pouring episodes needed to finish the task. Extra wall strength could be realized with the addition of corner blocks.

Erecting the roof was the last stage in the construction of the building's exterior. A flat roof was created when a wooden form was placed on top of the building and the concrete was poured in and left to set or dry. The wet concrete permeated the boards to such a degree that an impression of the grains in the wood was made in the concrete; this sometimes created the appearance of a wooden ceiling. It is rare that the boards used to create the bottom of the form for the roof were left in place. However, this was the case with the calaboose in Moore, Texas. Rebar is visible in the ceiling of the calaboose in Wellborn, and this is the only known example.

Buildings made of poured concrete were more likely to deteriorate faster when construction aggregate or rebar were not used to serve as reinforcement to add strength. Pebbles were commonly used, but when the ratio of pebbles to cement was too high the building was subjected to weathering that caused the structure to become unstable. This was the case of the calaboose in Frisco, and the city wisely chose to demolish it for safety reasons. No standard rebar was present; miscellaneous pieces of metal and horseshoes were used instead. Other types of aggregate that have been used to "stretch" concrete are a mixture of shell and concrete (a.k.a. shellcrete) and small pieces of brick. Rebar and other "retasked" metal bars or rods, like straps or railroad rails, are distinct from aggregate but serve the same purpose. However, it seems plausible that a permanent structure was not always the goal when building a calaboose. Additionally, the extra cost associated with a stronger building was probably a major factor in using materials that were cheaper and more readily available. The walls of some concrete calabooses were covered with concrete stucco or grout, a practice known to architects as rendering. This practice was sometimes used to protect surfaces that were starting to crack and deteriorate or as a cosmetic treatment. Some of the better examples of the use of rendering are found in the calabooses in Chillicothe, Glazier, and Royse City. Most of the poured concrete roofs were flat, but a few may be best described as a variation of the "barrel" or "barrel vault" roof. Other calabooses with barrel roofs are present in Gause, La Coste, Miles, and Rochester. Some of the concrete calabooses have pitched or sloped roofs. In most cases, the degree is relatively minor, but there are exceptions.

Brick

Brick is also a durable material that has been available for a very long time, but only twenty of the calabooses discovered through field investigations and archival research were constructed with bricks. Brick commercial buildings and storefronts are common in many Texas towns, especially along the main street. Calabooses made of brick represent the third-highest number in the sample, but only fifteen are known to be still standing. This figure seems to be low considering the apparent abundance of brick required to construct the other buildings in most towns. The main reason for this disparity was most likely associated with cost. The townfolk probably did not need or want a calaboose made of brick if it was more costly than one made of wood or poured concrete. The walls of a brick calaboose were sturdy and easy to construct when skilled bricklayers were available. As mentioned in prevous chapters, brick was readily available in towns like Desdemona and D'Hanis due to the close proximity of foundries. The brick walls were usually laid in two courses for extra strength and to make it more difficult for prisoners to escape. The floors and roofs of the brick calabooses were typically made of concrete. All of the brick calabooses in this sample have concrete roofs and floors. Most of the roofs are flat or exhibit a slight degree of pitch; the concrete roof in Rochester conforms to the definition of a barrel roof.

Stone

Ten calabooses made of stone are still standing. Others are known to have existed at one time but are no longer present. The number of standing stone calabooses seems low when one considers the fact that stone does not deteriorate like other building materials. In the deterioration of stone buildings, the major problem is the method of construction. Mortar is used to hold the stones in place, and over time, if not maintained, it can erode, causing stones to settle or fall. With proper care, a stone structure can last a lifetime and can serve many purposes after it outlives its original function. The walls were constructed in much the same way as those made of brick. The downside to this building material is the amount of time and labor needed to quarry, shape, and transport stone to the building site. Unlike the framing of a wooden building, mastering the art of stone masonry was not something a group of citizens could tackle on a whim and be successful.

Manufactured Blocks

The use of manufactured blocks was another way walls could be constructed with minimal effort, especially when compared to pouring concrete or handling heavy stones. In the 1930s, new machinery made it possible to produce large amounts of blocks faster and more economically than the earlier molded blocks. These modern smooth concrete blocks are commonly known these days as "concrete blocks" or "concrete masonry units." They were made from Portland cement mixed with a natural aggregate such as gravel. Other types were made using Portland cement combined with a cinder aggregate, usually coal cinders, and they are known as "cinder blocks." A few calabooses were made with blocks, but the specific type has not been identified.

Tin Siding

Covering a wooden frame with sheets of tin was an easy process. This material was available long before the early days of the twentieth century, and it became a popular choice during that time. "Yet, in many ways corrugated sheet metal is the archetypal modern material: humble, anonymous and unpretentious maybe, but cheap, strong, durable, easy to transport and erect, and recyclable. Statisticians calculate that it may have sheltered more people in the 20th century than any other building material."[2]

The Sanborn maps depict calabooses with a metal exterior over wood and refer to them as "ironclads." The maps, however, do not make a distinction between calabooses covered with iron and those covered with tin. The only calaboose discussed in this book that may be an actual ironclad is in Wallis. The commissioner's court in Wallis voted on August 12, 1908, to build a calaboose made of solid steel with only 1 cell."[3] The reference to "solid steel" probably refers to the use of sheet metal as siding on the Wallis calaboose.

Some of the wooden calabooses were falling into disrepair to such an extent that tin roofs were added. Tin siding may have been added on the walls for the same reason. Once the sheets of tin were cut to the desired size, attaching them to the walls would have been an easy process. The calaboose in Crawford was originally sided with wood, but it was replaced with tin when George W. Bush was elected president because the locals wanted a more attractive building that was sure to be seen by hordes of tourists passing through town. Examples of wooden calabooses with tin siding that may be original are those in Lorenzo (not discussed in this book) and Trenton.

Adobe

Adobe construction is sometimes referred to as earthen architecture because it is created from natural resources. As a building material, adobe is only practical in a dry environment. The use of natural raw materials such as clay, wood, and rock has been a mainstay of building construction in the arid Southwest for centuries. When properly constructed and maintained, such buildings can last for a very long time, as exemplified by the famous Casas Grandes ruins in the northern Mexican state of Chihuahua, bordering Arizona, that were made of "puddled earth" during the twelfth or thirteenth centuries; portions of these buildings are still standing. When the Spaniards arrived in the Southwest, they introduced the technique of making bricks of adobe, and this material became so commonplace that most buildings in some towns exhibit adobe construction. No calaboose made of this material is known to exist today. The fact that they were built is supported by examples depicted on certain Sanborn maps. The only standing adobe jail documented during this study is San Elizario in El Paso. It was built circa 1850 of adobe bricks and cottonwood logs around steel cellblocks. It exceeds the 300 square foot size associated with calabooses in this book.

5

Calabooses

Arp

Smith County

LOCATION: Private Property

OWNER: Paul Arnold

DATE BUILT: 1930s

SIZE: 128 square feet

Arp was a rather quiet East Texas town until the oil boom of the 1930s. The prospects for work it created brought large numbers of people to the area. Along with the influx of workers was an increase in crime. Early in the 1930s it became obvious that a jail was needed and that it should be located downtown. The city fathers authorized the construction of a new jail, and it was erected near the corner of Main and North Longview Streets in city block 22 sometime after 1931.[1] The door is in the center of this concrete structure, and it opens to a small room or vestibule that is flanked on each side by a single cell that is 57 square feet in size. The current door is a replica that the owner paid to have fabricated. The original door was wood with no window or opening of any kind.[2] The flat roof

Arp calaboose (photo courtesy of Rhonda K. Holley).

was poured with a slight pitch from front to back for water runoff. The primary source of direct light and ventilation was a small window on each side of the calaboose. The windows contained metal bars placed vertically within a wooden frame. Each cell had a small closet-like area that housed a toilet, and there was a small window that faced the vestibule. Electricity was provided for the common room or entry area but not for the cells. The only definitive information regarding the time this calaboose was used is found on the Sanborn fire insurance map that shows it in its original location in 1939.[3] Paul Arnold is the current owner of the calaboose, and he related the history of its move to his property.[4] In the early 1960s, the decision was made to demolish the Arp State Bank and build a new one on a different site that would impact the town calaboose. Before the new bank could be constructed, the old calaboose had to be demolished or moved. The first option would create an enormous pile of rubble, and that was considered undesirable. Hugh Anderson was the chairman of the board of Arp State Bank, and he came up with the idea of moving it to a different location. He was convinced that the large oil trucks could handle the job. Loys Arnold told Mr. Anderson that if they could get it onto his trucks it could be put on his son's farm approximately one and a half miles from town. They were successful, and today it, along with the old bank vault, rests in a pasture owned by Mr. Arnold.

Bartlett

Williamson County

LOCATION: Behind the Chamber of Commerce at 140 Clark Street in Bartlett

OWNER: City of Bartlett

DATE BUILT: Unknown

SIZE: 361 square feet

The entire calaboose is made of poured concrete with a flat roof. It is one of only three in the sample with three cells. This calaboose is not depicted on the Sanborn map dated 1912. Since it appears on the 1921 version,

Bartlett calaboose (photo by the author).

Entrance to one of the two rear cells at the Bartlett calaboose (photo by the author).

the date of the construction was sometime between 1912 and 1921.[5] The floor plan consists of one large cell that spans the entire length of the structure and two cells of equal size that adjoin the rear wall of the large cell. The door to the main cell is offset to the right and consists of heavy metal bars behind a solid metal door. This room has a window on each of the three exterior walls, and they have metal shutters that can be closed for extra security or to keep out bad weather. The small cells have doors that open to the outside. These cells have concrete platforms on which a mattress would have been placed for sleeping; this is one of only two calabooses in the sample with this feature. The small cells at the back may have been created with segregation by sex in mind. Amenities in the three cells include a sink and toilet, a rarity in a Texas calaboose.

An electrical fuse box is a later addition to the facade. Although electricity was readily available in town as early as 1905, it was not until 1935 that the Rural Electrification Administration loaned money to the Bartlett Community Light and Power Company to help bring power to rural areas of the county. Barbara Sandobal is a member of the local chamber of commerce, and she believes the calaboose did not have electricity until sometime in the 1930s.[6]

Joyce Jackson White is a local resident of Bartlett who remembers the jail during the war years (1941–45).[7] When she was in the fourth grade, she and some of her friends would often visit the jail to see if anyone was inside. She recalls a wooden cot in the large cell and an electric light. Sam Levins was the night watchman who enforced the law in the 1940s and 1950s. Sometime in the 1950s, Bill Brisbin patrolled the town as a police officer for the city of Bartlett. Ms. White also recalls the prisoners being fed hamburgers prepared by one of the local cafés.

Bedias

Grimes County

LOCATION: Corner of West and Main in Bedias

OWNER: Bedias Civic Club

DATE BUILT: 1920s

SIZE: 80 square feet

This one-room calaboose was originally located between the old ice house and State Highway 90 on the south side of FM 1696. It is a small wood-frame, gable-fronted building clad with rough-hewn horizontal siding held in place with wire nails. The one room floor plan has a single door in the gabled front with a small barred window to the left. There are small narrow barred horizontal windows on each subsequent side. Mackie Bobo-White is the mayor of Bedias and former co-owner of the calaboose, and she provided the following information.[8] The consensus is that it was built in the 1920s and used until the 1950s, after which time it was moved two blocks away to a site owned by the Williams family. They built a barn around the calaboose, and it remained hidden and forgotten until Mike and Mackie Bobo purchased the property. When the barn was being demolished, they were surprised to find the old calaboose inside. The Plaster family (Mackie Plaster Bobo-White, Nancy Plaster Cook, and Meredith Plaster Yarbrough) recognized its historical significance and donated it to the Bedias Civics Club, which is charged with the responsibility of maintaining it for posterity. After the discovery, it was moved to the grounds of the civic center by

Bedias calaboose (photo by the author).

some of the local town folks. The civic center is in the middle of town and only about 40 yards from the original location of the calaboose. The actual moving was primitive but effective. First, the building was hoisted and logs were placed under it. Then a tractor pulled the building very slowly while the workers continuously moved the logs that had been passed over to the front so that the building "rolled" on the logs as the tractor pulled it. McAdoo Plaster was the father of Mackie Bobo-White, and he told his daughter that this jail was used mainly as a place to lock up drunks on Saturday night, a task carried out by the local constable or sheriff.

Best

Reagan County

LOCATION: Private Property

OWNER: Unknown

DATE BUILT: 1920s

SIZE: 180 square feet

The following narrative, including the quotes, was taken from a history of Reagan County written by J. L. Werst Jr.[9] Best was an unincorporated town in southwestern Reagan County that was established in the 1920s ten miles west of Big Lake, the county seat. The growth of the town was due to the oil boom, but when oil was no longer a lucrative business the town slowly died. Now it is a ghost town with only the calaboose and one other known structure remaining. The year that the calaboose was built is not known, but it was probably there as early as 1924 when the railroad made its appearance, bringing with it temporary workers from other towns who surely contributed to the need for a lockup. The condition of this concrete structure is poor, and the walls are deteriorating due to an improper mixture of cement, water, and aggregate consisting of small pebbles. The door is missing, and all that remains of the window on the north side is a large hole caused by erosion and possibly vandalism. An electrical connection over the front door apparently provided power for a light fixture inside the door, but it is not known if that was installed when the calaboose was built. When the town was laid out, a lot for a

Best calaboose (photo courtesy of Rolland C. Reynolds Jr.).

jail was allocated. Robert J. and Margaret Kenney moved to Best in 1925 and opened a service station. Their memories of the town were of a "poor land . . . where wind, dust, greasewood, and 'gyp water' abounded. All things were said to stick, sting, or stink." They describe the calaboose as "a concrete building some ten or twelve feet square. . . . There was a door of iron bars and three small windows, one on each side, approximately fifteen or twenty inches square, with nothing but bars to keep out the heat or cold. . . . It was a pretty hot place to wake up after a night on the town." Cries of "please bring me some water" made Margaret "feel so sorry for the poor fellows she often carried over a picture of ice water."

Today, the weathered old calaboose appears even more remote and desolate then when it was being used. It is difficult to imagine spending time in such a place where temperatures have been reported as low as 29 degrees Fahrenheit in the winter and as high as 96 degrees in the hottest part of the summer. The town was portrayed in the Clyde Ragsdale novel *The Big Fist*. At the time of our visit, swallows inhabited the calaboose. They did not seem to mind the heat. Plus, they are free to come and go as they please.

Boling

Wharton County

LOCATION: Corner of Stith and Floyd in Boling

OWNER: City of Boling

DATE BUILT: Unknown

SIZE: 256 square feet

The arrival of the New York, Texas and Mexican Railway in 1900 was the catalyst for the creation of Boling. Sulfur, oil, and gas were discovered at Boling Dome in 1925, and the town experienced rapid growth. The population was only twenty in 1920 but by 1930 it had increased to 450.[10] It is a reasonable assumption that the boom of the 1920s was a major factor in the decision to build a calaboose. This concrete calaboose is in a residential neighborhood where it is subject to vandalism. The floor plan is an open room across the front facing two small cells that are equal in size. At the time of my visit, the door was missing. The wall between the

Boling calaboose (photo courtesy of A. C. Shelton).

Chimney for heater in the Boling calaboose (photo courtesy of A. C. Shelton).

cells and the entry room is concrete. The doors are metal and secured with vertical round bars strengthened with pieces of flat metal. The lock plate is a solid piece of metal with a hasp. The floor and flat roof are also concrete. This blocky structure contains a decorative treatment that consists of two courses of brick around the roof that created a modest parapet with a small arch in the center as a form of embellishment. The six barred windows are square in plan and equal in size. Two are on the sides of the entry room, and the other four are on the sides and back of the two cells. A brick chimney for a fireplace still stands in the corner of the main room, which probably served as an office for law enforcement officers. This is the only calaboose in the current sample with a feature like this. When the cells were crowded with prisoners, the main room could also have been used for incarceration or to give the prisoners more room to get some exercise by walking around in a larger area. At the time of my visit, it was being used as a most unusual doghouse. There was no Sanborn map for Boling at the time of this project.

Brownfield

Terry County

LOCATION: Terry County Heritage Museum at 600 East Cardwell Street in Brownfield

OWNER: Terry County Heritage Museum

DATE BUILT: Early 1900s

SIZE: 280 square feet

Part of the following was made possible by a discussion with Jane Blay of the Terry County Heritage Museum.[11] She said that this structure was the first jail in the county. In 1925, a new lockup was built on the second floor of the new courthouse, and this calaboose was no longer needed. The last owner returned it to the county, and today it can be viewed at the Terry County Heritage Museum. This building was constructed by attaching wooden siding to vertical supports, much like a typical house. The door is in the center and made of metal with flat bars arranged in a crisscross pattern, which allows light and ventilation into the interior. The windows are larger than most calabooses in the present book. The roof

Brownfield calaboose (photo courtesy of Rolland C. Reynolds Jr.).

is of the hip style and is currently covered with wooden shingles. This one-room structure was originally located on the northwest corner of the courthouse square. The interior contains a metal cage with two cells that was probably ordered from one of the major manufacturers of jails and cells. On entering the jail, there is very little room on the sides and back as the cell dominates the interior. The current condition of this structure is poor, but the city has plans to restore it to its original condition.

Burlington

Milam County

LOCATION: Behind City Hall in Rockdale at 505 West Cameron Avenue

OWNER: City of Rockdale

DATE BUILT: Circa 1910

SIZE: 72 square feet

The town was named Irish Settlement and Waterford before being changed in 1899 to Burlington, after the town of the same name in Vermont. The name change was the result of the efforts of the first postmaster, who moved to Texas from Burlington, Vermont. Growth was mainly due to the arrival of the San Antonio and Aransas Pass Railway, which first passed through town in 1891. The population of Burlington was at its zenith about 1914 when there were six hundred residents.[12] The original location of this calaboose was in downtown Burlington near Church Street. It was later moved to private property next to the post office at 14 Church Avenue. Billy and Frances Prescott donated it to the city of Rockdale, where it will rest permanently at the site of the new Rockdale police station. This move was made possible by the efforts of Zach Reeves (director of the Rockdale Public Works Department), Chris Whittaker, and many others. At the time of this negotiation, this wooden calaboose was leaning drastically and in danger of collapse. Its location in a small town also made it an ideal target for vandalism. Its exact age is not known, but the consensus is that it was constructed circa 1910. Its dimensions are 12 feet across the front and 8 feet on the sides. The distance from the ground to the roof is only 7 feet. The two windows are on the front and back walls. The bars were made locally of flat iron and are attached to the wall with bolts. The floor was dirt, and the flat roof consisted of wooden boards covered with tin. The boards are nailed to vertical beams with wire nails and average 9 inches in width. Leo Helpert was a native of Burlington, and his memories of this calaboose were during the period 1936–38 when he was in elementary school.[13] He said the original site of the calaboose was on Church Street, and there were two saloons nearby. Helpert said that it was not uncommon to see prisoners in the jail on Sunday morning after too much drinking or fighting the night before. When there was not enough room for everyone, some prisoners were shackled to trees. He also said that most of the offenders were seasonal workers hired to pick cotton and other similar tasks. The old cotton gin still stands, albeit in disrepair. Gene Klein is the fire chief of the Burlington Volunteer Fire Department, and he reported that Burlington boasted eight saloons during its heyday. Constable Carl Marberger oversaw law and order during those days. Much of Texas did not allow the sale of alcohol in the early days of the twentieth century. Mr. Klein recalled that it was a common event to see loads of passengers disembark from a train that left Fort Worth, where they had gone so that they could drink legally.[14] There are two historic photos of the calaboose in the Burlington Volunteer Fire Department archives. One is an aerial view taken in 1928 (not pictured here) that shows the building

Burlington calaboose in original location (photo courtesy of Jack Brooks).

Burlington calaboose not in original location (photo courtesy of Gene Klein).

in its original location. Virtually all the buildings in this photo have been demolished. The other photo was taken in the 1970s at its 1910 location. The photo reproduced here is used courtesy of Gene Klein. This calaboose has been moved to Rockdale, where it has been restored for future generations to view.[15]

Caldwell

Burleson County

LOCATION: 200 block of South Hill Street behind the old fire station in Caldwell

OWNER: City of Caldwell

DATE BUILT: 1935

SIZE: 187 square feet

This city constructed this calaboose in 1935. According to the *Caldwell News and Burleson County Ledger*, "The jail will cost approximately $200. Old lumber from the old fire station is being used to construct the forms for the concrete." It was made of "concrete throughout with heavy reinforcement of steel."[16] It measures 23 1/4 feet across the front and 8 feet on the sides. The floor plan consists of a rectangular structure with three rooms. There is a common room or vestibule in the center that was probably used by law enforcement officers and possibly as a holding area when the cells were full. The two end rooms are cells. Each one had a toilet, sink, and two metal bed frames arranged in bunk bed fashion. The two metal pipes extending from the roof above the cells served as a source of ventilation for a stove in the middle room; the only source of light was a single fixture in this room. The entry door is solid metal with a window that allowed law enforcement officers to view the interior without unlocking the door. The bars in the window are arranged in a circular pattern that allowed someone to poke their head inside and look to the right and left as well as straight ahead. A similar window is in one of the doors in the jail in Jayton, Texas. A solid metal door is positioned in front of the window so that when closed there would be no possibility of looking through the window. Louis Hudson was a student at Texas A&M University in 1940. One night as he was walking across the courthouse lawn on his way to

Caldwell calaboose (photo by the author).

catch a ride to College Station, he was arrested and put in the Caldwell calaboose. The next morning, he was asked if he had any money in his possession, and when he gave up eight dollars and some change he was released and driven to the depot where he caught a train to the university.[17] Graffiti on the cell walls of the current calaboose are dated 1960, 1972, and 1978. It is not known if the graffiti was created by prisoners or vandals after the calaboose was no longer in use. Visitors to Caldwell can also view the Classical Revival courthouse constructed in 1927.[18]

Cameron

Milam County

LOCATION: Corner of East Main and South Fannin across from the county courthouse in Cameron

OWNER: City of Cameron

DATE BUILT: 1892

SIZE: 200 square feet

The first jail in Cameron was a log cabin built over a dungeon.[19] Unfortunately, little information is available regarding the size and date it was constructed. The first formal county jail in Cameron was designed by architects Larmour and Klerke and constructed by Jackson and Arnold in 1875. The Pauly Jail Manufacturing Company provided the metal cells and door.[20] The first Sanborn map for Cameron was published in 1885, and it depicts this two-story brick jail at the corner of Belton and Edwards Streets in city block 11.[21] By 1893, it was considered obsolete, and it was replaced by a new three-story county jail in 1895. The calaboose discussed here was built in 1892 by the firm Westmoreland and

Cameron calaboose (photo by the author).

Mullinax for $262.50.[22] A likely scenario for the construction of the calaboose is that it provided much-needed additional space for prisoners while the new jail was being built. This is a one-story wood structure that occupies a footprint of 10 feet by 20 feet and reaches a height of 12 feet. The four-inch-thick wooden walls were formed by the placement of 2-inch by 4-inch timbers laid flat on top of each other, and the floor is of similar construction. It is rectangular in plan, and the door at each end allows access to the two individual cells. There are two windows, one for each cell, and they have two sets of iron bars. Twelve round bars are built into the facing of the window, and nine flat bars are attached on the inside. Wooden shutters were added to the outside to keep out the rain, and they could be lowered and locked with iron bars as an added method of security. Its original location is not known, and it does not appear on any of the Sanborn maps through 1931. The US Census does not list any prisoners in the Cameron calaboose as of January 1, 1910. Eight prisoners were committed in 1910. Six were white and two were African Americans.[23] Visitors to Cameron can also view the Renaissance Revival courthouse made of stone in 1892[24] and the 1895 county jail.

Camp Wood

Real County

LOCATION: Behind City Hall at
105 West Fourth Street in Camp Wood

OWNER: City of Camp Wood

DATE BUILT: 1928

SIZE: 162 square feet

A Real County Centennial marker on the front of the calaboose states: "In August of 1928, the Real County Commissioners' Court ordered that A. G. Wells, be authorized to enter into Contract with P. Northcutt and Less Allen to build one Concrete Calaboose at Camp Wood, Texas, at a cost of $635.00."[25] Eighteen episodes of pouring concrete were needed to construct the slab, walls, and flat roof. The aggregate used to add stability to the concrete was small pebbles. No sign of rebar was observed. This calaboose has a floor plan of three rooms. The front room spans the entire

Camp Wood calaboose (photo courtesy of Darryl Pearson).

width of the structure. This area was used by law enforcement as an office and for other administrative duties. No furniture was present but a water faucet extends upward through the slab at the front of the room. There is only one door to the outside and it consists of two parts. A solid wooden door covers the metal door with bars, presumably to be shut during cold or rainy weather. There are two barred windows of equal size on each side of the door and two windows on the back wall that are centered on the two cells located behind the entry room. When the outer door is closed, these four windows are the only source of ventilation and light. The four windows are equal in size and they measure 12 by 27 inches. The two cells are equal in size and are entered through solid metal doors. A window with metal bars above each cell door provided light from the main room and allowed law enforcement officers to hear any suspicious sounds from within the cells. There are two metal pipes on the back wall that protrude from the top above each window at a 90-degree angle. Their function is not known. The walls of the cells are decorated with graffiti left behind by former prisoners. The two most legible dates are "Oct. 2/35" and "May 31, 1941." Jack Lockhart was one of the members of the construction crew.

He used his wages to purchase moonshine and, thus, had the honor of being the first prisoner in the calaboose he helped build.[26] A prisoner who had escaped from jail in Brackettville, Texas, told his girlfriend who was visiting him that no man could escape from this "stalwart little building."[27]

Carbon

Eastland County

LOCATION: Private Property

OWNER: Unknown

DATE BUILT: circa 1919–21

SIZE: 79 square feet

Madge Burgess is a longtime resident of Carbon and former owner of the structure; she related some of the history told here.[28] She said that the first jail in town was constructed in 1905 and made of wood. It was destroyed during a jailbreak when the brothers of a prisoner tied a rope to the building and pulled a wall down. This calaboose was its replacement and was built of poured concrete sometime between 1919 and 1921. It was a primitive facility with no restroom, lights, or heater. On the rear wall is a heavy metal ring that could have been used to shackle prisoners. There are no windows, and the only source of light and ventilation is a row of three metal pipes on each side. A most unusual feature of this jail is the presence of a cast iron, nonstructural pediment above the door. Architects describe this type of feature as a "broken" or "open" pediment because the two decorative elements on each side do not connect. Instead, there is a space in the middle that contains a relief sculpture of the head of a lion on a vase that is typical of classical, neoclassical, and baroque architecture. The use of cast iron as a decorative element on a concrete structure seems incongruous at best, and its origin is not known. It bears a strong resemblance to those that adorn bank vaults. Don L. May moved to Carbon as a boy with his family in 1936 and they stayed there until 1942.[29] He lived about three blocks from the calaboose and never saw anyone in the jail. During that time prisoners were taken to the county jail in Eastland. The old door was always open, and May and his friends often played inside and around the old 'boose. He remembers evidence of fires that he believes were used by hobos and transients who used it for

Carbon calaboose (photo courtesy of Roger G. Moore).

shelter. Mr. May believes the calaboose was constructed during the oil boom in Eastland County that occurred around 1919. He said that there was an influx of some pretty rough people looking for work, and a lockup was badly needed. There are no documents that confirm either date. Mrs. Burgess recalled that during the war years, it was used as a place to store papers and other items that were collected for the war effort. She also said that the original door is missing, and the current door is a reproduction.

Castroville

Medina County

LOCATION: On the west side of the Medina County Emergency Services building at 800 Madrid Street in Castroville

OWNER: City of Castroville

DATE BUILT: 1920s

SIZE: 152 square feet

Castroville calaboose (photo courtesy of Darryl Pearson).

This calaboose is owned by the city, and informants at city hall said it was built sometime in the 1920s.[30] It has two cells of equal size that are secured by iron doors with windows that could have been used to feed or view the prisoners inside. This calaboose is unique in that the windows on the doors are not the same size or located in the same part of the door. Most of the wall that separated the cells was removed so that the entire space could be used for storage. The window on the northeast side was removed, and a new door was added as the new access point. "Medina County, Flammable Product Storage Area" is written on the door facing. This calaboose is made of large bricks that closely resemble some of the types made by the factory at D'Hanis. The flat roof has a slight pitch from front to back. The height at the front is 9 feet and 7 inches, and the height at the back is 8 feet and 5 inches. Also, the roof extends outward from all four walls about 12 inches. The front doors were welded shut at the time of my visit. The only access is through the door on the northeast side. The door to the left is 30 inches wide by 6 feet and 10 inches high and flush with the face of the building. The window in the center of the door measures 11 inches wide by 15 inches high. The door on the right is recessed into the front of the building about 4 1/2 inches. It measures 32 inches wide by 8 feet high. This is only the second calaboose in the current sample with doors that are not equal in size. The other is in Quemado. The only surviving window is on the northwest side, but the metal bars are missing. It appears that part of the opening for the window was closed in at some point, but this has not been confirmed. Most of these calabooses with two cells are symmetrical in terms of placement of doors and windows.

Chillicothe

Hardeman County

LOCATION: Private Property

OWNER: Unknown

DATE BUILT: Post-1921

SIZE: 194 square feet

Entry to this concrete calaboose is through a door to the right of center. What appears to be the original entry door was lying on the ground, where it will slowly deteriorate and become unrecognizable. The facade features columns on the corners that create the appearance of a recessed wall. The

Chillicothe calaboose (photo courtesy of Celeste Littlecreek).

View of parapet on the Chillicothe calaboose (photo courtesy of Celeste Littlecreek).

walls rise above the roof to form a parapet on three sides that contains coping as a decorative element. The floor plan consists of a vestibule that spans the length of the structure. Behind it are two cells with metal bars and doors. The cell doors are attached to vertical panels of concrete. The interior of the cells was littered with trash and modern graffiti. There is a small metal plate on the door that has tiny perforations, the likes of which have not been seen on any of the other calabooses in the current sample. Each cell has one window for ventilation and light that is centered on the sides of the building. The walls are coated or rendered with a coat of cement stucco. There is a metal flue on the front wall that connected to a heater on the inside. The date this structure was built is not known, but it would have been constructed sometime after 1921 because the Sanborn map for that year shows a one-story brick jail at that site in 1921.[31] An interesting side note is that I first noticed a small structure that I mistook for the calaboose. While examining it, I saw the real one in the background. The other building was a bank vault, and it is the one that alerted me to the fact that many old vaults are still standing.

Clifton

Bosque County

LOCATION: 120 Clifton Art Alley

OWNER: Kaye Callaway

DATE BUILT: Unknown

SIZE: 363 square feet

This concrete calaboose is in an alley and not visible from the main street. It contains three rooms that occupy a footprint of 363 square feet and is the second largest in the current sample. Fifteen episodes of pouring concrete were required to create the walls, and an additional two episodes resulted in a slab 10 1/2 inches thick. The flat roof was the final phase of construction using concrete poured into a wooden form. A metal threshold is attached to the entry beneath the door. The wall covers part of the threshold, and only the letters "——LTON" are visible. The single door

Clifton calaboose (photo courtesy of Roger G. Moore).

Interior of Clifton calaboose (photo courtesy of Roger G. Moore).

Cell Block (photo by the author).

is on the west wall and made of solid metal with no window. This door is offset to the left and opens to a common area that was used by law enforcement officers. It parallels the two cells that occupy the south end of the structure. At one time, this room had electricity, as evidenced by an antiquated fuse box on the north wall. Each cell was furnished with a metal bed frame, concrete platform for a toilet, and metal brace for a sink. The sinks drained to the outside, and the pipes were still present. Each cell has a window on the side and back walls, and the main room also has two windows. The windows that provide light to the entry room are larger than those for the cells. At one time, this calaboose had the only public telephone in town. Mary Orbeck of Clifton related the following story about a young lady named Dorothy who was eight months pregnant when she arrived on the train from Maryland to Clifton to visit family:[32] There was nobody at the station to meet her so the local night watchman took her to the jail so she could use the phone. When she told her friend that she was calling from the jail, her friend thought that she had been locked up and she was very upset. Fortunately, she was talking on a party line, and one of the ladies on the line interrupted the conversation and told her friend that she was calling from the jail because it was the only place in town with a phone. Jerry Hill said that the jail was still being used in the 1970s when he was constable, and the main room was often used by locals as a place to play dominoes.[33] The current owner was concerned about the future of this old jail, which she remembered as a youngster, and she decided to purchase it and turn it into something special and keep it as original as possible.[34] The result is a very upscale room for rent called the Cell Block. The cells remain in place, and it has been very well restored, including a deck on the roof for relaxing under the stars.

Comfort

Kendall County

LOCATION: Adjacent to the city water tower at Main and Seventh Streets in Comfort

OWNER: City of Comfort

DATE BUILT: Unknown

SIZE: 99 square feet

Comfort calaboose (photo courtesy of Rhonda K. Holley).

This brick calaboose is covered with a veneer of plaster. It consists of two cells of equal size arranged side by side. Each cell has three windows. The bars in the windows were made from rebar inserted into a wooden frame. The doors are solid steel with no windows or vents. They appear to be original, but this has not been confirmed. The flat roof is probably made of poured concrete and has a slight overhang on all sides. The height from the ground to the top is 8 feet. Entry is not permitted due to the presence of canisters of chlorine gas inside. One of the windows on the front has been altered to prevent the escape of gas from the inside. An unusual feature of this calaboose is the border around the walls and doors. This is the only calaboose in the current sample with this treatment, at least to this extent. Carmen M. Hernandez is a native of Comfort; she remembers seeing drunks spending the night in the calaboose until they were released the next day or transported to the county jail in Boerne.[35] There were no Sanborn maps available for Comfort at the time of this study.

Crandall

Kaufman County

LOCATION: Private Property

OWNER: Privately Owned

DATE BUILT: Unknown

SIZE: 69 square feet

Crandall developed along the Texas Trunk Line Railway that passed through town in 1880. The right-of-way for the railroad was donated by C. F. Crandall, and the community was named in his honor. The highest number of recorded residents was 750 in the middle of the 1920s. The local economy was largely dependent on cotton and the local gristmill.[36] This tiny brick calaboose is the smallest freestanding calaboose in the current sample. The flat roof with wooden trim and corrugated tin is also unique. The floor is concrete, and there was no plumbing or electricity.

Crandall calaboose (photo by the author).

The only window is on the rear wall. It is small and measures 14 by 18 inches. Between the opening on the door and the window very little air flow and light is possible. The door is wood with metal bars and is unlike any of the other calaboose doors I have seen. The lock was made by Collie Fastener Company with a patent date of 1912. There is additional writing, but it was obscured by a thick coat of paint.

Crawford

McLennan County

LOCATION: 6688 North Lone Star Parkway behind Security Bank in Crawford

OWNER: City of Crawford

DATE BUILT: Unknown

SIZE: 171 square feet

Crawford calaboose (photo by the author).

The community moved two miles to the west in 1881 to be near the Gulf, Colorado and Santa Fe Railway. Because of the railroad, shipping became a major source of income and jobs, along with cotton, corn, and wheat production. In 1910, the population rose to six hundred supported by thirty-five businesses.[37] Raydean Damon, Margie Thomas,[38] and Earl Booker[39] are residents of Crawford, and they provided the following information. The original location of this calaboose was across the railroad tracks near the current grain silos and outside the city limits. It was a wooden one-room structure that housed a metal cage containing two cells resting on a concrete slab that was put in place before the wooden structure was constructed. A metal plaque on one of the cells states that they were built by the Pauly Jail Building Company of Saint Louis, Missouri, a firm that is still in business. Each cell has two metal bed frames on opposite sides of the center wall. The two windows on the back wall have metal hinges that may have supported shutters. It is not known if other windows were once present. The door is offset to the left and appears to be a replacement. It was moved to its current location around 1999. The wooden siding was removed and replaced with the tin that is present today.

D'Hanis

Medina County

LOCATION: Private Property

OWNER: Privately Owned

DATE BUILT: Circa 1907

SIZE: 200 square feet

The D'Hanis Brick and Tile Company was founded in 1883 and used local clay to produce its early handmade bricks. In 1905, kiln-fired bricks were being produced in D'Hanis. T. Lindsay Baker's book, *Building the Lone Star*, discusses civil engineering marvels around Texas and contains examples of structures made with D'Hanis brick.[40] The exterior walls, floor, and partition between the two cells were made of this brick. On the rear wall rows of milled lumber were fastened to wooden supports with wire nails and bolts. W. H. Hearne was the constable in 1907, and he told a newspaper reporter that a subscription list was being circulated in

D'Hanis calaboose (photo courtesy of Darryl Pearson).

D'Hanis for erecting a calaboose.[41] The article also said that "Mr. Hearne has been 'making it hot' for lawbreakers at D'Hanis and as a reward the law-abiding citizens of that town will build him a 'cooler.'" Unfortunately, this wonderful building was virtually destroyed by a tornado on October 30, 2015. The following information was collected while it was still standing. The roof was a wooden frame covered with tin and slanted at a rather steep angle from front to back. The two doors were equal in size, and each had a small window in its approximate center that contained three circular metal bars placed vertically within the doorframe. One of the bars was missing from the door to the left. The other door is a replica created by Pat McGraw of D'Hanis, who used modern rebar to simulate the bars found in the other door.[42] Ventilation and light were provided by two windows centered on the back wall behind each cell. The windows were held in place by a wooden frame, and security was provided by metal bars. The interior was in poor condition. Virtually the entire brick wall between the two cells had collapsed, and the brick floor was nonexistent. John J. McGraw was the constable responsible for putting the bad guys in the D'Hanis calaboose.[43] He defeated E. L. Brod by a narrow margin in 1942 and became the constable, JP, for precinct 4.[44] His son, Pat McGraw, said that there was a saloon on Front Street. He remembers being told that it was not unusual for Sunday morning passersby to hear the voices of men who had been arrested the night before for minor offenses such as drinking too much or fighting.[45] Pat also stated that the windows were not that securely attached, and there was an incident where two prisoners pushed out one of the windows and escaped. They were later caught. The owners are considering restoring it to its original appearance as closely as possible.

D'Hanis calaboose after tornado (photo courtesy of Dottie and Ray Wolff).

Deport

Lamar County

LOCATION: 100 block of Monroe Street in Deport

OWNER: City of Deport

DATE BUILT: Unknown

SIZE: 100 square feet

Thomas and Nanalee Nichols are the owners of the *Deport Times*, and they were the source for most of the information regarding the history of this calaboose.[46] They believe it was built in 1937 when the town was incorporated. Originally, it was in another part of town, but the Deport Community Service Club hired a house mover in the 1980s to transport it to its current location. During the move, some restoration was done to the roof, exterior siding was replaced in some areas, and the building was placed on a cement slab. In its original location, it sat on logs. A feature unique to this jail is the presence of a metal pipe in the wall that was reportedly used as a urinal. At the time the jail was in use, the pipe was tilted upward and

Deport calaboose (photo courtesy of Lawrence DeVoto).

passed through the wall to the outside for drainage. New siding was placed on the outside and covered the drain hole. The pipe is in the original hole on the inside. This jail was constructed using two-by-four boards laid flat on top of each other to form a strong 4-inch-wide wall. These boards were covered with shiplap siding. The jail is equidistant on all sides, and this has resulted in a pyramidal or square hip roof covering an area of 100 square feet. These types of roofs slope downward to the walls on all sides, usually with a gentle slope. Buildings with this roof type have no gables or other vertical sides. There is a small window with bars in the door. Additional small windows are present on the sides, but there is no window on the back wall. The roof is metal, and the floor in the jail before it was moved was dirt. There were no Sanborn maps at the agencies visited for Deport, Texas, at the time of this study.

Desdemona

Eastland County

LOCATION: Private Property

OWNER: Privately Owned

DATE BUILT: Unknown

SIZE: 111 square feet

Desdemona was first referred to as Hogtown because of its proximity to Hog Creek, but later the name was changed to Desdemona after the daughter of an area justice of the peace. During the latter part of the nineteenth century and early part of the twentieth century, the economy was based largely on agriculture, with peanuts being the major cash crop. Everything changed in 1918 when the Hog Creek Oil Company struck oil. The town immediately boomed, and an estimated sixteen thousand people rushed to the area between 1919 and 1922.[47] Desdemona was a lawless town during that period with at least four gambling parlors; prostitutes were available at the Lone Star Hotel on Main Street. The first lockup had been overturned by an angry mob during the riot of 1919, and the need for a more substantial jail was obvious. The current one was erected sometime following the riot.[48] The jail standing today was made from brick manufactured by the Green and Hunter Brick Company of Thurber, Texas. This enterprise

Desdemona calaboose (photo courtesy of Lawrence DeVoto).

began in the late 1890s under the leadership of Colonel Robert Hunter and mining superintendent W. K. Gordon, and the company was one of the leaders in terms of numbers of bricks produced at the time.[49]

Some of the streets in the Eastland county seat are paved with Thurber brick, and it was probably a logical decision to use the same brick to build the local jail. Being incarcerated in the Desdemona calaboose must have been an awful experience. The only source of light and ventilation was through six vertical slits in the door and eight horizontal slits in the single small window. The door is atypical in that it is made in two pieces that open outward. Today, Desdemona is a virtual ghost town with only a few businesses still in operation. There were no Sanborn maps at the agencies visited for Desdemona, Texas, at the time of this study.

East Bernard

Wharton County

LOCATION: Southeast corner of Ray and Wallace Streets across the railroad tracks from Main Street (a.k.a. Alternate Highway 90) in East Bernard

OWNER: City of East Bernard

DATE BUILT: Unknown

SIZE: 175 square feet

East Bernard is a town that developed because of the arrival of the Buffalo Bayou, Brazos and Colorado Railway in 1859.[50] It was named for its original location on the east bank of the San Bernard River. The local economy was based on agriculture, and its population was made up largely of German and Slavic immigrants who began settling there in the latter part of the nineteenth century. Towns with close ties to the railroad often

East Bernard calaboose (photo courtesy of A. C. Shelton).

Bed in East Bernard calaboose (photo courtesy of A. C. Shelton).

attracted migrant workers and other transients. Therefore, some place of incarceration was an unfortunate necessity. The brick calaboose discussed here conforms to one of the more common floor plans identified during this study, two cells of equal size, side by side with separate doors. The doors consist of two parts, a wooden door on the interior and a metal door with bars on the outside. There are two windows for each cell, one on the side and the other on the back. They are like the doors in that there is a wooden double-hung window framed into the wall; metal bars are affixed to the outside for security. Sleeping accommodations were provided by metal frames across the back of each cell that served as platforms for mattresses. This is the only calaboose in the current sample with a bed fastened to a brick wall. A brief attempt at restoration was performed circa 2000 by a local Boy Scout who replaced the roof as part of an Eagle Scout project.[51] There were no Sanborn maps at the agencies visited for East Bernard at the time of this study.

Eden

Concho County

LOCATION: In an alley behind city hall located at 120 Paint Rock Street in Eden

OWNER: City of Eden

DATE BUILT: Unknown

SIZE: 225 square feet

This concrete calaboose faces south. It is one of three in the current sample with three cells, and the only one less than 300 square feet in size. The facade is embellished with two elaborate metal doors side by side that allow entry into two rooms. The room on the right extends from the door to the rear wall and measures approximately 7 by 15 feet. The door to the left opens to a room that is the same width but is half the size of the large room on the right. This is because the left side of the calaboose contains two cells of equal size. Entry to the rear cell is through a solid metal door on the wall between the cells. This is the only calaboose that has been documented with this floor plan. Light and ventilation was made possible by two windows on each of the side walls. The larger cell has two windows

Eden calaboose (photo by the author).

while the two small cells have one each. The windows are secured with metal bars and an exterior metal shutter that can be closed to keep out rain. Each cell had a toilet, and all three are along the same wall that was created by building a wooden frame and covering it with metal screen and stucco. This was done to make the installation of the plumbing easier. In addition, a concrete platform for a mattress was constructed along one of the walls in each of the three cells. The only other calaboose that has similar bed platforms is the one in Bartlett, also a structure with three cells. The doors were manufactured by Aetna Iron Works of Quincy, Illinois. Later modifications to the doors are horizontal slits that were cut through the metal to allow minimal air flow and light. The top and middle hinge on the right door appear to be factory originals. A possible attempt to change out the middle and bottom hinges is demonstrated by broken hinges that were attached by the process known as "running a bead." The door on the right has been personalized with the addition of the word "SLIM" and the date 10-8-45. A possible scenario involving these doors is that they were recycled from another building and were never intended for use on a jail. Perhaps "Slim" was responsible for the alterations in 1945. Other oddities

Toilet in Eden calaboose (photo by the author).

Manufacturer's plaque on the Eden calaboose (photo by the author).

are: the doors are not equal in width and the lintel above the larger door is bent. This suggests that the damage occurred before it was installed at this calaboose. Electricity was present at one time, but it may not have been part of the original design. Metal pipes run through the building and exit on the west wall. Apparently, a heater was once present, but this appears to be a later modification as well. Lines in the ceiling show that the forms for the concrete were placed at right angles to the general floor plan and that metal rebar was used. Steel I beams crisscross the ceiling for support. This is another feature that has not been observed in other calabooses. Perhaps the most unusual feature of this structure is the presence of terra cotta tiles on the rear wall that were covered with a hard substance that resembles plaster. The span of time that this calaboose served the town is not known, but the method of poured-in-place concrete construction began sometime in the early part of the twentieth century, and there are two dates associated with this structure. Modifications to the doors, and possibly the rest of the building, may have taken place in 1945, and graffiti dated 1950 shows that it continued to be used for another five years after the renovations. Unfortunately, the walls were covered with stucco or plaster and painted, and most of the graffiti is illegible. At the time of my visit, the structure was being used for storage.

Fayetteville

Fayette County

LOCATION: Fayetteville Heritage Museum at 117 North Washington Street in Fayetteville

OWNER: City of Fayetteville

DATE BUILT: 1887

SIZE: 96 square feet

This is another fine example of a well-preserved wooden calaboose that will last a very long time because it is inside a building where it is protected from the weather. Some of the following information was obtained through a personal interview with Liz Cubage, vice president of the Fayetteville Chamber of Commerce.[52] The calaboose is located inside the only example of a precinct courthouse in Texas with a four-sided Seth

Fayetteville calaboose (photo courtesy of Rolland C. Reynolds Jr.).

Leg irons in Fayetteville calaboose (photo courtesy of Rolland C. Reynolds Jr.).

Bed in Fayetteville calaboose (photo courtesy of Rolland C. Reynolds Jr.).

Thomas clock that keeps time. This impressive Greek Revival structure was built in the 1880s and served precinct 2 in Fayetteville. In 1887, the calaboose was constructed on the second floor. The cost, a meager $11 by today's standards. It was made using milled lumber attached vertically to the frame. It has double walls that probably were designed for stability and security. The wood used in its construction appears to be cedar. A higher level of security was provided by a chain attached to the floor with leg irons to keep prisoners from being able to move about; they are still in the calaboose. This is also the only example in this book of exterior vertical boards over horizontal milled boards. The facade is different from any other calaboose in the current sample in that both windows are to the left of the doors. Additional windows of the same size and design are on the sides as well. These windows are larger than average, and that translates to better ventilation and natural light. Another anomaly involves the window design. In contrast to many of the other calabooses encountered during this project, the six windows are not all equal in size, although the difference is never more than 2 inches at their width. Each window is secured by three metal bars spaced equally apart and housed in a metal frame. However, some of the windows have round or circular bars and others have bars that are angular in shape. The cells had wooden platforms to support mattresses for sleeping. There is nothing elaborate about this structure, but it appears to be well made. The calaboose and courthouse as well as information about the town of Fayetteville can be found in an article by Wayne Stewart in *Texas Farm and Home*.[53]

Flatonia

Fayette County

LOCATION: Rail Park at 114 East South Main in Flatonia

OWNER: City of Flatonia

DATE BUILT: 1890

SIZE: 236 square feet

The exterior of this wood calaboose consists of a facade with two doors, two windows, and a sign that reads "Old City Jail of Flatonia" centered above the doors. The exterior walls were constructed using milled boards and battens attached vertically to the wooden frame with wire nails. The resulting effect is described as the board and batten method of construc-

Flatonia calaboose (photo courtesy of Judy Pate).

Graffiti in Flatonia calaboose dated March 9, 1916 (photo courtesy of Judy Pate).

tion. The gable roof is covered with tin that may not be original to the structure. Four very tall narrow windows are secured with metal bars; two are on the front and two on the back. There are two cells of equal size, each with its own door that opens to the outside. Each door has a small barred window. The iron bars and hasps on the doors appear to be hand wrought. The interior walls consist of wooden boards attached horizontally to the frame, also with wire nails. The resulting double wall added strength to the structure and would have made escape more difficult. The wall separating the two cells was constructed like the exterior walls but was never painted. The vertical battens on the cell walls are adorned with copious examples of graffiti that bear the dates 1900, 1901, 1902, 1903, 1904, 1916, 1948, and 1953. Judy Pate is the director of the E. A. Arnim Museum in town. She said that there are numerous nail holes in the other interior walls that suggest vertical boards, possibly with more graffiti, have been removed.[54]

Construction of this calaboose was the subject of several articles in the local newspaper. “The new calaboose is beginning to loom up and will soon be finished.”[55] “The new hotel Jamison is finished and ready to receive boarders. In comparison with the old one, it looks quite inviting.”[56] “Mr. Jamison took charge as marshal on last Thursday, and can be seen, accompanied by his deputies, Toad and Mingo, perambulating our streets.”[57] It was referred to as the “Hotel Jamison” because Mr. Jamison was the marshal at the time. The Sanborn map dated 1891 depicts this calaboose in an alley between South Main and Sixth Streets.[58] It was in city block 49 and city lot 10. City hall and the Masonic Hall were in the southeast corner of the same block at 505 Market Street. A wooden lockup is depicted on the 1912 Sanborn map in the same location, but it was not unusual for mappers to refer to calabooses by other names at different times.[59] On May 9, 1950, local citizens presented the city commissioner with a petition asking that the jail be moved. They complained that it was a fire hazard, inmates disturbed the peace, it did not have proper sanitary facilities, and it was too far from the night watchman’s station.[60] On June 13, 1950, the city commissioners voted to move it to block 51, lot 18, in the City Addition, but it was not moved until 1952.[61] In 1984, it was relocated to its current home at Railroad Park.

Florence

Williamson County

LOCATION: 304 East Main behind the Florence Police Department

OWNER: City of Florence

DATE BUILT: Unknown

SIZE: 85 square feet

Following the Civil War, cattle became a major part of the local economy along with wheat and cotton. Growth was due in large part to the Bartlett and Western Railway, which served the town from 1912 until 1935. The population reached its peak in 1927 when there were one thousand recorded residents.[62] This structure is one of the smallest in terms of square feet in the current sample. The police department found it useful as a storage building. It has been painted but the lines marking the episodes of

Florence calaboose (photo courtesy of Darryl Pearson).

Curved bars on window of Florence calaboose (photo courtesy of Darryl Pearson).

poured concrete are still visible. The current door is a replacement. This is a one-room calaboose with no furniture present at the time of my visit. The only window is at the back and centered behind the door. The bars are curved inward; this is the only calaboose in the current sample with such bars. There were no Sanborn maps at the agencies visited for Florence at the time of this study.

Fort Griffin

Shackelford County

LOCATION: Private Property

OWNER: Privately Owned

DATE BUILT: 1878

SIZE: 118 1/2 square feet

The military fort was established in 1867 to protect settlers from hostile Indians. Soon after construction of the fort was completed a new town appeared. The town of Fort Griffin was often referred to as "Griffin" to

Fort Griffin calaboose (photo courtesy of Julie Elrod).

Fort Griffin calaboose in original location (photo courtesy of Jane Lenoir).

distinguish it from the fort, and it was also called "The Flats" because of its topographical position below the imposing hill where the fort stood.[63] The "Fort Griffin Civil Jail" was constructed in 1878 in the Veal's Addition on Griffin Avenue.[64] J. M. Cupp and Brother was awarded the contract, and the cost to the community was $150.[65] A man named Douglas was the stonemason, and he was also the first person to be held in the jail he helped build.[66] Prior to the construction of the calaboose, offenders from town were locked up in the post guard house of the fort.[67] The town was known as a lawless frontier town, and the little building often held the likes of gamblers, trail drivers, buffalo hunters, and mule skinners. It is reported that as many as eighteen men at one time spent a night there.[68] In 1881, the flag was lowered on the fort, and most of the businesses in town moved to Albany. During that time, the little jail served as a shed for cows.[69] The only photo of this calaboose before its move to Albany was taken in the 1930s, and it shows how its condition had deteriorated in the preceding fifty years. In 1954, William Graham Webb Sr. was instrumental in getting the county commissioners to move the jail to Albany, where it was placed on the grounds of Webb Park. The building was dismantled, and the stones were put back in their original position.[70] The roof was repaired, and the same prickly pear that had taken root on top of the jail was returned to its original spot. The cost to the community was $150.[71] The Texas Historical Commission awarded Historical Marker 1987 to this structure in 1974 when it was in Albany, fifteen miles to the south. The marker refers to it as the "Fort Griffin Civil Jail" as a way of distinguishing it from the jail at the fort with the same name. This imposing little calaboose occupies a footprint of only 80 square feet. It was made from limestone quarried from nearby hills. The type of original door is not known. Unless it had openings for light and ventilation, the only source of these luxuries would have been the two narrow windows on each side that measure only 4 inches wide by 24 inches high. The interior is an open room with a dirt floor, and the rock walls are about 1 foot thick. As part of the restoration, metal bars span the length of the interior of the building for support. An inscription is carved in a stone above the door that reads as follows:

> Fort Griffin
> Jail 1867
> C. M. Akard

Per Fort Griffin State Historic Site employee Jane Lenoir, this stone is not part of the original structure and 1867 is not the date of construction.[72] She said it was moved from Albany to Fort Griffin by Lynne and Clifford Teinert, who are the current owners.

Frisco

Collin County

LOCATION: Replica at the Frisco Heritage Center—6455 Page Street

OWNER: City of Frisco

DATE BUILT: 1912

SIZE: 180 square feet

On April 8, 1911, a committee was appointed "to look into the feasibility of building a city calaboose and selecting a site for same." The contract was awarded to the West Collin Grain and Elevator Company of Frisco in 1912 to be built at a cost of $225.[73] The city financed this project in payments. The only Sanborn map available for Frisco at the time of this

Frisco calaboose (photo by the author).

Windows on the side of the Frisco calaboose (photo by the author).

Replica of Frisco calaboose (photo courtesy of Lawrence DeVoto).

study was published in 1949, and it depicts this structure on the west side of the same block as the H. C. Richey Cotton Gin at 210 Main Street.[74] It was made of concrete, referred to on the Sanborn map as Fire Proof Construction, and consisted of two cells of approximately the same size. The cells were separated by a brick wall covered with plaster. Because the rest of the structure was made with concrete, the presence of a brick wall suggests a possible later addition, possibly when prisoner segregation was necessary. The original steel door, forged by local blacksmith John Gaby, is no longer present. Part of the floor is covered with a thin layer of what appears to be cement, and the rest is dirt. This calaboose was never equipped with lights, heat, or water. There are only two windows for sunlight and fresh air. At the time of my visit, it was in very poor condition with large cracks in the walls. The primary reason for this is the result of an improper mixture of cement and aggregate, which consisted of small pebbles and miscellaneous pieces of metal such as horseshoes, bedpost fragments, and pieces of unidentifiable metal. Susanne Kerley, a spokesperson for the Frisco Heritage Center, stated that it was used to house drunks, troublesome teens, and others on their way to the county jail until sometime in the 1950s.[75] An interesting event involving the calaboose occurred one

Halloween in 1944 or 1945 when Sonny McSpedden was locked up as the result of a prank. He was eighty-seven years old at the time I talked with him, and he related the following story:[76] Frisco was a small town at the time with a population of about six hundred, and boredom was often relieved by various pranks. On that night, around 10:00 p.m., he and some of his teenage friends decided to blow the whistle at the local volunteer fire department. Jarvis Hays was the night watchman, and he was close by when this happened. As a result, the boys were immediately apprehended. After giving them a lecture, he marched them to the calaboose on the edge of town and locked them inside. At the time, the calaboose was over thirty years old and seldom used. Its condition was already poor, and the boys could loosen the bars in one of the windows and effect their escape. The calaboose was on the same block as the cotton gin. The boys would sit on a bale of cotton and watch for Mr. Hayes. When they saw him coming, they would go back inside. Around midnight, he let the boys go after they promised to go home and stay out of trouble. This is the only recorded jail break from the Frisco calaboose, and the locals still refer to it as the "Calaboose Jail Break." Mr. McSpedden described this building as most unpleasant, as it had no electricity or plumbing. He said that it was rarely used, and the only times he knew of anyone being inside was because of drinking. He recalled one time when someone was put in it on a Saturday night and not let out until Monday morning. He would holler at people in the area for water.

Because of its deteriorated condition and safety concerns, the city decided it needed to be removed. Following its demise, a replica was constructed on the grounds of the Frisco Heritage Center in 2013 using as much of the original materials as possible.[77] Its original location was on a vacant lot that was a very desirable location for development.

Gause

Milam County

LOCATION: Private Property

OWNER: Privately Owned

DATE BUILT: 1920s

SIZE: 88 square feet

Gause calaboose (photo by the author).

Gause owes its existence and growth to the arrival of the International-Great Northern Railroad. The local economy depended largely on production and export of cotton, cottonseed oil, and corn. By 1915, the town reached the peak of its growth with a population of one thousand residents. The area began to experience a decline in population and number of businesses, and the bank closed its doors in 1927.[78] This calaboose is one of the smallest in the current sample, and it exemplifies the simplicity of jail construction that was practiced by towns across Texas. This structure was created by pouring concrete into wooden forms and adding a metal door and barred windows. The ominous looking edifice rests directly on the ground. Although the windows are large enough to provide adequate light and ventilation, a night inside could have been very unpleasant in bad weather, such as thunderstorms and freezing temperatures. There was no electricity or plumbing available to those who were unfortunate enough to be incarcerated there.

The door has been missing for a long time, and not one of the locals I interviewed can remember how it looked. Darlene Anglen is a member of the local historical society. She told me that Adrian McCowen was the night watchman in Gause; he regularly locked up drunks and other criminals in this jail.[79] He was also a Texas Ranger from 1921 to 1924. There were no Sanborn maps at the agencies visited for Gause at the time of this study. The owner of this structure has offered it to the city if they would arrange for it to be moved.[80]

Glazier

Hemphill County

LOCATION: Eastern edge of town on the north side of US Highway 60 (no physical address)

OWNER: Hemphill County

DATE BUILT: 1912

SIZE: 168 square feet

Local historian Wallace Forrest has conducted research regarding the history of this calaboose, and he has taken an active part in efforts to protect it. Most of the following information was obtained from a personal interview with him.[81] He researched the minutes of the commissioners' court and learned that the calaboose was constructed on May 18, 1912.[82] At the time, it was in the main part of town. However, a tornado passed through on April 9, 1947, and destroyed all the town's buildings except the calaboose and bank vault. Since that time, only a few residences remain. The businesses have relocated to Canadian, ten miles to the southwest, or Higgins in Lipscomb County, fifteen miles to the northeast. This structure is made of concrete covered with stucco and has a flat roof with a slight pitch from front to back. The modest false front contains a lip that extends over the facade. Entry from the outside is through a solid metal door. A segment of metal pipe that served as ventilation for a heater extends from the roof, but the heater is no longer present. This calaboose has an entry room that leads to the single cell in the back; the cell is less than 45 square feet in area. A concrete wall and a barred metal door divides the two rooms. Two windows that are on the sides of the structure provide the only source of light. Preservation efforts that have taken place to date include applying a new coat of stucco that closely matches the original surface treatment,

Glazier calaboose (photo courtesy of Wallace Forest).

replacing the window glass and wooden frames, and constructing a new roof. The glass windows are covered with metal bars affixed to the exterior of the wall, much like those on the calaboose in East Bernard.

Goldsmith

Ector County

LOCATION: 205 North Midland Street in Goldsmith

OWNER: City of Goldsmith

DATE BUILT: 1938

SIZE: 236 square feet

This concrete building is divided into two cells of equal size with a door of metal bars securing each cell. At one time, there was another door in front of the bars and a wooden frame around the windows, but they are no longer present. The interior contains two small bathrooms; the resulting floor

Goldsmith calaboose (photo courtesy of Dustee Craven).

plan of the interior is the only one of its kind in the current sample. A metal pipe extends from the top and there are two small vents on the back wall. The vents were associated with small rooms that housed toilets. Small gravels were used as aggregate, and metal cable was added to reinforce the concrete. A metal bed was present in each of the cells. The following information was taken from a marker the city placed at the site:[83] This calaboose was constructed in 1938 at which time Randolph Gillispie was the Justice of the Peace and Punck Burns was the Constable. A three-room house was constructed south of the jail [and] served as office and living quarters for Mr. Gillispie and his family. Prisoners were fed the same food and at the same time as the Gillispie family. Mrs. Ozelle Gillispie was the wife of Randolph and she prepared the meals.

Goree

Knox County

LOCATION: On the corner of East Oak and North Fifth Streets next to the Memorial Building in Goree

OWNER: City of Goree

DATE BUILT: Unknown

SIZE: 170 square feet

In 1905, the town was established when it was learned that the Wichita Valley Railroad was coming to the area. Track was completed in 1906, the same year that Goree was incorporated. Also in that same year the first cotton gin was built, and a second followed in 1920. The number of residents was greatest in 1920 when the population was recorded as 614.[84] This structure is one of three brick calabooses in the current sample with two cells side by side. The others are in D'Hanis and East Bernard.

Goree calaboose (photo courtesy of Donna Hyatt).

The walls extend about 1 foot above the flat roof to form a parapet. The door measures 2 1/2 feet by 6 1/2 feet and is solid steel except for two small windows with bars that measure 7 by 8 inches. The other windows measure only 8 by 11 inches and are on the back wall and centered behind each cell. The doors were welded shut at the time of my visit, and the interior could not be viewed. The interior walls that divide the cells in the calabooses in D'Hanis and East Bernard are brick. It is, therefore, assumed that this is the case with the one in Goree. The building rests on a concrete slab that extends about 4 feet from the west side, and the purpose of the extension is not known. One plausible explanation is that there was not enough leftover concrete to use elsewhere at the time so the slab was extended beyond the proposed footprint of the calaboose. It is also possible that the plans for the calaboose were for a larger structure but for some reason the final product was smaller.

Granger

Williamson County

LOCATION: Private Property

OWNER: Privately Owned

DATE BUILT: Unknown

SIZE: 432 square feet

Granger is a town that derives much of its income from cotton. As early as 1890, there were five gins in town along with a college and hotel. Incorporation came in 1891, and the population grew to 841 by 1900. In 1910, the population doubled and there was a combined cotton compress and cottonseed oil mill, electric light plant, ice factory, and waterworks. The Granger gin was one of the largest in the country at the time. In 1912, it was the only town in Texas with paved roads and a population less than five thousand.[85] This concrete calaboose is one of three in the sample with three cells, and it is the only one with the cells arranged side by side. There is a similar building in Comanche, but it is described as a jail because of its larger size. Each cell has metal bars in front of a solid metal door. The door in the middle has an opening that could have been used to hand food and other objects to a prisoner. This calaboose is only one of a very

Granger calaboose (photo by the author).

few with awnings over the doors. There are three windows, one centered on each wall on the back. Amenities included a small wall sink and toilet. The age of this calaboose is not known, but it is depicted on the Sanborn map dated 1910.[86] In that year, it was in the eastern half of city block 16 (lots 14 and 15) near the corner of Granger and Broadway Streets. It was still in use in 1921, and the address was 130 1/2 Granger.[87] One reason many of these calabooses have survived is that they provide a good building for storage, and that is the case with the one in Granger. One of the inmates known to have been housed in the Granger calaboose was George Tate of Holland, Texas, who had been indicted for the murder of Henry Duncan in 1910. Constable Lee Allen put him in the calaboose where he stayed until Sheriff Dan Crow took him to the Bell County jail the next morning.[88] The newspaper article does not give the results of his trial.

Grapeland

Houston County

LOCATION: City Park at Oak and Chestnut Streets in Grapeland

OWNER: City of Grapeland

DATE BUILT: 1906

SIZE: 116 square feet

The town of Grapeland owes its beginnings to the Houston and Texas Railroad, which set aside 1 square mile to become a town in 1871. The railroad was completed in 1872, and the name of the town was changed from Grapevine to Grapeland in 1873 when it was learned that another town in Texas already had the former name.[89] Local resident Jayne Stuart provided the following information.[90] She stated that the prevailing opinion is that this jail was built by private subscription during the first incorporation of the town in 1906. Its original location was across the railroad tracks near the home of Catherine Howard Pridgen, a longtime resident of Grapeland. When Mrs. Pridgen was young, she saw young boys on bicycles stopping by the jail where they would talk to the prisoners through the windows. Sometimes they were given money to go and buy cigarettes for the prisoners. Sometime during the 1930s, the jail was no longer being used, and it became the property of Mrs. Pridgen. It was placed in her back yard and used as a chicken coop. In 1972, Grapeland celebrated its centennial and Mrs. Pridgen graciously donated it to the city so it could be preserved for future generations, and it was moved to Main Street. At the time, a modest restoration project took place, and wooden shingles replaced the deteriorating roof. A consulting engineer advised the city to proceed as soon as possible or it may be too late to save the structure. The Grapeland Economic Development Corporation and private citizens worked together to complete the restoration, and it is now on display in the city park. This tiny building is divided into two cells with doors at each end. It was built using vertical board and batten over horizontal boards. At the time of my visit, the hip roof was covered with wooden shingles. Each cell had two windows secured with metal bars placed horizontally in a wooden frame. In 1972, the Houston County Historical Commission published *Crossroads to Progress: Grapeland, the Queen City of the Sand Flats*. This book documents the history of the town and references the calaboose.[91]

Restored Grapeland calaboose (photo courtesy of the Grapeland Historical Society).

Grapevine

Tarrant County

LOCATION: Southwest corner of West Franklin and South Main at a city bus stop in Grapevine

OWNER: City of Grapevine

DATE BUILT: 1909

SIZE: 80 square feet

This town has been called by a variety of names, but Grapevine was probably chosen because of the abundance of wild grapes in the area and nearby Grapevine Creek. In 1890, the town had eight hundred residents, four churches, three gristmills, several cotton gins, and a public school. With the arrival of the Saint Louis Southwestern Railway circa 1900 the town began a period of growth that reached a peak of 1,200 residents in 1914. Incorporation did not occur until 1936.[92] It was during this period of

Grapevine calaboose (photo courtesy of Sallie Andrews).

Grapevine calaboose restoration by Buddy Hall (photo courtesy of Pam Price).

growth that city marshal W. T. Bigbee was authorized to construct the first calaboose in Grapevine. The year was 1909. City mayor B. R. Wall deeded the land, and the concrete structure was erected on the southwest corner of Barton and Texas Streets near the site of the current water tower.[93] The door opens to a single room of 80 square feet in size and only 8 feet of headroom at its highest point. With a metal door, tiny windows, and 1-foot-thick walls, this was a very secure calaboose. Several calabooses in the current sample have roofs that fit the description of barrel or barrel-like, but the roof on the Grapevine structure is by far the best example of this shape. This forbidding structure was used to house petty criminals until the early 1950s. The night watchman at the time was W. T. Bigbee, who served in that capacity from 1909 to 1911. In 1956, a chief of police replaced the night watchman position.[94] The city of Grapevine is in possession of a photograph taken by the *Airport News Advertiser* of the calaboose at its original location in 1967 before it was moved and restored. This image is also available on the website The Portal to Texas History and at the Tarrant County College NE, Heritage Room. In 1994, the calaboose was relocated to the southwest corner of West Franklin and South Main Streets where it was restored and remains today. The restoration was a labor of love carried out admirably by city of Grapevine employees. The Sanborn Company mapped the town of Grapevine in 1921, but not one of their maps includes the site of the original jail. The only known map that depicts it is titled "Grapevine and Area, Late 1800s–1920." This map was created by W. D. "Ted" Willhoite, and it hangs on the wall in the Donald Schoolhouse Museum in Grapevine at 627 Church Street. This old calaboose is a landmark in town; students love to visit it during their class's Main Street Walking Tour. The restoration project carried out by the city of Grapevine has not only preserved an important structure but it has also increased awareness and interest in the kinds of jails that were present during the early years of the twentieth century.

Hermleigh

Scurry County

LOCATION: 900 East Coliseum Street adjacent to the grounds of the Western Texas College Coliseum in Snyder

OWNER: City of Snyder

DATE BUILT: Circa 1913

SIZE: 80 square feet

The following historical narrative was provided by interviews with area residents[95] and the text on the Texas Historical Commission marker awarded to this structure.[96] The unincorporated community of Hermleigh was surveyed in 1907 to serve as a shipping point on the railroad. At the time, the citizens of Hermleigh decided that they needed a local lockup. The county seat of Snyder was twelve miles distant, and since the roads were poor it was sometimes not possible to transport a prisoner to the county jail. Therefore, this small wooden structure served as a holding facility. Prior to the 1920s, law enforcement was the job of the town constable. The cost of construction was financed by the citizens of Hermleigh and the structure was probably built with volunteer labor. The size of the finished calaboose was 10 feet across the front and 8 feet on each side. The roof was made

Hermleigh calaboose (photo courtesy of Rolland C. Reynolds Jr.).

of wood covered with tin, and it slopes to the back at an angle of 17.4 degrees. This degree of pitch classifies it as a shed roof or single pitch roof with a pitch greater than 10 degrees. The door is to the right and allows entry into an open room. The method of construction consisted of placing two-by-fours laid flat on top of each other. In order to make the building sturdier, the corners were cut and fitted, resulting in notches similar to log cabins made with hand-hewn timbers. The juncture of the corner boards is referred to as butt joints. There was one small window on each side, and a single bed was placed inside for the prisoners to use for sleeping, and it is still there. The calaboose was never painted. There is a pole in the center to help support the roof. It is reported that the D. R. Layman family wanted it for storage space, and they obtained it in exchange for a cow. The Historic Society, Inc. purchased it and moved it to Snyder, where it remains today. The state of Texas designated it a Recorded Texas Historic Landmark in 1972 (marker number 1946). In 2016, the marker was reported missing. There were no Sanborn maps at the agencies visited for Hermleigh, Texas, during this study.

Holland

Bell County

LOCATION: Behind city hall at the corner of West Travis and Front Streets in Holland

OWNER: City of Holland

DATE BUILT: Unknown

SIZE: 150 square feet

The walls of this calaboose consist of blocks, but the type of block is not known. The flat roof and foundation were formed with concrete. The floor plan is that of two cells side by side. These cells are secured by metal doors that are not equal in size and method of construction. The cell to the left is larger and has a solid metal door behind one that is constructed of a heavy wire mesh. The other door is narrower in width and was made of flat strips of metal cold riveted in a cross-hatch pattern. The resulting square

Holland calaboose (photo by the author).

Holland calaboose, window detail (photo by the author).

openings offered the only source of light and ventilation at the front of this calaboose. Truck wheels on each end provided ventilation with two bars welded or bolted in place across the circular center opening. If the bars are welded to the wheel (ventilator) then this would mean that the jail was likely constructed after World War II since welding of metals did not become commonplace until that time. Prior to World War II, metals were riveted or bolted.[97] Local resident Wayne Deaver remembers the jail being used as late as 1968.[98] A deputy sheriff in the town of West who wished to remain anonymous said he transferred a prisoner to the Holland calaboose in 1973.[99]

Holliday

Archer County

LOCATION: Private Property

OWNER: Privately Owned

DATE BUILT: 1925

SIZE: 200 square feet

Holliday calaboose (photo courtesy of Amy Boyd).

Holliday was another Texas boomtown that owed its early success to the discovery of oil in the early 1920s. The promise of money to be made created such an influx of people that "border-trained Texas Rangers came in to ride their horses up and down the streets and alleys."[100] Two rangers were quoted as saying that people were so thick on the streets that "the law had to move them out so wagons and cars could get by."[101] The first jail was reported to have been a dugout before this concrete calaboose was built. The town was incorporated on September 16, 1925, and Judge G. A. Halloway was largely responsible for the new calaboose.[102] This calaboose is equally divided into two cells that are separated by a concrete wall and protected by massive metal doors. There is a large crack in the rear wall. Because the rest of the structure appears to be intact, this flaw could be the result of the ground shifting. The doors are most unusual. Fred Maier is a longtime resident of Holliday, and he stated that the doors were originally solid sheets of metal, but a local welder cut circular holes in each one to provide ventilation to prisoners who were complaining about the temperature inside.[103] The two small windows on the back wall are centered on each cell. Plumbing and electricity was not available to the prisoners. In the 1950s, Mr. Maier recalled that the jail was privately owned and used to house chickens. At the time of my visit, it was across from the post office in a vacant lot and not being used for any special purpose. Early photographs of this jail can be found in the *History of Holliday* by Hodge[104] and *Trails through Archer: A Centennial History, 1880–1980* by Jack Loftin.[105]

Hubbard City

Hill County

LOCATION: In an alley between Second and Third Streets behind a row of brick buildings in the 200 block of Magnolia Street in Hubbard City

OWNER: City of Hubbard

DATE BUILT: Unknown

SIZE: 178 square feet

The first documented jail in Hubbard was a small one-story ironclad structure described as a lockup. It is depicted on the 1904 Sanborn map at 215 Magnolia in city block 81 next to an alley.[106] In 1916, it was still in

Hubbard City calaboose (photo courtesy of Amy Boyd).

Bed in the Hubbard City calaboose (photo courtesy of Amy Boyd).

Toilet in the Hubbard City calaboose (photo by the author).

the same location, but at that time it was labeled as a jail at 208 Magnolia Avenue.[107] The most recent Sanborn map for Hubbard City that I could review was published in 1935.[108] The ironclad jail had been replaced by a one-story concrete calaboose of "fireproof" construction in city block 53, the subject of this discussion. This structure was built to accommodate prisoners in two separate cells of equal size. In the cell on the right there is a metal bed that appears to be very old, and it may likely be one that was present when the calaboose was being used. Both cells have toilets but only one is in good condition. It only lacks the seat to be complete. There are a few examples of graffiti, but some appear to be modern. The two names that may represent actual prisoners are Ophen Davis and Edward Barree. Another possibility is "Chris was here" in the cell with the bed. The doors are made of steel with bars that allow light and visibility from the outside. The windows are located on the side and back walls of the cells, and they can be closed from the outside with metal shutters that are still in place. The bars are flat metal and consist of four vertical and five horizontal pieces. The facade and side walls extend about 6 inches above the flat roof to form a parapet. On the roof, there is a cast iron vent pipe and two metal hooks. The purpose of the hooks is not known. The exterior is covered with stucco, a technique used for decoration and protection of the walls against the weather.

Jewett

Leon County

LOCATION: 200 block of Division Street inside a fenced area behind city hall in Jewett

OWNER: City of Jewett

DATE BUILT: Unknown

SIZE: 144 square feet

The walls are brick, and the roof conforms to the pyramid style and consists of tin over wooden rafters and supports. The exact date of construction is not known, but a local informant at city hall said it was built sometime during the early part of the twentieth century and was still in use in the 1960s.[109] The two windows have been boarded up, and there is a concrete

Jewett calaboose (photo by the author).

lintel above the windows and door; a similar feature was placed beneath the windows. According to the same informant, a friend of her husband was locked up in the calaboose during the winter and had no blankets or heater to keep him warm. Her husband tied a chain to his car and yanked out the bars from one of the windows so his friend could get out, and this damaged the wall. This event happened sometime during the 1960s. A large tree growing very close to the west wall will eventually affect the structure.

Kemp

Kaufman County

LOCATION: Corner of East Eleventh and South Main behind city hall in Kemp

OWNER: City of Kemp

DATE BUILT: 1912

SIZE: 131 square feet

Kemp, Texas, was a railroad town that began its development in the 1880s. In 1912, the commissioners' court ordered that a calaboose be built at a cost not to exceed $200. This order was the result of a petition submitted to the court by Constable J. B. Duncan and other citizens.[110] This one room calaboose is made from well-fired brick and has a massive door made from quarter-inch steel. There are two small windows, one on each side, with two rows of horizontal bars. The ceiling, as viewed from the interior, is made from quarter-inch iron C channel. On the outside of each corner are metal bars, but their function is not known. A metal ring on the inside

Kemp calaboose (photo courtesy of Lawrence DeVoto).

was probably installed to shackle unruly prisoners. There is a wooden electric pole at one corner that appears to date to the early twentieth century because of the presence of brown ceramic insulators. However, there is no evidence that electricity from this pole was available inside the calaboose. The calaboose at Kemp became well known throughout East Texas when Bonnie Parker and Ralph Fults were arrested and spent a night there.[111] "Clyde Barrow was with them, but he escaped capture. Bonnie and Ralph were charged with mule theft, auto theft, and burglary on April 20, 1932. Fults identified himself as Jack Sherman of Tulsa, and Bonnie told authorities that her name was Betty Thornton of Dallas. The calaboose was surrounded by armed men and there were many curious visitors." One of the memories of this event was related by Abbie Lou Williams of Kemp, who said, "I remember my momma going down there to look at Bonnie Parker. Bonnie got so mad, she spit in my mother's eye. This really tickled my father. No one ever had the nerve to stand up to my mother before."[112]

Kyle

Hays County

LOCATION: San Marcos Baptist Academy—2801 Ranch Road 12 in San Marcos

OWNER: The Friends of the Hays County Historical Commission—Preservation Associates, Inc.

DATE BUILT: 1884

SIZE: 138 square feet

The calaboose discussed here was built in 1884 with money donated by Hays County. The construction was performed at a cost of $100 by Clyde Herald.[113] The little calaboose remained in Kyle until 1964 when it was purchased by Aquarena Springs, an amusement park with a "Texana Village."[114] Texas State University acquired the springs, and the calaboose was given to the Friends of the Hays County Historical Commission—Preservation Associates, Inc., a countywide, nonprofit organization. Now it is on the grounds of the San Marcos Baptist Academy. Current plans are for it to be moved to the site of the 1884 jail in San Marcos, which

Kyle calaboose (photo by the author).

is being restored. Then, restoration of the calaboose will begin.[115] This calaboose was constructed by placing boards measuring 2 by 4 inches flat on top of one another to form a more secure wall. The boards interlock at the corners for added strength. The floor plan is two cells of equal size separated by a wall of similar construction to the exterior. Entry to the cells was provided by doors made of milled boards nailed to horizontal boards. A small window in each door was probably used to pass food and other items to the prisoners. There is one small window on the back wall of each cell that measures 10 by 12 inches. They are secured by a frame of round metal bars that consists of three vertical bars and one horizontal bar. The gabled roof is covered with modern tin over wooden shingles. During its stay at Aquarena Springs, it was damaged by a fire, and there is good reason to suspect that the current roof is not original. The only Sanborn maps for Kyle were published in 1896, 1902, 1907, 1912, and 1936, and this calaboose was not depicted on any of them. Visitors to San Marcos can also view the Beaux-Arts-style courthouse constructed in 1908[116] and the two-story limestone county jail built in the Italianate style in 1884.[117]

La Coste

Medina County

LOCATION: Private Property

OWNER: Privately Owned

DATE BUILT: 1915

SIZE: 129 square feet

This calaboose contains two cells separated by a heavy metal door made of strap iron attached to a wooden frame that may not be original. The door was fashioned from a solid sheet of metal and the hinges are massive. A 6-inch-long key was needed to operate the lock.[118] The arrangement of two cells in a linear pattern is not a common floor plan among the calabooses in the current sample. The calaboose was constructed by pouring concrete mixed with aggregate into wooden forms. However, the exterior has been covered with a grout-like substance that covers the horizontal lines that emerge from between the wooden forms in structures constructed this way. The concrete was strengthened by pieces of metal wire and small

La Coste calaboose (photo courtesy of Darryl Pearson).

pebbles. The domed roof and beveled outer walls have an unusual and very distinct architectural style. Ventilation for the front cell was provided by two long narrow windows on each side. The back cell also had windows of the same size on the sides and one on the back wall. The walls are 1 foot thick and slowly crumbling. Each window was imbedded in the concrete with metal bars placed horizontally and vertically. It is not known what furnishings were inside, but a plaque on the front says, "Bathroom facilities were primitive in keeping with the times."[119] Yvonne Chandler Ludwig is a local historian, and she provided the following information regarding the history of this structure:[120] When this calaboose was built, the railroad required that only businesses be built on the street facing the tracks. Therefore, the jail was built on the back part of one of the lots owned by the city. The temporary workers the railroad employed frequented the local saloons, and it was not unusual for drunkards and people charged with rowdy behavior to spend a night in this calaboose along with those charged with more serious crimes. William Marcus Collins was the contractor hired to design and build the current structure in 1915. Materials needed for the construction were brought to the area by wagon. Collins was charged with constructing a "two-cell, escape proof jail." Apparently, the two cells were required in case males and females were locked up at the same time. In the front, there is a small area for the constable. Meals were prepared at the constable's house and brought to the prisoners, and the cost was borne by the county. Ms. Ludwig said that the last known occupant was locked up in 1960 for disorderly conduct. When the calaboose was no longer needed, the city sold the property and included it in the sale. This historic building received a plaque cast by Yvonne and Lester Ludwig on December 9, 2006, for its distinctive style, manner of construction, and the part it played in the history of La Coste.

La Grange

Fayette County

LOCATION: 171 South Main next to the chamber of commerce in LaGrange

OWNER: City of LaGrange

DATE BUILT: Post-1921

SIZE: 164 square feet

La Grange calaboose (photo courtesy of Roger G. Moore).

Ed Blackburn Jr. writes that the first jail in town was completed in 1838 at a cost of $460.[121] He believes it was a wooden structure, and he states that in those days "it was the custom to place prisoners in irons and chain them to a large stone or piece of timber inside the jail."[122] This structure was used for ten years before it was abandoned and the city began paying citizens $3 per day to board prisoners in their homes.[123] In 1854, the town had a new two-story brick jail that measured 23 by 34 feet and contained four rooms.[124] It was used until replaced by a larger and more elaborate county jail in 1882. This structure was created in Victorian Gothic style and designed by architects Andrewarthe and Wahrenberger.[125] It was located at the corner of Main and West Crockett Streets and functioned as a jail until 1985. Today it is the home of the local chamber of commerce. The first Sanborn map available for LaGrange was drafted in 1885; it depicts a brick calaboose at 626 Main Street next to the county jail.[126]

This building was still standing in the 1960s. It was not uncommon for calabooses and county jails to coexist and serve the county as places of incarceration, especially when the newer county jails were not finished. In 1890, this building was still standing but no longer labeled as a calaboose.[127] Sometime between 1912 and 1921, it was repurposed as a jail annex.[128] The concrete calaboose discussed here appeared in 1921 or later. The reason the county decided to construct a calaboose next to a county jail that was still in use is not known. This structure consists of an open room with only one window. The front door is metal with bars, but the city has installed a wooden door on the outside for protection from the weather. An opening at the bottom of the door allowed food to be passed to the prisoners. In the center is a light fixture, but it is not known if electricity was provided when the jail was built or if it was added later. According to Catherine Poppe of the Fayette Electric Cooperative, the courthouse in La Grange had electricity as early as 1892, and by 1921 the entire town had service.[129] This suggests that the light fixture in the calaboose may be original. There is a vent in the ceiling that may have been connected to a heater. Near the front of the building there is a metal pipe attached to the outside wall on the east side that extends through the roof. The purpose of this fixture is not known. The ceiling on the inside is flat but the roof is gabled. Visitors to LaGrange can visit the county courthouse built in Richardsonian Romanesque style in 1891[130] and the Gothic style jail that served the county from 1882 to 1985.[131]

Lakeview

Hall County

LOCATION: Private Property

OWNER: Privately Owned

DATE BUILT: Unknown

SIZE: 109 square feet

This concrete calaboose was constructed using the poured-in-place method for the floor, walls, and flat roof. The floor plan consists of an entry room with a cell to the left. The wall that separates the cell from the other area was made of two-by-fours fashioned in a checkerboard pattern that allows visibility from each side. The cell door is no longer present, but a board across the floor suggests that it was made of wood also. The only other

Lakeview calaboose (photo courtesy of Shari Watson).

Interior of the Lakeview calaboose (photo courtesy of Shari Watson).

calaboose in the current sample known to have had a wooden cell wall is in Plaska, but the only remnants are a two-by-four on the floor. These two calabooses are very similar and could have been built by the same person, especially since the two towns are only about nine miles apart. Terry Watson is a resident of the area, and he provided the following memories: The current door is a replacement of the original wooden door.[132] There is one window on each side. He recounted that his father (B. P. Watson) remembered seeing prisoners in the jail in the 1930s, mainly on Saturday night.

Leonard

Fannin County

LOCATION: 100 block of West Grayson in Leonard

OWNER: City of Leonard

DATE BUILT: 1919

SIZE: 117 square feet

According to local resident Joe Sudderth, this calaboose was preceded by a tiny wooden calaboose that stood in the same area.[133] On May 20, 1919, a committee was appointed to "have the jail erected." Members of the committee were O. H. Black, W. H. Chapman, and W. T. Stevens. The city council met on June 15, 1920, and it was decided to "sell the dilapidated jail on city lot for best cash price."[134] The city paid C. J. Felmet $98 for moving it to make room for the new jail.[135] Mr. Sudderth was unable to find any information regarding who built the new jail and at what cost. He estimated the price to be about $300 based on expenditures believed to have been allocated for this project.[136] This calaboose faces north and is in its original location. It was made of concrete using the poured-in-place method. The result was a rectangular structure on a slab 1 foot thick and walls 9 inches thick. The roof is best described as domed. The door is offset to the right, and the interior consists of two rooms of equal size. Other calabooses with this floor plan are described as having only one cell with the entry room having been used by law enforcement officers. However, the presence of a barred window in the main room suggests it was also used as a cell. If this was the case, this structure is the only example of

Leonard calaboose (photo courtesy of Lawrence DeVoto).

this floor plan. The door consists of vertical metal bars in a metal frame. A flat metal strip across the center adds strength and support to the door. The amount of light and air flow that was able to enter a calaboose varied greatly from those with no windows to structures with windows that appear to have been more than adequate. The windows in this calaboose are larger than most, and the barred door was another source light and air flow. The first room occupies one-half of the structure, and it is separated from the second cell by a wall of metal bars created in the same pattern as those on the door. It has a window on the wall opposite the door that consists of six bars placed vertically in the concrete. There is no window on the west wall. The formal cell has windows on each of the three walls. It was common for simple furniture such as cots or bed frames to have been available to prisoners, but none was present at the time of my visit. A feature that helped protect prisoners from rain is the presence of awnings over the door and each window. They are made of wood covered with tin, and they extend from the walls in an angle of approximately 90 degrees. In 1930, repairs were made to the structure. A toilet was installed in the entry room, and it is still in place. Also, concrete grout was used to cover the exterior and create a smooth surface. The workers who did the repairs etched the date—July 28, 1930—into the grout on the front of the calaboose. In 1997, Joe Sudderth replaced the awnings on the door and windows, and a concrete threshold was added to the base of the door to prevent water from entering the building.[137]

Linden

Cass County

LOCATION: Behind the chamber of commerce at the corner of Rush and Taylor Streets at the city water plant in Linden

OWNER: City of Linden

DATE BUILT: Unknown

SIZE: 102 square feet

Linden calaboose (photo by the author).

This calaboose is located behind a chain link fence along with the city water tower. An interesting feature is a brick retaining wall and steps that lead directly from the street to the calaboose. This small one-room structure rests on a concrete slab. The single door is offset to the right and made of milled lumber attached vertically to a frame for support. The walls consist of two courses of brick, and they support a mono-pitched roof made of wood and covered with tin. The front and rear walls were stopped short of one or two courses of brick at the top to create a shelf that supports large wooden beams. Flat milled boards were placed across the beams at a right angle, and the roof was covered with tin. There is a pitch of 1 1/2 feet from front to back. There is a window on each side, and each is held in place by a wooden frame. Each window has four metal bars placed vertically in the frame. Although the door appears to be old, it may not be original to the building. In the concrete floor is an oval-shaped area approximately 3 feet in diameter. There are four small holes in this area that suggest something was bolted to the floor. The shape suggests that there may have been a toilet present, but no evidence of plumbing was observed. At the time of my visit, this building was being used by the city to house equipment associated with the water plant, and there were no plans to get rid of it.[138]

McGregor

McLennan County

LOCATION: 202 South Jefferson between West Second and West Third Streets in McGregor

OWNER: City of McGregor

DATE BUILT: 1922–38

SIZE: 140 square feet

McGregor was well established by 1884 with a variety of businesses and several hundred residents. The town adopted a city charter in 1886, and around the turn of the century it was the commercial center and shipping point for most of the western part of the county with a recorded population of 2,081 in 1920.[139] My first introduction to this calaboose

McGregor calaboose (photo courtesy of Dinah Mills).

was a telephone interview with longtime resident Pat Fehler, who recalled passing by it many times as a child. She said that it was used mostly on weekends and holidays.[140] She accompanied me during my visit; it was the first time she ever saw the inside of the cells.

This concrete calaboose has two cells of equal size and one window per cell. The grains of the wooden boards used as forms for the roof are visible in the ceiling. The doors consist of two parts: a solid metal door with a smaller door cut into it that covers a door made of metal bars. Ronnie Moe said that there were several saloons on Main Street in the 1940s.[141] Soldiers from Fort Hood frequented these establishments. McGregor was the nearest town where liquor was allowed, and many of the occupants of the local calaboose were soldiers arrested by the local constable during that time.[142] The interior walls of the cells are festooned with graffiti, with the most recent dated 1951. One of the more interesting writings is dated September 23, 1938, and says, "Hope to be out by the 24th."

Marble Falls

Burnet County

LOCATION: Across the street from the Marble Falls/Lake LBJ Chamber of Commerce at 916 Second Street in Marble Falls

OWNER: City of Marble Falls

DATE BUILT: Unknown

SIZE: 238 square feet

This town was named for the falls on the Colorado River that were recognized by travelers as a landmark to identify their whereabouts while traveling. The town's beginnings were in 1887 when Adam Rankin Johnson chartered the Texas Mining and Improvement Company. In 1889, the Austin and Northwestern Railroad extended their line from Granite Mountain to Marble Falls.[143] The floor plan of this concrete calaboose is two cells of equal size. The barred metal door allows access to the first cell, which is separated from the second cell by a concrete wall. The door to this cell is missing. The shape of the building is rectangular with a flat

Marble Falls calaboose (photo courtesy of Darryl Pearson).

roof. The walls on three sides extend above the roof to form a parapet. The front wall is higher and could be described as a false front or a stepped parapet adorned with coping along the top. The brick chimney on the roof may have served as ventilation for a heater, but this has not been confirmed. Also, there is a concrete feature on the roof, and its function is also not known. Squares are cut into the ceiling, probably for ventilation. The front door is attached to three hinges and is the only one of its kind in the current sample. The outer door was constructed using parts of plows that bear the manufacturer's names: "Shunk—Bucyrus Ohio and Southern Plow Co. Columbus, GA." Behind it is a wooden door that is recessed 1 foot from the front wall of the jail. This door may be a replacement. The front cell has one window on each side wall, while the rear cell has windows on the side walls and one on the back. The windows are narrow and are secured by eight metal bars embedded vertically in the concrete. They measure 8 inches high by 32 inches wide. Electrical fixtures are present and, if original, could date this building to sometime in the late 1920s when power was first available in Marble Falls. This calaboose was preceded by one that burned and took the life of William Lacy, the son of a wealthy stock man, who was locked up for intoxication.[144] According to Sarah Cummings at the Marble Falls Chamber of Commerce, the city considers this structure to be an important part of the history of the town, and it needs to be preserved.[145]

Marion

Guadalupe County

LOCATION: City Property

OWNER: City of Marion

DATE BUILT: Unknown

SIZE: 282 square feet

Before the town was created, the area was a camp for railroad workers associated with the Galveston, Harrisburg and San Antonio Railroad, which arrived in 1877. During the 1880s, Marion had a steam mill, gristmill, sawmill, two cotton gins, four general stores, and a population of 250. Incorporation did not occur until 1941.[146] This structure is on city property and not available to the public without permission because of safety concerns. The original structure was made with two-by-fours laid on top of one another. The exterior walls and gable roof are covered with tin. The floor plan is two rooms or cells divided by a wooden wall and doors at each end, similar to the calabooses in Cameron and Grapeland. The difference between this one and the others is that there is an opening between the two rooms that may have supported a door. Each wall has two windows with vertically placed metal bars that were measured at 3 feet 3 inches wide by 2 feet 10 inches high. These windows are directly opposite those on the other wall. Two metal vents in the roof suggest heaters were present at one time. The cell at the front has two metal bunks attached to the back wall. There are two identical bunks on the opposite side of the same wall. The upper bunk in both rooms is high enough from the floor that a ladder would have been needed to reach it. This structure was moved to its current location with the intention of restoring it. Unfortunately, its original location is not known. Currently, it rests on the ground with no floor, possibly the result of a rotted sill plate. The tin on one side is bent under the weight of the building without a floor to support it. This calaboose is in very poor condition and if it is not saved its lifespan is not long. The floor plan is based on the assumption that the wall dividing the two cells

Marion calaboose (photo courtesy of Darryl Pearson).

had no door. The opening is considered to be the result of later changes. At the time of my visit it was being used for storage. The city has decided it's a liability and it will be razed.

Marquez

Leon County

LOCATION: Between Pearl and North Commerce and about 100 feet west of the intersection of Pearl and Elm in Marquez

OWNER: City of Marquez

DATE BUILT: Unknown

SIZE: 196 square feet

Marquez calaboose after restoration (photo by the author).

Marquez was a station on the International-Great Northern Railroad in 1871 and was named for Maria de la Marquez, the owner of the land at the time. In 1884, there were 150 residents along with a cotton gin, gristmill, saloon, two general stores, and a hotel. The population in 1925 is reported to have been at a high of seven hundred.[147] This tiny structure was constructed using vertical boards as studs and attaching wide boards onto them facing the inside of the building. Narrow boards cover the cracks between the larger boards, and this creates a horizontal board and batten effect. There is a small window on each side, but only one has bars remaining. It is possible that there was a third window in the back, but too much of the wall is missing to know for sure. It is not known if the tin on the outside is original to the structure or was added later. If it was original, there would not have been a third window. In 1907, Norman Calloway broke into the home of W. J. Dean on Christmas Eve. He was later captured and put in the calaboose at Marquez. A mob took him from the jail and lynched him.[148] At the time of my visit, this structure was in very poor condition and on the verge of collapse. In 2016, the city commissioned a resident of Marquez to stabilize it. He used as much original wood and tin as possible, and the rest of the wood was obtained from an old barn in town. The bars in the other window were made from rebar.

Mason

Mason County

LOCATION: Private Property

OWNER: Privately Owned

DATE BUILT: 1857

SIZE: 255 square feet

The following information regarding this calaboose's physical appearance was provided by Darryl Pearson, who visited the site.[149] The date 1857 is carved in the facade. If this date of is correct, this would be the oldest documented standing calaboose in the current sample. There is one in Gatesville that is reported to have been constructed in 1855, but it is a dungeon-type jail where prisoners were put underground through a trap door.[150] There is a potential problem with the date that is carved in the

Mason calaboose (photo courtesy of Darryl Pearson).

Door to Mason calaboose (photo courtesy of Darryl Pearson).

wall. The first three digits were carved deeply into the plaster, and the last one only scratched the surface. The door is offset to the right and made of solid metal except for a small window that allowed a view inside when opened. There is a window on each side, and each one is secured by metal bars in a wooden frame. Seven circular bars about the size of rebar are placed vertically and equidistant from each other and three square pieces of metal placed horizontally. The rocks in the walls are pieces of limestone of various sizes. They were not cut and shaped like many of the rock buildings in the area. Instead, they were joined together with mortar, much of which has eroded. The current roof appears to be a later addition as its wooden construction contrasts markedly with the rock walls. The ceiling consists of sheets of plywood, and some of the walls are also covered with the same material. There is a metal cable stretched 360 degrees around the building and angle iron is at each corner. The reason for this is probably to keep the walls from collapsing. It is currently being used for storage. Visitors to Mason can also view the Classical Revival style courthouse made of sandstone in 1909[151] and the two-story sandstone county jail built in 1898.[152]

Miles

Runnels County

LOCATION: 100 block of North Boykin Street at the city water tower in Miles

OWNER: City of Miles

DATE BUILT: Post-1921

SIZE: 135 square feet

Miles has also been known as Miles City. It was named for Jonathan Miles, who donated money for the extension of the Santa Fe Railroad, which passes through the town.[153] Towns dependent on the railroad often attracted various workers and transients, which contributed to the crime rate, and the presence of these types of folks may have been a contributing factor to the construction of a calaboose. The only two Sanborn maps available at the time of this study were published in 1908 and 1921. The post-1921 date of construction for this calaboose is based on its absence

Miles calaboose (photo by the author).

Barrel roof on Miles calaboose (photo by the author).

on the 1921 version. This concrete calaboose has two cells of equal size side by side, and each cell has its own door consisting of two parts. The outer doors were made of flat strips of metal riveted together in a crisscross pattern, and the interior door is wood with no openings for light or ventilation. When the wood door was closed, the only relief from the elements were the two small windows on each end of the building. The roof is an example of a barrel vault roof with an overhang of about 6 inches. This calaboose is located inside a fenced area and is being used by the city for storage. No furnishings were observed on the inside. There is a large tree that is so close that part of its trunk touches the back wall. Eventually, it may pose a threat to the stability of this structure.

Monahans

Ward County

LOCATION: Million Barrel Museum at 1500 East Sealy Street in Monahans

OWNER: Ward County

DATE BUILT: 1928–29

SIZE: 192 square feet

The following information was taken from a memorandum by Edd E. Cox titled "First Monahans Jail,"[154] and from *Just Visitin': Old Texas Jails*, by Joan Upton Hall.[155] Monahans experienced an oil boom in 1927 with the result that the promise of work attracted outsiders and turned the town into a "tent city full of roughnecks." There was no jail or calaboose in Monahans, Pyote, or Wink prior to 1929. At that time, prisoners were chained to telephone poles on the streets of all three towns. On January 1, 1927, F. I. Dryer became the sheriff of Ward County, and he began a campaign to have a jail or lockup built in Monahans. The town was incorporated on May 18, 1928. The first city election was held on August 6, 1928, and Fred P. Gibson was elected mayor. The new jail was constructed sometime between October 1928 and April 1929 at the southwest corner of what is now North Main Street and A Street about 150 feet north of the old Monahans well. The builder was Jim Wylie and/or Sam Keithley. It was constructed using 2 inch by 12 inch boards for the walls, and the

Monahans calaboose (photo courtesy of Rhonda K. Holley).

Monahans roofline (photo courtesy of Rhonda K. Holley).

exterior was also covered with 2 by 6 boards. A tremendous amount of size sixteen common nails was used, and the resulting wall was very strong and 4 inches thick. The footprint is oblong at 16 feet across the front and 12 feet on the sides. At each end, there is a small window 30 inches wide and 6 inches high with two bars made of 1-inch pipe over each window. The roof was formed using milled boards over rafters that slope from front to back at a pitch of 17.4 degrees, which formed a roof commonly referred to as a shed or a single pitch roof with a pitch greater than 10 degrees. This calaboose was used for approximately three years, or until 1932. At the time this information was published by Cox, it had been moved to the northeast corner of Allen and D Streets on county property. Finally, it was moved to the museum where it resides today under a protective roof.

Moore

Frio County

LOCATION: Private Property

OWNER: Privately Owned

DATE BUILT: Unknown

SIZE: 170 square feet

In its early days, Moore was a station on the International–Great Northern Railroad. The local economy was based largely on cotton. In 1910, the town had an estimated population of three hundred, and it was one of the largest towns between Laredo and San Antonio. A boll weevil infestation during the 1920s and early 1930s caused a major decline in the town's economy.[156] The date this concrete calaboose was constructed is not known, but it is likely that the event occurred during the early 1900s when the town was most prosperous. This structure has one open room and a concrete floor. The door consists of flat metal bars arranged in a crisscross pattern. A wooden frame around the door contains metal bolts that suggest there was a second door that was probably closed in bad weather. The roof is flat with a very slight pitch from front to back. There is a metal bed on the inside, but it could not be determined if it is original to the structure. The door was welded shut. A most interesting feature of this calaboose is the ceiling. When the roof was constructed the boards were placed on a

Moore calaboose (photo courtesy of Darryl Pearson).

ledge and left in place. The only materials observed that were used to keep the concrete intact were small pebbles, and there are places where erosion is taking place and threatening the structural integrity of this building. It was in an area of very thick secondary growth. Small trees and brush had to be cut away to get satisfactory photographs. In the summer, it is barely visible from the road.

Moran

Shackelford County

LOCATION: 200 block of Fisher Street at northwest corner of Fisher and Ground Streets in Moran

OWNER: City of Moran

DATE BUILT: Unknown

SIZE: 85 square feet

In the latter part of the nineteenth century, Moran was served by the Texas Central Railway and was a shipping center for local farmers and ranchers. In

Moran calaboose (photo courtesy of Julie Elrod).

Moran calaboose, corner construction detail (photo courtesy of Julie Elrod).

1910, natural gas was discovered and the town became an oil field service center.[157] The original location was next to the blacksmith shop on West Ground Street one block from its current location.[158] The city moved it to a city park and placed it on a cement slab, where it can be appreciated by the public. This small building is rectangular in plan. The door is centered on the front wall and has no opening that could have been used to pass food and other items to the prisoners. The locking mechanism is crude and may have been created by the local blacksmith from a spare part; this type of activity would be consistent with using available materials to save money. The wall construction consists of two-by-fours lying flat on top of each other, and the spaces in between were filled in with shorter boards. The siding is milled boards attached to the walls vertically with wire nails. This type of nail was available during the latter part of the nineteenth century and later. Therefore, their presence cannot be used to place this jail in a specific time. Wooden shingles that appear to be original cover the gable roof. There is a window on each side wall. The bars are strips of flat metal in a crisscross pattern, and there are wooden shutters that could be closed to keep out rain and cold.

Odell

Wilbarger County

LOCATION: It is in a vacant lot at the site of the old town of Odell northwest of that part of Cooper Street that lies between Halloway and Thompson Street North.

OWNER: County of Wilbarger

DATE BUILT: Post-1908

SIZE: 101 square feet

Odell owes its existence to the Kansas City, Mexico and Orient Railway, which arrived in the area in 1908. A post office was established in 1909. Ten years later there were thirty businesses, including two banks and a picture show.[159] This sturdy concrete building is one of the few surviving structures from the days when Odell was a prosperous North Texas town that relied on cotton and oil for its success. The thick concrete walls are in excellent condition, and its blocky appearance creates a formidable image.

Odell calaboose (photo courtesy of Celeste Littlecreek).

The door is missing, but the metal bars are still in place in the two small windows. Although the metal bed frame on the inside may have provided some comfort to those unfortunate enough to be on the inside, the absence of plumbing and electricity combined with very little ventilation from the windows suggest it was not a pleasant place to spend the night. Eight pouring episodes were needed to complete the walls, while the flat roof and floor were created with only one.

Pilot Point

Denton County

LOCATION: 106 West Division Street in Pilot Point

OWNER: City of Pilot Point

DATE BUILT: 1920s

SIZE: 117 square feet

Pilot Point was a thriving community in 1890 with a population of 1,090. The Texas and Pacific Railway and the Missouri, Kansas and Texas contrib-

Pilot Point calaboose (photo courtesy of Lawrence DeVoto).

uted to the growth that depended largely on oil and the shipping of cotton, grain, and hides. It was incorporated in 1866 and was reincorporated in 1906. By 1914, the population had reached 1,371 residents and the town boasted an electric plant and water works.[160] This building was probably constructed sometime between 1912 and 1922 when the property was acquired by the city. It is in a fenced area that serves as the water works plant for the city. The concrete exterior is covered with a thick layer of stucco. The gable roof is different from most of the other calabooses I have documented in that it is also poured concrete covered with stucco. The door is centered on the front wall and is made from flat pieces of iron that are attached vertically and horizontally to form a crisscross pattern. This pattern created square holes for light and ventilation. The bars are attached to the frame and each other with rivets. There are two large pieces of metal attached to hinges that provide hasps for locking. The front door opens into a room that was probably used by law enforcement personnel. A massive wall of flat metal bars with a matching door separates the entry area from the single cell. The only source of direct light is a window centered on the back wall of the cell that is 16 by 19 inches in size. It is not known if any furniture was present for the comfort of the prisoners; it was not unusual for the city to provide at least a metal bed. Electricity and plumbing were not available.

Plaska

Hall County

LOCATION: Private Property

OWNER: Privately Owned

DATE BUILT: Unknown

SIZE: 142 square feet

The first Plaska post office was established in 1905 when the town was called Lodge. Cotton was the backbone of the economy, and there were three gins operating in 1908. The current name, Plaska, was given to the town in 1920. The population reached its peak in 1920 with two hundred residents. The Great Depression and highway improvements resulted in a general decline, and by 1933 there were only twenty recorded inhabitants.[161] Today, Plaska is a virtual ghost town. This calaboose was made of concrete reinforced with rebar. A segment of this material was observed because of the damage to one of the corners. The exterior is covered with a thick coat of stucco. The door is offset to the right and consists of vertical bars in a metal frame. The interior consists of an entry room for law en-

Plaska calaboose (photo by the author).

forcement and a cell to the left. Although the door allows ventilation and light through the bars, the cell is not in the direct path and receives these benefits only indirectly. Two small windows are the only source of light for the cell, and they are placed high on the front and back walls. There are wooden boards attached to the concrete floor, and these served as support for the cell wall, which was probably made of wood like the calaboose in Lakeview. When the flat roof was constructed, wooden boards were placed across the top as part of the form for the concrete. The grains of the wood are clearly visible on the ceiling. The facade has a false front that extends less than 2 feet above the front of the calaboose. The interior has been modified with shelves to hold paint and an electrical outlet that was no longer being used.

Port O'Connor

Calhoun County

LOCATION: Main and Sixth Streets next to the precinct 5 barn in Port O'Connor

OWNER: City of Port O'Connor

DATE BUILT: 1909

SIZE: 120 square feet

This is a very plain structure made of poured concrete. It has only one window, and there was no electricity or plumbing. The original door is no longer present, and the floor is concrete. Mr. and Mrs. Jess Reed have conducted extensive research regarding their town of Port O'Connor.[162] They believe the calaboose was built in 1909, the same time that Port O'Connor was incorporated as a municipality. The constable in the 1950s was Grady Malone (a.k.a. Jack Malone). His grandson, Henry Anderson, told Mr. Reed that he remembers riding around with Mr. Malone and listening to his stories. He has Malone's badge and blackjack that he carried but no historic photos. Deputy Leonard Moss Fisher once locked up twenty-two men in the jail at the same time. In a building of only 120 square feet, that would have been a very crowded situation. Those who lived near the calaboose reported that there was a lot of noise at dusk when the mosquitoes arrived in swarms. Another informant said that there was a homeless

Port O'Connor calaboose (photo courtesy of Darryl Peason).

family who lived in a tent adjacent to the jail during the late 1920s and sometime during the early 1930s. Judge Nancy Pomykal is a longtime resident of the town, and she said the calaboose has been in the same location since 1909.[163] She also said when Hurricane Carla destroyed much of the town in 1961, the calaboose survived.

Powell

Navarro County

LOCATION: Petroleum Park on South Twelfth Street in Corsicana

OWNER: Navarro County Historical Society

DATE BUILT: Circa 1923

SIZE: 83 square feet

This wooden calaboose was built for use in the Powell Oil Field circa 1923. Work in the oil fields was hard and drinking and fighting were common occurrences among the roughnecks during their time away from the rigs.

Powell calaboose (photo courtesy of Darryl Pearson).

Lockups like this were necessary to maintain civility in harsh conditions. For about seven years, the Powell Oil Field was one of the most productive in the country.[164] After the decline of the oil boom, the property on which it stood was acquired by a Mr. Emerson. He moved it to his barn where it remained out of the elements, and that is the reason for its excellent condition today. The move was made by placing logs beneath the structure and pulling it with a horse.[165] This calaboose was made using very wide milled boards that would be a specialty item today. They are attached vertically, and the seams are sealed with bats in the style of board and batten construction. The doors are extremely well made and secure. The windows in the door are tiny at 25 square inches, and the metal bars attached to the outside of the doors are atypical of most wooden calabooses. There are two larger windows on the back wall that measure 144 square inches each. The bars are round pieces of metal inserted into holes drilled in the wood. The original roof was tin. Harriett Emerson is the daughter of Mr. Emerson, and she graciously donated the calaboose to the historical society; the members placed it at Petroleum Park in Corsicana where it can be viewed by the public. Visitors to Corsicana can also view the Beaux-Arts and Prairie style courthouse constructed of brick and marble in 1905.[166]

Presidio

Presidio County

LOCATION: 109 Jail Street at the corner of Jail and Madero in Presidio

OWNER: County of Presidio

DATE BUILT: Circa 1925

SIZE: 264 square feet

This concrete calaboose has been covered with stucco. The footprint is 22 feet across the front and 12 feet on the sides. The flat roof and floor are also made of concrete. The structure contains two cells of equal size with doors in the approximate center of the cells. The interior doors are made of flat metal in a crisscross pattern that created square openings for light and ventilation. The exterior doors are solid sheets of metal with no openings. When closed, the only light and air flow would have been through the windows. The two cells are divided by a concrete wall. There are three freestanding metal army cots and a mattress in the cell on the left, but

Presidio calaboose (photo courtesy of Brad Newton).

Toilet and sink in the Presidio calaboose (photo courtesy of Brad Newton).

it is not known if they were used by prisoners. Each cell has a porcelain sink and toilet. Both cells are adorned with graffiti; at the time of this writing, it was protected from vandals by a wire fence. This calaboose has six windows. Two are on the front, centered above the doors; one is centered on each side wall; and two are on the back wall and centered on the cells. These windows are larger than most in the current sample and are higher above the ground than those on most calabooses. Another feature of the windows is the presence of heavy mesh wire behind the bars. This has only been observed on two other calabooses so far. Brad L. Newton interviewed Edmund Nieto, who was ninety-seven at the time. Mr. Nieto stated that the jail was built in the late 1920s or early 1930s when he was a teenager. He said that "as kids, we would watch for the lights to come on. We would go peek in to see who they had locked up."[167] He also said that the local teens did not want to be in that place. Mr. Nieto's grandfather, William Russell, was the first sheriff in Presidio. A regular "guest" in those days was Ramon Baraga. When he got paid he would drink until someone would call the law and put him in the calaboose A possible special arrest occurred on January 14, 1942, when Tomas Castenada and Jose Chavez were arrested for smuggling by Sheriff Juan Ochan and two Texas Rangers. This jail was commonly referred to by the old timers as *el Bote*, which translates as "the Can." The walls are adorned with graffiti written in chalk and pencil with dates from the 1930s to as late as 1969.

Quemado

Maverick County

LOCATION: Private Property

OWNER: Privately Owned

DATE BUILT: 1937

SIZE: 124 square feet

The town received its unusual name because it was in the Quemado Valley, an area that the Spanish explorers believed had been parched by volcanic activity. Many of the early settlers came to this area in the late 1800s to escape the drought in the Texas Panhandle. Hans Lahrman started the business of beekeeping, a trade that became an important industry in the area in the early 1900s. The greatest period of growth was in the 1930s when the Maverick County Irrigation Canal provided a dependable source of water and made truck farming and livestock raising possible.[168] This concrete calaboose has two cells of equal size arranged in a side-by-side pattern. The barred doors are covered with modern tin to keep out rain.

Quemado calaboose (photo courtesy of Rhonda K. Holley).

This is one of three calabooses in the current sample that has doors of different sizes. Other examples are in Eden and Holland. The door on the right measures 36 by 82 inches and the door on the left measures 36 by 84 inches. The two windows are very small, located on the back wall, and centered on the cells. The flat roof has a slight pitch from front to back, ostensibly for water runoff. At the time of my visit, this structure was being used for storage. There is a concrete feature on the inside that may have served as a platform for a toilet. Although the aggregate is small pebbles, the structure was also strengthened by the use of round metal bars that were observed protruding from one of the walls. Overall, its structural integrity is poor. There were no Sanborn maps for Quemado at the time of this study. In a county where the July mean temperature is 100 degrees Fahrenheit, this building must have been a very uncomfortable place day or night.

Riesel

McLennan County

LOCATION: Behind the old Masonic Lodge located on the corner of Frederick and South Wiebusch Streets in Riesel

OWNER: Riesel Historical Society

DATE BUILT: 1910

SIZE: 77 square feet

Riesel is another small Texas town tied to the railroad and cotton production. The Houston and Texas Central Railway built a section house called Roddy circa 1880. W. H. Riesel built a cotton gin in 1890, and the town was named after him. In 1900, the population was 268, and banks were opened in 1906 and 1910. By 1930, Riesel boasted 420 residents and twenty businesses.[169] This calaboose was moved from its original location in Mart, Texas, to its current site on private property on September 27, 1910. On October 14, 1910, it welcomed its first prisoners: a black, a Mexican, and a person of Greek descent. In 1911, the first female prisoner was in town with the Kennedy and Booger Red's Show, which was there for a performance. She did something that caused her to spend a night in the calaboose, but her crime was never revealed. She is quoted as saying

Riesel calaboose (photo courtesy of Darryl Pearson).

that she was not "over pleased" with Riesel's hospitality.[170] This tiny building was constructed using very wide milled boards to create the exterior walls. The roof is slanted to the back and consists of wide boards covered with corrugated tin. The wooden door on the exterior covers two metal doors with bars. These doors provided entry to two cells of equal size. They are connected to the building by three large metal hinges and a metal bar across the front that can be locked to provide additional security. There are only two small windows, and they are on the back wall. Each window contains three vertically placed flat metal bars. The walls are covered with thin sheets of very rusty metal. The bars on the windows are fastened to the wall on the inside, and that is a feature I have not seen before. The structure rests on a concrete slab and is supported by modern concrete piers. There were no Sanborn maps for Riesel at the time of this study. Its original location in Riesel has never been confirmed, but resident researcher Ruth Foster believes that it used to be on property occupied by the cotton gin in operation at the time. That would put it somewhere between North and Frederick Streets and east of Main Street.[171]

Ringgold

Montague County

LOCATION: Downtown Ringgold on Highway 19 between Fifth Street and the intersection of Highway 19 and Loop 19 in Ringgold

OWNER: County of Montague

DATE BUILT: Unknown

SIZE: 83 square feet

Ringgold became an organized community in 1892 when the Rock Island Line extended service to the area and intersected with the Missouri, Kansas and Texas Railroad. Ringgold became a major market center for the area due to the location of the town at the intersection of the two railroads. During the 1920s, the population had grown to four hundred, and eighteen businesses had been established.[172] This calaboose is one of the few remaining structures in the old downtown area. Max Brown is a resident

Ringgold calaboose (photo courtesy of Max Brown).

of Ringgold and an active participant in the movement to save the local calaboose. He provided the following information:[173] At the time it served as a calaboose, it was behind the McCall Company hardware store that faced Main Street; the store was owned by Will Hawkins and others. The key to the jail was kept in the store, and it is believed that it was lost in 1939 when the store was destroyed by fire. The date 1934 carved in the west wall is not an indicator of when it was built, but it shows that it was still in use during that time. Local resident Bill Rushing remembers climbing on top of the old calaboose sometime in the late 1930s after it was no longer used as such. His maternal grandfather, William Hawkins, was the town marshal during the 1920s, and he told Bill that most people who spent time there were arrested for minor infractions such as public intoxication, fighting, and disturbing the peace. This is the only calaboose in the current sample that was constructed using a mixture of concrete and stone. The flat roof is concrete and was made using the poured-in-place method. The opening for the door is centered on the front wall and measures 32 inches wide. Unfortunately, the door is no longer present. There are two small windows with round metal bars. They were placed on the north and east walls. The floor is dirt and below ground level. It varies from 76 inches below the ceiling in the front to 70 inches below the ceiling at the back. There is no evidence that the jail had a wood floor or other amenities such as plumbing or electricity. The walls are approximately 1 foot thick. A hole in the northeast corner measures 8 by 11 inches and is irregular in shape. The purpose for this opening is not known, but Mr. Brown suggested it might have been for ventilation if there had been a heater inside. The pattern of the boards used to create the form for pouring concrete for the ceiling is visible on the inside, and it is possible to count the number of boards that were used. This historic structure is being protected by the county and will serve as a memorial to the early days of the town.

Rochester

Haskell County

LOCATION: Inside the fenced City Water Plant at the corner of Fourth Avenue and Main Street in Rochester

OWNER: City of Rochester

DATE BUILT: Unknown

SIZE: 120 square feet

Rochester was founded in 1906 when the Kansas City, Mexico and Orient Railway was constructed. In 1915, it had a population of four hundred, and incorporation occurred in 1922.[174] This brick calaboose is unique in that it has a concrete roof that was poured in a barrel shape. Other brick calabooses have concrete roofs, but they are usually flat or have a slight pitch. The floor is also concrete. There are three windows, one on each

Rochester calaboose (photo courtesy of Jo Brown).

side and one on the back. Another unique feature is the placement of the windows. The two on the sides are 35 inches from the ground, and the one on the rear wall is only 29 inches from the ground. The bars are secured in wooden frames and run parallel to the ground, a feature not common in most calabooses. The walls have two courses of bricks for strength. Overall, this structure is in very stable condition. The city uses it for storage.

Rosebud

Falls County

LOCATION: 217 West Avenue D in Rosebud

OWNER: City of Rosebud

DATE BUILT: Post-1914

SIZE: 177 square feet

Rosebud calaboose (photo by the author).

Rosebud was developed by the Texas Townsite Company in 1889. The town experienced rapid growth following the construction of the San Antonio and Aransas Pass Railway in 1892. On November 7, 1905, Rosebud was incorporated. Cotton raising provided the major form of employment; cotton grew successfully due to the rich black soil. In the 1920s, there were seven cotton gins and a cottonseed mill.[175] The year this concrete calaboose was built is not known, but it is likely that it coincided with the growth during the 1920s. Its two cells are arranged side by side. The entrance to each cell is secured by a solid metal door in front of a door with bars. There are four windows, one at each end and one behind each cell on the back wall. The windows are unique in that they are covered with sheet metal that has been perforated to create a grate-like appearance. This is covered with another piece of metal with diagonal-shaped openings. This is one of the few calabooses where the windows are not secured with bars. At one time, all four windows had wooden shutters or doors that allowed them to be closed off from light and air. The gable roof was created with poured concrete. A metal pipe behind the structure extends above the roof, but no connection with the interior of the calaboose could be detected. The city recognizes the significance of this structure and is working on plans to best protect it and make it available to the public.[176]

Rosser

Kaufman County

LOCATION: Private Property

OWNER: Privately Owned

DATE BUILT: Unknown

SIZE: 76 square feet

Rosser is another Texas town that owes its growth to the railroad. In 1872, construction on the Texas and Pacific Railway began, and people looking for work flocked to the area. The result was a town of tents. Local commerce was tied to cotton and was augmented by a sawmill and gristmill. The population increased from 128 in 1904 to 350 in 1925. It is likely that the local calaboose was built during that time. Many residents left Rosser in the 1940s for wartime jobs in urban areas.[177] The floor plan of

Rosser calaboose (photo by the author).

this calaboose is two side-by-side cells. One of the unusual features is that the cells are not equal in size. The doors were in the center of the structure and virtually next to each other. This arrangement has only been seen in two calabooses, with the most notable example the one in Riesel. There are two small windows for each cell, and each one has three round metal bars placed vertically and evenly spaced. The doors to the cells and the roof are missing. The floor is concrete, and the roof was probably made from the same material. The aggregate used to bind the concrete structure consisted of small pebbles that are visible in areas where they have become exposed due to weathering. Including the foundation, eleven pouring episodes were required to reach the desired height. Some furniture may have been present, but there was no plumbing or electricity. No Sanborn map for Rosser was available at the time of my visit.

Rowena

Runnels County

LOCATION: Private Property

OWNER: Privately Owned

DATE BUILT: circa 1910

SIZE: 110 square feet

Rowena was laid out in 1898 by Paul J. Baron and named Baronsville in his honor. The Santa Fe Railroad was a major factor in the growth of this town. In 1904, the population was fewer than one hundred, but cotton production and an influx of immigrants created a boom that resulted in a population between four hundred and six hundred in 1908. The town reached its peak number of residents in 1930 with eight hundred people living there.[178] Beverly Teplicek is a member of the Runnels County Historical Commission and a resident of Rowena.[179] She provided me with

Rowena calaboose (photo by the author).

much of the information regarding the history of this historic structure. The exact age of this building is not known, but there is a sign on the front that reads "Town Jail—Circa 1910." According to Mrs. Teplicek, this date may be based solely on hearsay. This structure is in poor condition but it is not in immediate danger of collapse. It was constructed using milled boards over a frame that created a double wall, probably to make escape more difficult. Wire nails appear to have been used throughout the construction. I was unable to inspect the interior, but I saw no furniture or other amenities through the door, and Mrs. Teplicek is not aware of any having been there in the past. The foundation is pier and beam. The boards on the exterior measure 11 to 12 inches in width and are about 1 inch thick. This structure consists of only one room. The door is metal and consists of a frame with vertical, horizontal, and diagonal bars secured with rivets. The two metal features on the right side of the door may have served as hinges for an outer door that is now missing. This structure is covered with a gable roof framed of wood and covered with tin. Some panels appear to be replacements. There is one small opening on each side, but the one on the north side is the largest and, because it has been framed, it appears that this calaboose may have had only one small window that would have been 12 inches square. Because of the absence of bars this is only conjecture. There were no Sanborn maps for Rowena available at the time of this study. The infamous Bonnie Parker was born in Rowena on October 1, 1910, the same year that this calaboose was supposedly built.

Royse City

Rockwall County

LOCATION: Between 217 East Main and 305 East Main where Main Street intersects with Plum Street in Royse City

OWNER: Royse City

DATE BUILT: Between 1911 and 1921

SIZE: 129 square feet

Settlement in the area began in earnest when it became known that the Missouri, Kansas and Texas Railroad would be constructed in the area. The first business was a general store, and it opened its doors in 1885. By

Royse City calaboose on a foggy day (photo courtesy of Daniel Stahl).

Royse City calaboose in the twilight (photo courtesy of Jack Palmer)

1890, there were one thousand residents in town along with two cotton gins, a gristmill, and twenty businesses. In 1906, the community was officially incorporated. In 1914, the town boasted 1,300 residents and forty businesses.[180] This calaboose contains two cells that are equal in size and side by side. The concrete exterior was covered with stucco. The use of stucco was considered to be a cosmetic treatment, but it also protected the underlying concrete from additional cracking and deterioration. Similar stucco treatments were applied to buildings that were constructed from 1910 through the 1930s. In some areas where the stucco has peeled away, the joints between the layers of poured concrete are exposed. There is no visible evidence of rebar in the wall profiles. A higher than normal ratio of aggregate to cement was used, and this is probably the reason for the settling and ultimate crumbling of the walls. Since it does not appear on the Sanborn map dated 1911,[181] but is depicted on the map dated June 1921,[182] it was built sometime between those years. Millie Jean Coppedge writes, "no one can be found who remembers when it was built or even the exact date of when it was no longer used."[183] Zaner (Robinson) Benetin has been quoted as saying that in 1942 it was no longer being used as a jail.[184] At one time, there was a movement to destroy it. Ms. Benetin was in the Rotary Club, and this organization was able to preserve it, and they are responsible for its maintenance. This area was turned into a park and is now called the "Royse City Old Jail Park." At the time of this writing, Julia Bryant of the local chamber of commerce was leading the effort to preserve this historic structure, and some progress has been made.

Santa Anna

Coleman County

LOCATION: Next to the old Fire Department building at 610 Avenue B in Santa Anna

OWNER: City of Santa Anna

DATE BUILT: post-1921

SIZE: 192 square feet

Santa Anna is located at the juncture of the Atchison, Topeka and Santa Fe Railway and several major US highways. The town was incorporated in

Santa Anna calaboose (photo by the author).

1906. By 1910, it had a population of 1,453 and a city water system. Four years later, there were three cotton gins two banks, churches, telephone service, electric lights, and gas. The Texas Glass Company opened in the 1930s and provided an extra boost to the economy.[185] The date that this interesting calaboose was constructed is not known, but it would have been sometime after 1921 based on its absence on the August 1921 Sanborn map. It was moved to its current location in 1927.[186] The Sanborn map dated May 1930 appears to confirm this statement in that it is depicted in city block 11 (lot 11) facing an alley and behind a brick building that housed city hall, the Fire Department, and the Water Department at 143 Second Street.[187] It is described on the map as made of fire-proof construction and concrete throughout. This structure was fabricated of concrete mixed with small pebbles and pieces of unidentified metal for strength. This mixture appears to not have been adequate because there are several places where erosion is seriously affecting the integrity of this calaboose. The doors are a very unusual feature of this structure. There are two sets of metal doors, each in two pieces that open in opposite directions. The exterior doors open outward while the interior set opens inward. This is the only calaboose in the current sample like this. Neither set of doors has any windows or openings that could have been used to pass food and other items to the prisoners. Use of these doors may have been prompted by their availability, which would have saved the city the cost of making or buying new doors. The only source of light and ventilation would have been the two windows, one on each side, and they have metal bars placed vertically and horizontally in a metal frame that is embedded in the concrete. The floor of the structure is also concrete, and no furnishings were observed on the inside. The roof is best described as flat with a slight pitch from front to back. Local resident Montie Guthrie recalled that at one time there was a metal cot for the prisoners to use.[188] The exact year that the local calaboose was no longer used is also not known. However, Mickey Dodson remembers it still housing bad guys as late as 1969.[189] Following its usefulness as a jail, it served as an office for the justice of the peace, Earl Irick, and as an office for the city's public scales. Gary Patterson, another resident of Santa Anna, confessed that he might be the last person alive to have been locked up in this calaboose.[190] He related a humorous story that involved the night watchman. They could pull the door open enough for the smallest to slip out and go get the night watchman who had forgotten to let them out. According to the research conducted by Gladys Hunter,[191] this building was mainly used for punishing the perpetrators of petty crimes, and the local constables had jurisdiction. During Christmas and other special occasions, extra night watchmen were hired. Hunter writes that seventeen boys were locked up at one time for shooting off firecrackers. They called out for matches, cigarettes, and water. During the 1950s a curfew bell sat atop the roof. Local historian Ralph Terry shared his knowledge of this building and other happenings in the county.[192]

Seadrift

Calhoun County

LOCATION: 104 East Houston near the entrance to the Seadrift Sports Complex Park in Seadrift

OWNER: City of Seadrift

DATE BUILT: circa 1914

SIZE: 163 square feet

Seadrift calaboose (photo courtesy of Darryl Pearson).

The town existed since 1891, but it was not until 1911 when development took off. A. D. Powers offered five acres outside the city limits for each lot purchased in the city limits. The next year incorporation took place and the first city council meeting was held. Two years later, the town had three churches, two banks, a telephone connection, four hotels, and 1,250 residents. On June 28, 1919, the town was severely damaged by a large hurricane and many residents moved. The population was only 321 in 1926.[193]

The sign placed at the site of the calaboose makes the claim that it was the first and only jail built in Seadrift and that it was constructed circa 1914. It stands today in its original location.[194] This is another example of the blocky concrete calabooses that were fairly common in Texas during the early part of the twentieth century. The flat roof is typical of these types of structures. Unfortunately, the original door is missing. However, the metal bars in the two windows are still present. One rare feature in the calabooses I have encountered is the presence of wire mesh behind the bars; it is present in this structure. These windows are a decent size for adequate light during the day and air flow at all times. The floor is also concrete. During the city's centennial celebration in 2012, two cells made of wood and chicken wire were constructed in the interior. Some murals were painted on the exterior but they are now faded.

Sealy

Austin County

LOCATION: Santa Fe Museum Park at 211 East Main in Sealy

OWNER: Sealy Area Historical Society

DATE BUILT: 1887

SIZE: 140 square feet

This town has prospered because of its junction with the Missouri, Kansas and Texas and the Atchison, Topeka and Santa Fe Railroads. Because of the proximity to these railroads, Sealy became a major shipping center, and a post office was established in 1880. Unfortunately, a flood involving the Brazos River in 1899, the relocation of the Gulf, Colorado and Santa Fe Railway division headquarters to Bellville, and the hurricane of 1900 were major disasters that had to be overcome. In 1931, the future looked better, with an estimated two thousand residents and ninety

Sealy calaboose (photo courtesy of Nancy Naron).

Interior of the Sealy calaboose (photo courtesy of Nancy Naron).

businesses that included the Sealy Mattress Factory and the Engleking Brothers Broom Factory.[195] The first jail in Sealy was built in 1884, but it burned after only a few years of use. The one discussed here was built in 1887, and some of the boards from the previous structure were salvaged and used in its construction. The next jail was built in 1928.[196] Therefore, this calaboose could have served as a lockup from 1887 until 1928. Unfortunately, no Sanborn maps for Sealy were available at the time of this study. The walls of this building are covered with milled boards placed in a vertical position over boards that were attached horizontally. This method provides stronger walls for security against escapes. Narrow strips of wood cover the spaces between the boards to create the board and batten look. The door is offset to the left and is not original. The gable roof is covered with tin. This calaboose consists of two rooms and is the same basic floor plan as the one in Wallis. Just inside the door is an open room that was used by law enforcement officers, and it probably had a desk and other pieces of furniture. The cell is behind a wooden wall and measures 71 square feet. The boards in the front room are planks that were measured at 1 by 12 inches. Wooden planks used to create the floor are exposed in the front room. The floor in the cell was covered with a layer of thin sheet metal, and there is a metal ring in the center of the floor that could have been used to shackle prisoners. The metal also covered the walls to a point just below the ceiling. It was attached to the walls with massive metal bolts. There are four windows. The two in the front room are the largest, and the two in the cell are very high up on the wall and are much smaller. To the right of the door that separates the front room from the cell there is a small window that allowed law enforcement a view inside the cell. The interior door was secured by a massive metal latch and was constructed of four layers of boards, which make it extremely strong. Wooden calabooses were common, but only a few have been documented during this study with walls to the cells made of wood. Other examples are Wallis, Lakeview, and Plaska. This calaboose was donated to the Sealy Area Historical Society by the Cletus Brown family of Brookshire, Texas, in 1991.

Skidmore

Bee County

LOCATION: Skidmore Historical Society Museum at Highway 181 and Sullivan Street in Skidmore

OWNER: Skidmore Historical Society

DATE BUILT: Circa 1898

SIZE: 147 square feet

The town was formed in 1886 when Frank O. Skidmore donated the town site, right-of-way, and land to the San Antonio and Aransas Pass Railway. In 1893, the town was moved to its current location south of Aransas Creek. By 1914, there were one thousand residents in town along with three saloons and eight stores. The growth of the town was hindered due to three large fires in 1913, 1918, and 1929 and the declining importance of the railroad.[197] This small calaboose was built in 1898 and was moved from its original location near the justice of the peace office to the museum as a permanent exhibit in the 1970s.[198] The walls are vertical board and batten, and the pyramid hip roof consists of wooden shingles. There are three windows, one on each side and one in the back. The windows on the sides are centered on the wall and low to the ground. They are covered with wooden doors that can be opened when light or ventilation is needed. If the existing door is original, these windows would have been the only places where air and light could pass through. The window on the back wall is also centered and low to the ground, but it is much larger and contains bars made of flat metal that are riveted together in a checkerboard pattern. It is probable that a wooden door at one time covered this

Skidmore calaboose (photo courtesy of Carol Dubois).

Skidmore calaboose, window detail (photo courtesy of Carol Dubois).

window as well. There is a metal bed inside, but its exact age is not known. There were no Sanborn maps at the agencies visited for Skidmore at the time of this study.

Somerville

Burleson County

LOCATION: Somerville Historical Museum at 742 Memory Lane in Somerville

OWNER: Somerville Historical Society

DATE BUILT: 1940s

SIZE: 163 square feet

Somerville was incorporated on March 19, 1913, and law enforcement in those days consisted of a city marshal. Confinement was to be in the "town prison/calaboose of the Town Hall."[199] Meals for the prisoners

Somerville calaboose (photo by the author).

would consist of bread and water.[200] Bubba Scott is a lifetime resident of Somerville, and he remembers a wooden outbuilding being used as a calaboose until a real jail could be constructed.[201] He also said that the concrete calaboose discussed here was made by a local contractor named Oscar Landolt sometime around 1940. The two cells are equal in size and divided by a wooden wall made of planks placed horizontally from front to back. This is the only concrete calaboose in the current sample where the cells are divided by a wooden wall. The floor is cement, and each cell was furnished with a sink and toilet. There were two doors to each cell. The exterior door is metal and consists of six round metal bars welded to the frame in a vertical direction. Added support was created by three pieces of strap iron welded to the frame in a horizontal direction. The interior doors were wood, but only one remains today. When the wooden doors were closed, the only light and ventilation would have been through the two tiny windows at the back that are centered on each cell. The flat roof is also concrete. During the 1940s, Kenneth Scott was the constable and Bob Massey was the night watchman.[202] Scott's deputy was Romeo Lewis, and he became the next constable after Mr. Scott left office. Bubba said

Toilet in the Somerville calaboose (photo by the author).

that Somerville was a rough town in those days with lots of saloons and billiards parlors.[203] Prisoners did not like being locked up in those tiny cells with no heat in the winter and little or no ventilation in the summer. Lonnie Ray is a former citizen of Somerville, and he remembers the calaboose still being used as late as 1969.[204] The sheriff was Milton Lewis who owned the city café next door to Boones's IGA grocery store downtown on State Highway 36. Lonnie Ray and the sheriff were good friends. Typically, prisoners only stayed there overnight or a few hours until they could be transported to the county jail in Caldwell or turned loose. It was usually used on weekends as people would get paid on Fridays from picking or chopping cotton and get liquored up and fight. There was a lot of knifing in those days, and Mr. Lewis was real busy on weekends. He knew many people who spent time in the Somerville calaboose, including some of his friends. Ann Guadango conducted research on Thomas Lannuzzi, who was in Somerville from 1948 to March 1949.[205] She said he was arrested by police officers from Newark, New Jersey, and placed in the Somerville calaboose. He was so well liked that during the time he was locked up people would bring him food; one time, over five hundred people gathered outside wanting to break him out. During his stay in town he supposedly worked as bartender and manager of the local honky-tonk. In 2003, the calaboose was moved from its original location to the museum grounds, where it will be preserved for future generations as an example of life in the early days of Somerville.

Spofford

Kinney County

LOCATION: Private Property

OWNER: Privately Owned

DATE BUILT: Unknown

SIZE: 73 square feet

Spofford calaboose (photo courtesy of Darryl Pearson).

Spofford is located on the Southern Pacific Railroad; a railroad depot named Spofford Junction was established there by the Galveston, Harrisburg and San Antonio Railway in 1882. The community became a shipping point for area ranchers. In 1896, the town had a population of 125 and numerous saloons. The town grew and by 1906 it had expanded south of the railroad. The population reached a high of two hundred by 1914, and telephones were present in some homes.[206] The calaboose at Spofford is an example of the use of metal cages placed inside structures. The cage rests on a concrete slab that appears to be original due to the presence of a groove around the edge that strongly suggests a former wooden structure. The exterior walls are no longer present. The cage is beneath a wooden roof supported by posts but it is not known if the roof and posts are original. No attempt was made to describe the form of the roof because of its collapsed condition. The cage has two cells of equal size. It has no windows because the doors and back wall are perforated with 4-inch-square holes. There are openings near the top of the doors that were probably used to pass food and other objects to the prisoners. The roof and floor are also metal. There is graffiti on the inside but much of it was not legible. It was difficult to get close to the cage in some places because of thick vegetation.

Stiles

Reagan County

LOCATION: Reagan County Park at 1205 Montana Street in Big Lake, Texas

OWNER: County of Reagan

DATE BUILT: Circa 1903

SIZE: 90 square feet

Stiles was founded in 1894 and was the only town in the area when Reagan County was organized in 1903 with L. M. Rankin as the sheriff. In 1910, the route of the Kansas City, Mexico and Orient Railway bypassed Stiles. Big Lake was established in 1911, and it became the new county seat in 1925 due to the proximity of the railroad and the oil boom near town. At that time, a new stone courthouse was built that contained a jail. The

Stiles calaboose (photo courtesy of Rhonda K. Holley).

above information was taken from Ed Blackburn's book on county jails of Texas.[207] The wooden calaboose discussed here was probably abandoned as a lockup for prisoners following the construction of the courthouse and jail. This structure contains two small windows on the sides that are secured by three round metal bars placed vertically and horizontally. The door was created by fastening boards vertically over a second set of horizontal boards. There is a small window in the door that contains three vertically placed flat bars apparently made of strap iron riveted to three similar horizontal bars. The hinges and lock are made of massive steel. The walls were constructed by placing boards in a flat position and stacked to the flat roof with interlocking corners. The tin roof and boards supporting it are replacements. It probably had a dirt floor and no electricity or plumbing. There were no Sanborn maps for Stiles at the time of this study. The calaboose was moved to the town of Big Lake from Stiles and placed in the county park for preservation. Today, it rests on a rock pad behind a chain link fence.

Stockdale

Wilson County

LOCATION: Corner of South Third and West Pearson Streets next to the city water tower in Stockdale

OWNER: City of Stockdale

DATE BUILT: Unknown

SIZE: 72 square feet

The town received its name from Fletcher S. Stockdale, who was the lieutenant governor when the town was established in 1863. The San Antonio and Gulf Railroad passed through town in 1898. This event spurred growth, and the population grew from three hundred in 1885 to nine hundred in 1914.[208] This concrete calaboose is one of the smallest in terms of square feet in the current sample. The date of its construction is not known, but it is likely that construction took place shortly after incor-

Stockdale calaboose (photo courtesy of Rhonda K. Holley).

poration in 1919. There are two windows that were placed on the side walls, and they have six horizontally placed round metal bars inserted into a wooden window frame. The only source of light and ventilation is the opening in the door and the two windows. The interior consists of one open room that was being used for storage at the time of my visit. The exterior is covered with stucco that created a smooth surface. A fresh coat of paint was added by the city to the walls and door. The roof is flat, but the builders went above and beyond the mere creation of a functional roof. The product is a most attractive structure adorned with a castellated parapet around the top. This architectural expression is created by the construction of crenellations or battlements with alternate raised or lowered sections. Banks Akin is the city manager, and he said that the last time it was known to have been used as a jail was circa 1952.[209] He also said that this calaboose is one of the destinations for the Geocache game, and it is frequently visited. The key was lost some years ago, and entry is not possible without damaging the lock. There were no Sanborn maps at the agencies visited for Stockdale at the time of this study.

Thorndale

Milam County

LOCATION: Private Property

OWNER: Privately Owned

DATE BUILT: 1930

SIZE: 140 square feet

The city incorporated in 1929, and the Thorndale Independent School District was formed the same year. Its population at that time was 1,500, but the onset of the Great Depression caused a decline. An employee of the International–Great Northern Railroad who had passed through named the town for the abundant thorny vegetation in the area.[210] In 1930, the local calaboose was on railroad property. The Thorndale City Council met on July 14, 1930, and one item on the agenda was the building of a new jail.[211] On July 19, 1930, a second meeting was held, and the motion to build a new jail of concrete at a cost not to exceed $375 was approved.[212] The city contracted with G. W. Gunn to remove the old calaboose and

Thorndale calaboose (photo by the author).

be responsible for the construction of the new one. The lot for the new calaboose was obtained for a sum of $50, paid to V. F. Norris. At the city council meeting on August 11, 1930, the installation of a light at the new jail was approved.[213] The city marshal at the time was R. L. Ratte Jr.

This structure is made of concrete and covered with plaster. The floor is also concrete, and the roof is best described as domed. It is one of the few calabooses with three rooms and only the second with rooms in a straight line. The solid metal door opens into the first cell, which has two metal bed frames on the east wall. The middle room also has two metal bed frames on the east wall. The second and third rooms are separated by a wall and metal door with bars. The third room still contains the original toilet and a sink, another rarity in Texas calabooses built during this period. Ventilation and light is provided by four windows made up of four vertically placed round bars over flat bars set into the window frame in a diagonal pattern. Three windows are on the east side, and one is on the west side opposite the third window on the east side. On the back of the jail is a metal pipe that probably provided ventilation for the bathroom. There is a circular feature made of cement with a metal band around the top on the east side that may be related to the sewer system that serviced the jail. The writing on the metal band states that it was made by the Dallas Foundry, but not all of the writing is legible. At the time of my visit in 2013, the front room was being used for storage. There were no Sanborn maps at the agencies visited for Thorndale at the time of this study. This calaboose is privately owned; the city has tried without success to purchase it and move it to a place where it can be preserved.[214]

Tioga

Grayson County

LOCATION: Corner of Main and North Lamar in Tioga

OWNER: City of Tioga

DATE BUILT: Circa 1906

SIZE: 228 square feet

Tioga was founded in 1881 when the Texas and Pacific Railway came through town. At the time, the community already had two churches, a school, cotton gin, grocery, general store, pharmacist, carpenter, and blacksmith. The population was a meager sixty inhabitants. The town

Tioga calaboose (photo courtesy of Lawrence DeVoto).

became well known in 1884 when the blacksmith, Matt Rains, discovered medicinal qualities in the local water. Companies marketed the water, and trainloads of health seekers reportedly came to Tioga each day. Incorporation took place in 1906. In 1925, the population peaked at 777.[215] This calaboose was made using local brick. The gable roof is covered with tin and may not be original. The door is heavy-gauge metal with perforations for light and ventilation. There are windows on the other three walls, but they are very small. In 1914, this calaboose is depicted on the Sanborn maps as being located at 317 College.[216] In 1922, the street was called College Avenue, and the calaboose was still at the same location.[217] College Avenue is now known as North Lamar. These are the only maps available at the time of this study. Local historian James Hilliard recalled that the jail was still used in the 1970s but mainly to lock up drunks.[218] He said that at one time there was a hole in one of the walls, and the offenders could escape in the morning when they were sober. That hole has since been repaired. Ross Estes related his memories of living in Tioga to Robert J. Duncan who compiled and edited what he said for a book titled *I Remember Things: An Informal History of Tioga, Texas*. The following quote is from that book:[219] "Ol Doc got drunk one time and they put him in this little old calaboose out here. Had an iron door to it, and they locked him up in there. He'd got drunk, cussin'; the law took him down there and put him in that calaboose. It 'us hot in there. He 'us big and fat anyhow, and it 'us summertime. They was some little boys around there, and Doc, he looked out them little windows. He hired them boys to carry him water up there. They carried him water 'til 12 o'clock. They 'us just kids and they got sleepy and wanted to go home. He got them to go up to the house, then, and wake his wife up, and tell her to give him water 'til after daylight."

Tivoli

Refugio County

LOCATION: Refugio County Museum at 102 West Street in Refugio

OWNER: Refugio County

DATE BUILT: Unknown

SIZE: 192 square feet

Tivoli calaboose (photo courtesy of Darryl Pearson).

Tivoli was founded by Preston Rose Austin in 1907 and named after his Tivoli ranch. In 1912, a branch of the Saint Louis, Brownsville and Mexico Railway was extended through town, and river traffic was no longer the major artery for transporting goods. The arrival of the railroad caused rapid growth, and the town became a shipping point for cotton farmers and ranchers. The population had increased to four hundred in 1914, and a bank and telephone service were available to the residents. The population reached its peak in 1928 at seven hundred but decreased in the 1930s due to the Great Depression and decline of the cotton industry.[220] The Reverend Mack Williams, of the Mount Galilee Baptist Church in Tivoli, purchased the calaboose for $25 in 1993.[221] He wanted to repair the old jail, so he moved it to Garza Grocery on Interstate Highway 35 in Tivoli. When the reverend passed away, the folks around town knew that he wanted it "fixed up" and made into a museum. They moved it to the museum in Refugio behind the fire station where it sits today. Mr. Wales said that the museum has plans to restore the building when and if funding can be obtained. This is a rectangular structure with only one door. The floor is wood, the hip roof is covered with wooden shingles that are not original, and the walls consist of boards stacked horizontally like the logs of a cabin. These boards measure 2 by 8 inches and 2 by 10 inches. The current board and batten exterior may have been added in the 1940s when the structure underwent repairs. The interior is divided into two rooms with the front room occupying about two-thirds of the area. The rooms are divided by a wooden wall. The door in place now may not be original. It has been reported that prisoners were sometimes shackled to metal hooks on the wall and/or rings on the ceiling, and some of the hooks and rings are still in place. Each side wall has two windows. Three of these are small and secured with round metal bars in a vertical position. On one side a large opening is covered by a wooden shutter. The back of the building has no doors or windows. The only door is on the front.

Trenton

Fannin County

LOCATION: Corner of West Saunders and Pearl Streets in Trenton

OWNER: City of Trenton

DATE BUILT: 1930s

SIZE: 120 square feet

The information here was obtained from the online version of the *Handbook of Texas*;[222] a personal interview with Tom Mac Holmes, editor of the *Trenton Tribune*;[223] and a document by Janice Golden Smith.[224] In 1875, Trenton was a thriving community that experienced rapid growth with the arrival of the Denison Southeastern Railroad (later the Missouri, Kansas, and Texas Railroad) in 1881. The town was platted by Dr. W. C. Holmes (also known as the Father of Trenton) who was a pioneer physician and editor of the *Trenton Tribune*. By 1885, the population had reached two hundred and the town had a score of businesses. There was also a town marshal, jail, and several doctors. In the early 1930s, the town experienced more growth due to the large-scale production of cotton and onions. The increase in population and arrival of migrant workers hired to work in the fields probably created the climate for an increase in crime that led to the need for a jail. The walls were constructed with 2- by 6-foot boards lying flat on top of one another, and tin was used for the walls and roof. Only

Trenton calaboose (photo courtesy of Lawrence DeVoto).

one small window on the rear wall is present for light and ventilation. It consists of seven metal bars placed vertically in a wooden frame. The roof is an example of the pyramidal style. D. H. Glen was the person in charge of keeping law and order in those days, and he was often referred to as the night watchman. In the 1930s or 1940s, pranksters tied the calaboose to a boxcar with a rope or chain, and when the train pulled out it dragged the calaboose along with it. The city rebuilt it using as much of the original lumber as possible. Later, it was returned to its original location where it sits today. There were no Sanborn maps at the agencies visited for Trenton, Texas, at the time of this study.

Turkey

Hall County

LOCATION: Private Property

OWNER: Privately Owned

DATE BUILT: 1924

SIZE: 170 square feet

Turkey calaboose (photo courtesy of Shari Watson).

Turkey is at the intersection of two state highways and the Burlington Northern line. In 1900 the post office was opened, and the town was platted in 1907. Incorporation came in 1926, and there were an estimated six hundred residents in 1927. When the Fort Worth and Denver Railway came to town in 1928, Turkey became a major shipping point for farmers and ranchers. In 1929, there were two banks and a population of one thousand.[225] This calaboose is a rectangular shaped structure made of poured concrete with a flat roof. Its exact age is not known, and I was unable to find a Sanborn Fire Insurance Map for the town. The date 1924 is painted on the door, as that is when the locals believe it was constructed. It consists of two rooms. The front room is open and larger than the one at the back. Because of the size of the front room, it is assumed that it may have also served as a lockup area. At the back of the structure a small room is defined by metal bars and a door. Since entry to the calaboose was not possible at the time of our visit, we estimated that the cell is about 8 by 10 feet based on a change in the roof line at this distance. The metal door at the entry is solid metal. There is one very small window and it is on the rear wall.

Interior of the Turkey calaboose (photo courtesy of Shari Watson).

Wallis

Austin County

LOCATION: City Barn at 17402 Railroad Street in Wallis

OWNER: City of Wallis

DATE BUILT: 1908

SIZE: 170 square feet

The community now known as Wallis was first referred to as Bovine Bend. This changed when the Gulf, Colorado and Santa Fe Railway constructed a spur through the area and the settlement became known as Wallis Station in honor of J. E. Wallis, director of the railroad. The San Antonio and Aransas Pass Railway reached Wallis Station in 1887. In 1911, the name was shortened to Wallis. In 1925, the community was inhabited by eight

Wallis calaboose (photo courtesy of Rhonda K. Holley).

Shackle on the floor of the Wallis calaboose (photo courtesy of Rhonda K. Holley).

hundred citizens.[226] Donnie Marek, a resident of Wallis, has conducted research regarding this calaboose, and he found the following quote in the courthouse records: "Commissioners' Court voted on August 12, 1908 to build a calaboose made of solid steel with only 1 cell."[227] It is the consensus of the local residents that the original location of this calaboose was near the Wallis gin on Southern Pacific Railroad property off Guyler Street. Constable Joe Recnicek had metal skids attached to the bottom of the structure so it could be moved to a more desirable part of town, where it could be in the shade and not be as uncomfortable for the prisoners. It is divided into two rooms that are approximately the same size. The constable used the front room, and the room behind it was the cell. This calaboose is made of wood and covered with sheet metal. Until the city decided to paint it, Mr. Marek described it as "very rusty." The exterior walls consist of framing covered with 2- by 4-inch milled boards placed vertically. Entry is through a solid wooden door that is offset to the left. The only source of light for the constable's room is a window on each side wall. The wall between the two rooms was made using two-by-fours that were also placed vertically. The metal door that separated the two rooms was being stored in the cell at the time of my visit. Above this door is a small window with bars. Two small windows allowed light into the cell. There were two folding metal beds on the right wall and no other furniture. In the center of the floor is a heavy metal ring that could have been used to shackle the unruliest prisoners. This calaboose was used as a jail until the late 1950s. Eventually, the city decided that it is an important part of the town's history, and it was moved again around 2000. This time it was taken to the site of a water treatment plant and city hall pending its restoration and future home. The city has modified the building, and it was used as an office and storage for several years. In the front room, paneling was added and the building was wired for electricity. The gable roof is covered with composite shingles that are not original to the structure. Mr. Marek said that local vandals often shot at the jail when driving by, and the dents in the walls were caused by their bullets.[228] The city is considering applying for a historical marker from the Texas Historical Commission. There were no Sanborn maps available for Wallis at the time of this study.

Weesatche

Goliad County

LOCATION: South side of Seiler Road (a.k.a. State Highway 884) and east of a row of wooden commercial buildings and post office on the north side of the road in Weesatche

OWNER: City of Weesatche

DATE BUILT: Unknown

SIZE: Not measured

In 1892, Weesatche had a population of two hundred, saloon, two steam gristmills and cotton gins along with a school, hotel, and churches. A major part of the economy was shipping cotton, wool, and hides. In the late 1940s, the population began to decline.[229] This building was used mainly as a place to lock up drunks on Saturday night, and this task was carried out by the local constable or sheriff.[230] The exact date this wood calaboose was constructed is not known, and I was unable to find a Sanborn Fire Insurance Map for the town of Weesatche. The vertical siding was attached to horizontal framing members. The siding is planed or milled boards, and the spaces between the boards are covered with strips of wood to create the board and batten look. The gable roof is covered with wooden shingles

Weesatche calaboose (photo courtesy of Darryl Pearson).

over a wooden framework. The door and attached hardware appear to be original. Some recent restoration is obvious due to the presence of modern screws holding the hinges and part of the locking assembly. Currently, the city is using it for storage.[231]

Wellborn

Brazos County

LOCATION: Private Property

OWNER: Privately Owned

DATE BUILT: Unknown

SIZE: 144 square feet

Wellborn began as a railroad construction camp of the Houston and Texas Central Railroad in 1867. In 1910, the town had a school, two churches, steam gristmill, cotton gin, and four hundred residents.[232] This blocky

Wellborn calaboose (photo by the author).

concrete structure with a flat roof and concrete floor would be like many others if it were not for the window on the west wall. The size and shape are typical and the single door in the front and one open room identify it as belonging to the most common floor plan. The window, however, is unlike any of the others in the current sample. It is the largest in any calaboose I have seen as it covers an area of 16 square feet. The size is even more imposing when one considers the four walls are only 12 feet wide. Another unusual feature is the presence of rebar placed vertically and even spaced as if to form the bars for the window only to be replaced at a later date by a well-made iron set of round bars and flat metal strips. The door is missing, and it is believed it was sold for scrap. In its heyday, this calaboose was located behind a local saloon, and today it is one of the few original buildings of the old town of Wellborn still standing. Its current use is that of a convenient place for storing hay.

White Deer

Carson County

LOCATION: In the eastern half of a city block bounded by Highway 60 on the north, West Third Avenue on the south, South Omohundro Street on the east, and South Doucette Street on the west in White Deer. The calaboose is in an alley in the eastern half of the block and faces west.

OWNER: City of White Deer

DATE BUILT: Unknown

SIZE: 216 square feet

This one-story concrete calaboose is located in downtown White Deer, Texas. The date it was constructed is not known but the technique of poured-in-place concrete began in the early part of the twentieth century and was still used until at least the 1940s. This particular one-room calaboose is unique in that its 216-square-foot size is atypical of those with only a single room or cell. It is rectangular in shape with dimensions of

White Deer calaboose (photo courtesy of Rolland C. Reynolds Jr.).

12 feet across the front and 18 feet on the sides. The height is 7 feet 8 inches. The roof is best described as flat, although there is a slight dome-like surface that probably aided in the runoff of water during heavy rains. The solid metal door is offset to the right, and there is a large window on the left of the facade. In many cases, an offset door was an indicator of an entry room with a formal cell opposite it. This is the only calaboose in the current sample with this arrangement of door and window on the front. A second window on one side is also larger than those observed in most calabooses. Randy Reynolds visited the site and is responsible for the excellent photos and measurements. The number of episodes needed to pour the concrete for the walls was eight, and they are clearly marked by the horizontal lines created when new wooden forms were added. The roof was poured in one episode and was the last step. The two windows are larger than most, and the placement of the metal bars in a horizontal pattern is also not typical.

Wortham

Freestone County

LOCATION: Behind the Police Department at 104 West Concho Street in Wortham

OWNER: City of Wortham

DATE BUILT: 1915

SIZE: 180 square feet

The city of Wortham has an original Sanborn map that shows this calaboose on West Rusk Street (now West Concho), and it refers to it as a fireproof concrete structure built in 1915 that was in an alley in lot 9 of city block 31.[233] This date is also stated by an article in the *Mexia Daily News*, which reports that it was constructed in 1915 and used until 1950.[234] The same article refers to it as the original city jail that was built by contractors from Fairfield, Texas. It was referred to locally as the "Old Wortham Calaboose"; it was used mainly to house drunks and minor lawbreakers. Roy (Crook) Calame (constable) and John Edwards (city marshal) were among those who locked up prisoners in this inhospitable place. Wrongdoers were not released until they paid their fines to justice of the peace

Wortham calaboose (photo courtesy of Amy Boyd).

Esaw Crouch. Serious criminals were also confined there until Sheriff Jim Sessons from the county seat in Fairfield could come and get them.[235] The article is illustrated by a photograph of the calaboose that was taken during the early days of its use. The date of the photograph is not stated, but it may have been taken sometime around 1922. This calaboose is made of concrete with small pebbles as aggregate and metal rebar for extra strength. The mixture appears not to have been a proper proportion because serious deterioration is present in the southeast corner at the bottom of the wall, and there are minor areas of deterioration elsewhere. The flat roof is also concrete and was created by pouring cement and aggregate into a wooden form at the top. When the boards were removed, the impression of the grains of wood were present in some areas of the ceiling; this created the illusion of a ceiling of wood. The walls on the front and sides extend above the roof to create a parapet. This structure consists of two side-by-side cells of equal size. The doors are secured with metal bars that are a mixture of flat iron (horizontal bars) and iron with a rounded side (vertical bars). Another unusual feature is the massive metal hinge that secures the door on the left. An identical hinge was present on the other door but it has been removed. Diana Echartea, retired director of the Wortham Chamber of Commerce, said that John Conn was the former owner of the calaboose.[236] It is believed that he built the doors from rims of old wagon wheels that were straightened. Paul Conn Jr. was given the job of hand drilling the holes in the bars for the bolts.[237] There is one small window for each cell that was placed on each side of the calaboose. They are unique in that they are secured with sheets of flat metal with circular holes for light and ventilation.

This is the only calaboose like this in the current sample. In the ceiling of each cell is an opening that leads to metal pipes protruding from the roof. The purpose of these pipes is not known but they may have served as vents for a small heater. It is likely that most of the metal pieces used in this calaboose were made by a local sheet metal company in town. The town sponsors an annual event called "War on Hogs" where they try to raise money to help control these animals, which are viewed as pests. The Police Department has cooperated by locking up people in the calaboose for a donation. The donors would ask for a certain person to be arrested for the very popular event.

6

Jails

Beeville

Bee County

LOCATION: 605 South Hillside next to the new probation office in Beeville

OWNER: Bee County

DATE BUILT: 1874

SIZE: 448 square feet

This structure is reported to have been the first jail in the county. It was built in 1874 at a cost of $1,381.74 and was guarded by local citizens.[1] The exterior is vertical board and batten with double walls. The wooden flooring consists of four layers of boards placed in a crisscross pattern for extra strength. This was a common method used in the construction of wooden jails because the extra layers made it more difficult for prisoners to effect an escape through the floor. The gable roof is covered with tin that may be a later replacement. Originally, there was an "iron box" near the door that was manufactured by Pauly of Saint Louis.[2] A metal box on the outside contains levers that allow the cell doors to be opened and closed

Jail in Beeville (photo courtesy of Darryl Pearson).

Metal box with levers for locking cells (photo courtesy of Darryl Pearson).

without entering the building. This is the only jail in the current sample with levers on the exterior of the building. This building is unique in that there are four windows of different sizes and shapes. One window has a massive metal shutter, another window has a small wooden shutter, and the others have no shutters. High up on the wall to the rear of the building is a small vent on each side. In 1893, the county hired architect Eugene Heiner to erect a two-story brick jail using the French Second Empire design.[3] The cells from the wooden jail were removed and installed in the new building. The old jail was considered to be an "eyesore, " but the new one was touted to be the finest of its kind in the state and perhaps the best and most substantial edifice in Bee County. In 1898, the old wooden jail was located at 522 Houston Street (city block 44) southwest of a wooden two-story courthouse in city block 38.[4] In 1904, it was being used as a dwelling.[5] Kay Mix is the chairperson of the Bee County Historical Society, and she provided the following information.[6] It sat for a time at the county yard on West Corpus Christi Street where it was used for storage. Sheriff Robert L. Horn found it and, realizing the historical significance of this building to the town of Beeville, orchestrated its transfer to the county lot next to the new county jail, which had been built in 1989. When the lot was sold in 2015, County Commissioner Dennis DeWitt acted to save the jail a second time. The county hired a company specializing in moving historical buildings to relocate it to 605 South Hillside Street. It now has a more secure foundation of cement piers resting on a cement slab as well as a new porch and steps. Visitors to Beeville can also view the Beaux-Arts-style courthouse constructed in 1912.[7]

Comanche

Comanche County

LOCATION: Private Property

OWNER: Privately Owned

DATE BUILT: 1940s

SIZE: 775 square feet

Christopher S. Till is an attorney in town and his office is in the old county jail at 302 West Central adjacent to this building. This interesting structure

Jail in Comanche (photo courtesy of Christopher S. Till).

resembles the three-cell calaboose in Granger, but it is much larger and, therefore, is classified as a tiny jail. Mr. Till purchased this building and the county jail to prevent their demolition. He stated that it was built in the 1940s as a place where women and children could be segregated from male prisoners.[8] Three metal doors open into the cells. The women's cells are on the left of the structure, and the doors open into a small entry area that separates the cells with metal bars and a metal door, also with bars. These are the only cells with windows on the front of the building. At the back of these cells is a partition that hides the sinks, showers, and toilets. The cell to the right was where male prisoners were supposedly housed. At the time the jail was being used, there may have been cots for sleeping. No plumbing was available to the men, and no electricity was provided. There are two rather large windows on the east side and one on the back that provided light and ventilation for the male prisoners. They are rather large, and the bottom of each one is at ground level. Like many of the buildings in Comanche and other towns in the area, this structure was made of native limestone. The original roof has been replaced with tin. Tommy Harvey at the Comanche County Museum told me that he remembers seeing prisoners inside the jail and walking around an enclosed fenced area in the early 1980s.[9]

Gail

Borden County

LOCATION: 141 East Wasson Street

OWNER: County of Borden

DATE BUILT: 1896

SIZE: 768 square feet

Borden County was organized in 1891, and five years later, a stone jail was erected next to the courthouse. It was made of hand-hewn native stone quarried at nearby Gail Mountain, and locals performed the masonry work. Mr. J. H. Smoot was a stonemason, and he hand cut the massive rocks. Others who helped with the labor were Jim Smith and W. K. Clark, who was hired because the great strength in his arms was needed for lifting the stones. The walls are 2 feet thick and touted as virtually escape proof. The bars to the windows and the steel door were deeply set into the stone. The Diebold Safe and Lock Company of Canton, Ohio, was retained to fabricate two metal cells and a holding cell at a cost of $4,500. They are

Jail in Gail (photo courtesy of Rolland C. Reynolds Jr.).

equal in size and made of one-third-inch case-hardened steel plate that is impervious to hacksaw blades. The doors are fastened with huge hasps and padlocks that require a six-inch key to open them. The sheriff at the time was T. D. Love. The above information was taken from Ed Blackburn's book on county jails.[10] The following information was taken from an article in the *Borden Citizen*.[11] The appearance of this jail has changed very little over time. The original door with metal bars was replaced with the current solid metal door. Because of problems with leaks in the roof, two courses of stone were removed from the top of the walls and a new roof was installed. At that time, plumbing was also added. The claim that this jail was "escape proof" was borne out by the workers who installed the plumbing. The steel floors of the cells are one-third of an inch thick, and cutting torches were needed to make holes for the pipes. Beneath the floor of the cells are huge blocks of stone that measure 4 feet square and 6 inches thick. The ceiling and walls of the cells are also made of the same steel plates pierced by two-inch-square holes for light and ventilation. The doors to the cells were secured by a series of huge hasps and padlocks. Each cell has a small opening through which food and other items could be passed to the prisoners. It still housed an occasional prisoner as late as 1967, but at that time it was more convenient and cheaper to board prisoners in Snyder. This jail was dedicated as a Texas Historic Landmark in 1967, and the architectural style is described as Classic Revival.[12] The marker also states that it is one of the oldest jails in use in West Texas.

Hearne

Robertson County

LOCATION: 200 block of South Cedar Street
next to the city water tower

OWNER: City of Hearne

DATE BUILT: 1911–25

SIZE: 483 square feet

This jail was constructed sometime between 1911 and 1925 based on a review of fire insurance maps prepared by the Sanborn Map Company. It

Jail in Hearne (photo by the author).

False front on the jail in Hearne (photo by the author).

measures 30 feet across the front and 16 feet on each side. There are two large windows on the front and two similar windows and a solid metal door on the back. The interior housed metal cells at one time, but they have been removed and placed in a different jail.[13] Architectural historian Adam Alsobrook considers this building as a possible example of the late Victorian period with both Romanesque Revival and Italianate details.[14] The brickwork around the windows is elaborate, and the portion that extends above the flat roof in front and back is described here as a double false front. There is an inscription on the door that warns visitors to not talk to prisoners without permission from the officer on duty. At the time of my visit the jail was filled to capacity with tires.

Henrietta

Clay County

LOCATION: Clay County Pioneer Museum at Fifth and Bridge Streets

OWNER: Clay County Pioneer Association

DATE BUILT: Unknown

SIZE: 304 square feet

The first documented jail in Henrietta was a "two-story wooden dungeon built in 1874."[15] The next lockup was a "two-story square stone fortress" that was built in 1878 and reputed to have been the first jail in Henrietta to have steel cages.[16] The jailer's residence was on the first floor, and the cells were on the second floor. The first available map for Henrietta was published in 1885. This map depicts the two-story wooden dungeon in city block 18 but refers to it as a calaboose. In the same block is the two-story stone fortress.[17] It appears that both structures were being used as lockups during the time the map was drafted. In 1890, a more elaborate brick county jail replaced the stone fortress. This building was erected by the Pauley Jail Building and Manufacturing Company of Saint Louis at a cost of $24,000.[18] Today, this impressive jail remains in its original location at the corner of Graham and Ikard Streets where it serves as a museum. The next available Sanborn map was published in 1891. The stone fortress is labeled as an "Old Jail," and there is a small one-story wood calaboose in the center of the block. The two-story dungeon was no longer

Jail in Henrietta (photo courtesy of Dee Ann Littlefield).

present.[19] In 1896, city block 18 had been divided into unnumbered lots. The calaboose was still present, and the old jail had been converted to a Chinese laundry.[20]

In 1902, a photo shop had replaced the Chinese laundry and a small one-story wooden building occupied what appears to be the same footprint as the calaboose, but it is not identified by function.[21] The 1907 Sanborn map shows the wooden calaboose present in 1896 in the same location with an address of 817 1/2 Graham.[22] A possible explanation for the absence of the calaboose in 1902 could be it was not known to the preparers of the map as a calaboose or it had been moved temporarily. It was still there in 1912[23] and 1922,[24] but this time it was on the opposite side of the alley that bisected the block from north to south. The Clay County Historical Society has a photo that confirms its location next to the 1890 jail. In 1934, the last available Sanborn map for Henrietta was examined, and it shows the wood calaboose as being used for storage.[25] Later, it was moved to the Clay County Pioneer Museum where it stands today. In 1962, the Texas Historical Commission awarded a medallion (#3707) to this building under the entry Old City Calaboose and designated it as a Recorded Historic Texas Landmark. There is no text associated with the medallion that is now missing. It has two small windows on each side and one centered on the back wall. There was a wooden floor but it is virtually gone today. The roof is pyramidal in shape and covered with wooden shingles. The overall condition is poor and there are no plans to restore it.

Jayton

Kent County

LOCATION: Behind the Kent County Courthouse on Harrison Avenue between East Fourth and East Fifth Streets in Jayton

OWNER: City of Jayton

DATE BUILT: Unknown

SIZE: 880 square feet

Jayton is the county seat of Kent County. The town was known as Jay Flat after a local ranching family. In 1907, the settlement was moved to its present location for improved proximity to rail service. It was officially renamed Jayton later that same year and incorporated in 1910. In 1954,

Rear view of the jail in Jayton (photo courtesy of Becky Arnold).

it became the county seat because the previous county seat in Clairemont was declining in population. Today, it is a virtual ghost town.[26] The jail was locked at the time of my visit. Therefore, the description of the interior is based on a conversation with county judge Jim White and photographs his office provided.[27] The age of this stone building is not known, but Judge White believes it was built during the early part of the twentieth century, possibly around 1910. The exterior consists of stonework that represents excellent craftsmanship. The facade and side walls extend above the flat roof to create a rather high stepped parapet. This jail is divided into three areas. Entry from the front provides access to a large room that spans the width of the building. It served as an office for law enforcement officials or as a reception area. There are two large windows on the front wall that are obvious recent replacements. The door, concrete porch, and sidewalk are also later additions. The two cells in the back of the entry room appear to be equal in size, and each one has its own door. These doors are solid metal with small windows that could be opened to communicate with the prisoners or pass food and other items. Some of these windows open to a curved metal cage that provides a panoramic view of the interior, much like those in the calabooses in Caldwell and Mason. Each cell has a window to the outside that measures 21 by 36 inches. The bars are a crisscross pattern of flat iron. The two cells are divided by a wall of concrete. The back room also has two cells of equal size. At the time of my visit, it was being used for storage and there was an electrical fixture attached to the ceiling that may not be original to the jail.

Marathon

Brewster County

LOCATION: Southwest Second Street at the corner of an unnamed street that runs north to Southwest First Street in Marathon

OWNER: City of Marathon

DATE BUILT: Late nineteenth century

SIZE: 648 square feet

The town was founded in 1882 by Albion E. Shepard, a former sea captain who had worked as a surveyor for the Galveston, Harrisburg and San

Jail in Marathon (photo courtesy of Rolland C. Reynolds Jr.).

Antonio Railway. He named the new town Marathon because the area reminded him of the plains of Greece. At the time, the area was part of Presidio County. A post office was established in 1883, and the town became a major shipping and supply point for area ranchers in 1884. When Presidio County was divided into Brewster, Buchel, and Foley Counties in 1887, Marathon became the county seat for Buchel County.[28] These counties were never organized and they became part of Brewster County. The first jail in town was a windmill on North First Street. Drunks and other petty offenders were chained to its legs while those charged with more serious crimes were taken to Alpine and locked up in the county jail. A one-room adobe house behind French's Store was used as a jail, but there were too many escapes.[29] The stone jail described here is a formidable structure. There are two windows on the front and one on the west wall. They were measured at 33 inches wide by 79 inches tall. These are among the largest windows on any jail or calaboose in the current sample. The front door opens into a large room that may have been for the use of law enforcement. At the back of this room is a solid metal wall that separates the cells from the rest of the jail. Not one of the windows appear to be in line with the actual jail area. There is a door on the west side that would have led directly to the cells, but today it is boarded up. The walls are covered with a hip roof covered with corrugated tin.

Memphis

Hall County

LOCATION: Private Property

OWNER: Privately Owned

DATE BUILT: 1920–31

SIZE: 350 square feet

The neighboring towns of Salisbury and Lakeview competed for the honor of becoming the county seat of newly organized Hall County in 1890, but Memphis was selected to be the county seat in a close election. A railroad depot was built in town, and people flocked to the area where a courthouse of homemade bricks was constructed in 1892. The first jail was built in 1890 by the Pauley Company of Saint Louis.[30] The one-story concrete jail was used to house state and federal prisoners who worked on projects such as picking cotton or repairing roads. The locals say it was also used to house German prisoners of war.[31] This jail strongly resembles a calaboose but it is classified here as a tiny jail because it exceeds 300 hundred square

Jail in Memphis (photo courtesy of Shari Watson).

feet in size and was not for the usual type of offender. It was made of concrete using the poured-in-place method. The forms were made using 6- or 8-inch boards. The floor plan consists of two cells equal in size that are divided by a concrete wall. Entry is through two metal doors that contain a shutter that when open exposes metal bars with an opening that was used to hand food to the prisoners. Light and ventilation was provided by a large and small window on the back wall for each cell. There are massive metal bars that cover the windows that consist of glass panes. Guards could reach through the bars and open the windows by pushing them inward to allow ventilation for the prisoners. There is a toilet in one of the cells, and there was probably one in the other cell as well. Electricity arrived in Memphis in 1901, and this jail had service.

Port Neches

Jefferson County

LOCATION: Across the street from the Port Neches Riverfront Park at 620 Grigsby Street in Port Neches

OWNER: City of Port Neches

DATE BUILT: 1917

SIZE: 351 square feet

This jail was the second lockup in town. The first was a wooden structure made of vertically placed two-by-fours. It was destroyed when a prisoner set a fire inside, and rescuers had to "chop the jail apart to keep the prisoner from burning."[32] This unusual jail resembles some buildings built when art deco was in vogue. The most obvious architectural embellishments are the pediment on top and the trapezoidal-shaped lintels above the door and windows. Although an impressive structure in its day, the years of inactivity have not been kind to this jail. In 1979, staff writer Jerry Winkler of the *Port Arthur News* wrote that "mildew spreads across the floor, walls, and ceiling while ivy climbs the bars on the outside of the windows like latticework. The present residents are termites eating away at the woodwork around the doors and windows with two opossum skeletons showing that they were the last two occupants of the jail in Port Neches."[33] The exact life span of this jail has not been verified but

Jail in Port Neches (photo courtesy of Leo Weeks Photographers).

graffiti dating to 1947 provides a window of twenty-nine years since its construction in 1917.[34]

Red Bellair was a former officer of the law in the town. He stated that serious crime was not a problem as the majority of prisoners were drunks, traffic violators, and those charged with minor offenses. In 1979, he visited the old jail hoping to find among the graffiti the name of a man he locked up "almost half a century ago." The man was locked up for being drunk, and he exclaimed to Bellair: "I won't be here in the morning." The next day he was gone. A friend had pulled out the bars in one of the windows with his vehicle. Bellair didn't consider the incident that important and did nothing about it. In fact, he hired the escapee to work for him while he was foreman at the B. F. Goodrich plant in Port Neches.[35] Homer Taylor, an officer of the law, also worked in Port Neches. On one occasion, he arrested a fellow townsman for drunkenness. He did not want to lock him up so he told the drunk to wait outside while he went for the key to unlock the jail. He took his time crossing the street and never looked back to check on the prisoner, figuring the drunk would escape given the opportunity. When he returned, the drunk was still there so he was forced to put him in the jail.[36] The history of most buildings includes accidents and repairs. In February 1935, the commissioners' court elected to buy a lock for the jail; it had been without this modicum of security for many months. It was also decided to install a new roof.[37] In April of the same year, the fire department was called to the jail to put out a fire to a mattress set by a prisoner.[38] An unruly prisoner kicked out a window and received an additional ten days to his sentence.[39] C. O. Smith was the county's building superintendent. He recommended that certain repairs be made to the jail; the court accepted the bid of W. A. Koch for $95.[40]

The jail had plumbing, and it appears it was also designed with electricity because some of the electrical boxes were built into the walls. The entry door opens to a foyer 5 feet wide by 6 feet deep. On either side is a restored cell. The doors to the cells are 27 inches wide by 75 inches high, and the cells are equal in size at 10 by 12 feet. The ceiling is 9 feet 6 inches high. The doors are still solid and largely without rust. The hinges are tight and swing freely. One cell door is missing its locking mechanism but the other one is intact. Light from the outside was plentiful due to the presence of windows on all four sides.[41] There was no inside heat, and one former prisoner remembers it as a "cold, damp stone jail."[42] One of the reasons for its demise was the construction of better roads in the county, which made it easier to transport prisoners to the county jail in Beaumont. The city put the jail up for sale because of frequent vandalism after it was no longer a public building; the city later offered to give it to anyone who would haul it away. The diligence of Mrs. Murray Ezell and Leo Weeks of Port Neches and Mrs. James Parish of Port Arthur in the 1960s saved the structure. Joseph Grigsby was the founder of the town, and his descendants were among the donors to pay for the restoration.[43]

Post

Garza County

LOCATION: North of the courthouse on Main Street in the middle of the block defined by North Avenue M on the west and North Avenue L on the east in Post

OWNER: City of Post

DATE BUILT: Unknown

SIZE: 418 square feet

Jail in Post (photo courtesy of Walter Perez).

Ed Blackburn's book on county jails provided the following information regarding jails in Post.[44] The first jail in the county was made of two-by-four-inch timbers laid flat on top of one another and secured with nails. The date this structure was put into service and its size is not known. In 1911, this early lockup was replaced with a small metal cell block purchased from the Southern Structural Steel Company of San Antonio. It was enclosed in a structure that measured 16 by 20 feet. The first formal county jail was constructed on the third floor of the courthouse in 1923. It contained two metal cells fabricated by the Southern Structural Steel Company that were purchased at a cost of $5,635. The jail is a brick structure on the north side of the courthouse that was built circa 1925 around the metal cell block purchased in 1911. It measures 19 by 22 feet, and its function was that of a drunk tank until the county decided to use it for storage. This is a one-of-a-kind jail in terms of its facade and cell floor plan. It faces south and is one of the tallest in the sample with the roof 14 feet above the ground. The only entrance is through a solid metal door with no windows or vents. Two very large windows are high above the floor and centered on each side of the door. They are secured with circular metal bars with nine placed vertically and three placed horizontally to add strength. No windows or other possibility of air flow or natural light exist on the sides or on the rear wall. The cell doors were opened and closed by levers enclosed in a metal box. On entering the building, there is a narrow empty space that spans the entire front of the jail. In line with the outside door is a metal door to a large cell that has four beds on the back wall. The second cell is to the right and accessed by a door at the bottom left corner just above an extension of the linear empty space mentioned above. Two beds are on the left wall. Another brick building was built in the 1970s by the city as a space for additional storage, and it adjoins the jail. It is very difficult to get good images of the interior of because of the large number of items stored therein. During the life of the jail, electricity was probably not available, but it was added later. Walter Perez, a maintenance worker for the city of Post, shared his photos, measured the structure, and answered my many questions.[45]

Sabinal-I

Uvalde County

LOCATION: Behind City Hall at 501 North Center Street in Sabinal

OWNER: City of Sabinal

DATE BUILT: Unknown

SIZE: 324 square feet

Sabinal is located on the Southern Pacific Railroad, which arrived in 1881. The population in 1906 when the town was incorporated was five hundred, and there were six operating cotton gins in the area. By 1911, Sabinal was a commercial and agricultural center with a population of 2,500.[46] Cotton and livestock were the main contributors to the economy. This is a one-story building made from concrete blocks resting on a concrete foundation. Concrete was also poured over a wooden form to create the flat roof. Entry is through a metal door that contains a small window with seven metal bars placed in front of a heavy wire mesh. A circular metal pipe attached to the door covers the lock. This could have been put there to make it impossible for prisoners to reach through the windows and

Jail in Sabinal (photo courtesy of Darryl Pearson).

Interior of Jail in Sabinal (photo courtesy of Darryl Pearson).

unlock the door. The interior consists of three rooms. A small area that spans the width of the jail's interior was used by the local constable, and his wooden desk is still in place. Behind this space are two metal cells that were manufactured by the Stewart Iron Works Company of Cincinnati, Ohio, circa 1898. The rear walls and floor of the cells are formed by solid sheets of metal joined by rivets. The front walls and doors and the wall between the two cells were made using the lattice design. A narrow area to the left of the cells is 31 inches wide; a very narrow space behind the cells was not measured. The original location of the cells was the basement of city hall in Uvalde.[47] When the building was demolished, the two metal cells were brought to Sabinal and placed in the building depicted here.[48] Each cell has one window, and they are located on each side of the jail. Each cell has a bed, toilet, and sink. The toilet, sink, and electricity were added after the move to Sabinal.[49] A fuse box and metal conduit for wire is attached to the outside of the front wall. This structure was used as a jail during the 1950s when Red Houston was chief of police, and it continued to house prisoners until sometime in the 1970s or 1980s.[50] At the time of my visit, it was being used for storage. Graffiti created by prisoners adorn the rear walls of the cell.

Sabinal-2

Uvalde County

LOCATION: Private Property

OWNER: Privately Owned

DATE BUILT: Unknown

SIZE: 324 square feet

This jail was constructed by placing corrugated tin over a wooden frame on the walls and roof. The door is encased in a wooden frame and consists of flat metal bars arranged horizontally with three vertical strips for strength. The exact date it was built is not known but local resident Rose del Bosque said that the consensus among the locals is that it was around 1898.[51] She said that there were two or more metal cells inside but they are no longer present. The condition of this jail is poor and its future is uncertain.

Jail in Sabinal (photo courtesy of Darryl Pearson).

Trinity

Trinity County

LOCATION: 100 block of North Railroad Street in Trinity

OWNER: City of Trinity

DATE BUILT: Circa 1895

SIZE: 610 square feet

According to Mayor Lyle Stubbs, this unique jail was built sometime around 1895 and was the city's only jail until 1975.[52] A door on the inside of the jail allowed passage to city hall. Stubbs believes that this allowed prisoners to and from trial in city court. The inside is unusual in that there is a separate cell that was used solely for women. This cell measures about 100 square feet and is located inside the main room that was used for male prisoners. Another unusual feature is the height of the structure. It is approximately 15 feet, yet the structure only had one story. The roof is missing but, based on a historic photograph taken in 1927, it was flat.[53] The facade is unlike any of the other jails I have visited. The two windows

Jail in Trinity (photo by the author).

are very large and protected by strap-iron bars placed vertically and horizontally. The bars above the door are wood. Also, there is an open space above the windows and light above the door. Most openings in jails are completely covered with bars. Overall, the jail is in very poor condition. The front door, some of the windows, and the roof are missing. The door to the women's cell is present but barely attached to the frame. At one time, the interior walls were covered with plaster. The 1909 Sanborn map does not show this part of Railroad Street. The 1925 Sanborn map depicts a very small one-story ironclad jail between 142 and 143 Railroad Street that preceded this brick building.[54]

Van Horn

Culberson County

LOCATION: This jail is at the corner of East Third Street and Culberson in a city park in Van Horn

OWNER: County of Culberson

DATE BUILT: 1912

SIZE: 397 square feet

Jail in Van Horn (photo courtesy of Rolland C. Reynolds Jr.).

Toilet in jail in Van Horn (photo courtesy of Judge Carlos Urias).

The Van Horn area was a popular resting place for travelers due to the presence of natural water wells twelve miles south of the current site of Van Horn. The town was named for Lieutenant Judson Van Horn, who was in command of an army garrison at Van Horn Wells.[55] The town owes its early growth to the arrival of the Texas and Pacific Railway in 1881. The first lockup in town was a primitive structure made from railroad ties that measured 12 by 14 feet.[56] The jail was constructed in 1912, one year following the organization of the county in 1911.[57] This is one of the more elaborate and unique jails in the current sample. The flat roof is not visible because the walls extend above it to create a parapet. The interior floor is poured concrete, and plaster covers the walls. There are two very large windows on the front on either side of the door and three on each side. The interior is in excellent condition and contains six metal cells as well as sinks and toilets. Judge Carlos Urias told me that the county plans a restoration project that will protect the jail for future generations. A very valuable source of historical data is in the graffiti on the inside walls; the large amount of graffiti documents those who were incarcerated as well as the years that they were written. It has been reported that prisoners occasionally escaped by digging through the brick walls. Use of this jail was discontinued in 1964 when the new courthouse and jail were constructed.[58] The only Sanborn map for Van Horn that was available at the time of this study was published in 1950; it shows the brick jail in the northeast quadrant of city block 22 at the corner of Culberson and East Second Streets.[59] It occupied the same city block as the courthouse. In 1950, this would have been considered a substantial and perhaps an expensive building, as the majority of structures in town were made of adobe.

7

Cages and Cells

Athens

Henderson County

LOCATION: East Texas Arboretum at 1601 Patterson Road in Athens

OWNER: East Texas Arboretum and Botanical Society

DATE BUILT: Unknown

SIZE: 76 square feet

Dolores Herrington of Athens found my website and wrote me about the metal cage in her town.[1] This one is interesting for several reasons. There is a major difference in the way it was fabricated. The doors and panels containing square holes for light and ventilation were cut from a single sheet of metal unlike those made by companies such as J. Pauly and E. T. Barnum who used narrow strips of iron that overlapped to get the "lattice" appearance.[2] These strips were cold riveted to keep them in place, a process that predates welding. Raised letters on the exterior appear to spell Carnegie, a name not associated with the manufacture of jail cells. The most likely scenario appears to be that the steel was made by Carnegie and sold

Athens cage (photo courtesy of Gowan Photography in Athens, Texas).

Metal toilet in Athens cage (photo courtesy of Dolores Herrington).

to the company that made this cage. Cages of similar construction exist in Dessau (Travis County) and Leakey (Real County), but they lack the Carnegie name. This is the only metal cage in the current sample with two locks on each door. Perhaps the most striking difference is that this cage came equipped with a metal bucket of sorts, which was the toilet. Other companies provided similar amenities at an extra cost. E. T. Barnum advertised corner commodes and sinks as well as folding bunks. This is the only cage in the sample with this type of convenience.

Blooming Grove

Navarro County

LOCATION: A. L. (Doc) Garrison Memorial Park on North Fordyce Street in Blooming Grove

OWNER: City of Blooming Grove

DATE BUILT: Unknown

SIZE: 64 square feet

Blooming Grove cage (photo courtesy of Cindie Phipps).

This interesting metal cage is located on the grounds of the city park in Blooming Grove, Texas. It is one of the smallest found so far at only 78 by 99 inches. Perhaps the most interesting feature is the small door that will not allow entry to someone standing up. It measures only 24 by 52 inches. It was moved to the park for protection, but its original location remains unknown. The date it was purchased and length of service was not known to officials at city hall.[3]

Crystal City

Zavala County

LOCATION: Private Property

OWNER: Privately Owned

DATE BUILT: Unknown

SIZE: 42 square feet

This cage is tied with the one in Helena for the distinction of being the smallest cage in the current sample. It also has the distinction of being the only cage with two metal beds on the rear wall. The bunks have chains that allow them to be raised. The walls on the back and sides are solid sheets of metal, as is the floor. The only source of light and ventilation was through the door and front portion of the wall. The comfort level of being inside this cage would have been related to the direction it was facing. A unique feature of this cage is the way the bars on the facade were constructed. The horizontal bars are threaded through the vertical bars. The ends of the vertical bars are twisted, allowing them to be bolted to the same frame and on the same plane as the horizontal bars. The threading process is cheaper, and perhaps faster, than connecting them with a rivet at every intersection, as was done with many of the metal cages and cells.[4] It is not known if this cage is in its original location.

Crystal City cage (photo courtesy of Darryl Pearson).

Dessau

Travis County

LOCATION: Private Property

OWNER: Privately Owned

DATE BUILT: Unknown

SIZE: 68 square feet

A sign on the front of the cage reads, this was Dessau's community jail; it dates to the late 1800s. It was loaded onto a wagon to transport prisoners to the state prison in Huntsville. The rest of the time it was used for minor offenses and left in place. On its retirement as the community jail, it was moved to the Dessau dance hall and used to house drunk and rowdy patrons. At some point, 18 inches was cut from the bottom. There is a bullet hole in the front that was fired from the inside. Unfortunately, the story behind this incident is not known. This is one of three cages documented in this book in which the holes for light and ventilation were punched or

Dessau cage (photo by the author).

Emory cage (photo courtesy of Floyd Kent).

stamped from a solid piece of metal. The others are in Athens and Leakey. The steel used to make the one in Athens was fabricated by one of the Carnegie companies. The similarity in construction suggests that the steel used to make these two may have also been provided by a Carnegie company. At the time of my visit, it was in a field next to the storied dance hall building, now known as El Gran Mexicano. The owner of this cage provided its history.[5]

Emory

Rains County

LOCATION: Emory Heritage Park at
191 Doris Briggs Parkway in Emory

OWNER: Rains County Historical Society

DATE BUILT: Unknown

SIZE: 130 square feet

This very fine metal cage was originally located where the Rose Community Center sits today near Quitman Street. From there, it was moved to the courthouse and housed in an annex building. In 1999, the county donated it to the park, where it was enclosed in a building for protection from the elements.[6] The door opens into a hallway to the right of two cells of equal size. A massive metal box on the front contains two levers that allow the cell doors to be opened and shut individually. This arrangement allowed law enforcement officers to release the prisoners from the cells into a larger area without going inside and having personal contact. Inside each cell is a piece of flat metal against the wall; this served as a platform for a bed. On the back wall are holes that were cut into the metal after it arrived. The size and placement of these holes are consistent with the plumbing needed to install a toilet and sink. In a pre-restoration photograph housed at the park, a sink reposes against a cell wall. Perhaps this was one of the early fixtures. The only cage with a similar floor plan is in Lampasas.

Falls City

Karnes County

LOCATION: Courthouse Museum in Helena at 8167 North Farm-to-Market Road 81

OWNER: Karnes County Historical Society

DATE BUILT: Unknown

SIZE: 49 square feet

The first permanent settlement took place in 1886 when the San Antonio and Aransas Pass Railway built a switch and depot; it was named Brackenridge after George W. Brackenridge, the benefactor of the railroad. The

Falls City cage (photo courtesy of Rhonda K. Holley).

name of the town was changed to Falls City after waterfalls in the area. The town became predominantly Polish when people from Panna Maria and Cestohowa, Texas, moved there to take advantage of jobs the railroad offered. This cage was moved from its original location in Falls City to the museum in Helena for display and preservation.[7] The door is made of very thick metal strips in a lattice pattern with a massive lock plate. There is one panel of lattice on the rear wall, while the rest of the walls and ceiling are solid metal plates. The small openings in the door and the one panel in the back provided the only source of light and ventilation. This cage sits next to a very similar one that was used in Helena and made by the King and Son Company of Cleveland, Ohio. The two towns are only fifteen miles apart. Therefore, it is possible that the same company fabricated them both.

Helena

Karnes County

LOCATION: Courthouse Museum in Helena at 8167 North Farm-to-Market Road 81

OWNER: Karnes County Historical Society

DATE BUILT: Unknown

SIZE: 42 square feet

The town of Helena was founded by Thomas Ruckman and Lewis S. Owings in 1852 at the site of a former Mexican trading post named Alamita. The name of the town was changed to honor Dr. Owings's wife, Helen. The area was so successful that Karnes County was organized in 1854, and a courthouse was erected. It was destroyed by a storm and replaced by a two-story stone building in 1873, which served the county until 1893.[8] During its heyday, the town boasted a church, Masonic lodge, drugstore, blacksmith shop, two hotels, saloons, and general stores.[9] This was a lawless town; some called it the "roughest town on earth." At one time, the town had thirteen saloons for a population that ranged from 300 to 500.[10] The need for a jail was obvious, and the first one was a wooden building that stood in the north corner of the courthouse square. Little information is available about this building except it housed four metal cages. A stone

Helena cage (photo courtesy of Rhonda K. Holley).

jail took its place and the cages were placed inside it. The dates associated with these two jails are not known. When the stone jail was no longer needed, it was dismantled. The cages were given to the four county commissioners who used them for storage related to their work. The stone courthouse, although in need of repair, still stands and is the focal point of the Courthouse Museum. One of the four metal cages that used to be in the Helena County jail is on the grounds of the museum, a gift by one of the county commissioners. The appearance of the three missing cages is not known, but it's likely that they were similar. The surviving cage sports a combination of wall panels. The facade has a lattice-style door between two solid sheets of metal with massive hinges. The other three walls have lattice-style panels that consist of flat strips of metal that overlap and are secured by rivets. The Helena cages were made by the King and Son Company of Cleveland, Ohio.[11] The cage that rests next to this one came from Falls City, only about fifteen miles distant. Although not known to be fact, it's possible that both cages were made by the same firm and perhaps shipped at the same time. This cage is tied with the one in Crystal City for the distinction of being the smallest cage in the current sample.

Hico

Hamilton County

LOCATION: Billy the Kid Museum, 114 North Pecan Street in Hico

OWNER: Billy the Kid Museum

DATE BUILT: Unknown

SIZE: 100 square feet

This metal cage was originally in a stone building that housed office space for the sheriff and a large room for prisoners.[12] Joan Upton Hall writes that high-risk prisoners were kept in an iron cage or cell in the same building. In 1928, city hall became the place of incarceration, and

Hico cage (photo by the author).

she states that the cage from the former jail was moved to that building. E. T. Barnum Iron and Wire Works of Detroit shipped a metal cage to Hico in 1928.[13] This order suggests that there may have been two cages in city hall. Today, a metal cage can be viewed in the Billy the Kid Museum in Hico. This cage is like Barnum's No. 7 Steel Lattice Jail Cage. The door is made using the same lattice pattern as the walls. At the bottom, a cutaway area allowed law enforcement officers to pass food and other items to the inmates. There are four metal bed frames that supported straw mattresses for the prisoners. They were arranged in bunk-bed fashion with two on each side. This is one of the few cages with four bunks and only one small room. One of the prisoners set fire to the mattresses in his cell. The two mattresses that are missing are the two that were burned.[14] Setting fire to mattresses was a common ruse designed to effect an escape.

Knox City

Knox County

LOCATION: City Hall, 902 East Main Street in Knox City

OWNER: Knox City

DATE BUILT: Unknown

SIZE: 73 square feet

The original location of this cage was a small building behind the old city hall. This is another tiny cage that provided cramped conditions and no personal space for its prisoners. The two cells are equal in size at 36 square feet, and each cell was designed to house two prisoners. Sleeping accommodations consisted of two metal bunks attached to a common wall. When not in use, they could be raised up and secured to the wall to provide more space inside the already restricted area. The walls and ceiling were made of the lattice-style construction that provided for excellent ventilation. Unfortunately, there are no known photos of the building that housed this cage, and the unrestricted flow of air into the cage could have been compromised by a structure with few windows. That this cage is affixed to a concrete slab is an indicator that it was probably ordered without a floor because it was destined to be secured to a slab or wooden floor. The city is to be commended for taking the necessary steps to preserve this piece of its history. Even though the date this cage was put into service is not known, there is good reason to believe that the year was 1909. This statement is supported by two articles in the *Knox County News* that were published in that year. "The citizens of the town are now taking a very commendable step in having erected a calaboose in which to put unruly characters. Heretofore there has been no place for this purpose and no officer could do his full duty without such a place. It is now under construction in the northwestern part of the business district, fairly well away from the business sections."[15] "Knox City has just built a calaboose for the accommodation of any obstreperous visitors who may pay them a visit. Right you are, but up to date it hasn't had an occupant."[16]

Knox City cage (photo courtesy of Jo Brown).

Lampasas

Lampasas County

LOCATION: In an alley behind the Keystone Hotel and Keystone Square Museum at 303 South Western Street in Lampasas

OWNER: City of Lampasas

DATE BUILT: Unknown

SIZE: 177 square feet

This is one of the more unusual cages in the current sample. It is rectangular in plan, and the door is at one of the ends and offset to the right. It opens to a small walk space that extends the length of the cage. The two cells are to the left and equal in size. The solid metal wall that divides the cells is four inches thick. The four metal beds that were attached to the walls in bunk-bed fashion are no longer present. One of the most unusual features of this structure is that each cell had a heater in the corner with a pipe on the rear wall that provided ventilation. The cell doors were opened and closed by a massive locking mechanism with levers on the outside. The exterior wall opposite the cells was constructed with flat metal strips that

Lampasas cage (photo courtesy of Rolland C. Reynolds Jr.).

created an area that provided excellent airflow and natural light. A narrow opening on each end of this wall was used to pass food to the prisoners. This suggests that those locked up were not constantly restricted to their cells. The walls behind the cells and at the opposite end of the door are solid metal. This cage had previously been in an older jail in town. The city plans to make it available to the public for viewing.

La Pryor

Zavala County

LOCATION: In a city park near the corner of Perez Avenue and State Highway 57 in La Pryor

OWNER: City of La Pryor

DATE BUILT: Unknown

SIZE: 107 square feet

This metal cage was moved from its original location to this park, where it has been restored and made available for public viewing. Most of the metal

La Pryor cage (photo courtesy of Rhonda K. Holley).

Locking mechanism at the La Pryor cage (photo courtesy of Rhonda K. Holley).

cages that exist today have a patina of rust. However, this one was painted as part of the restoration process and placed on a concrete slab with a brick walkway from the street to the cage. The city has done an excellent job of maintaining it and making it easy to view. This cage has two cells that are side by side and equal in size. Each one had two metal bed frames arranged in bunk-bed fashion and attached to the exterior walls on the sides of the cage. They measure 5 feet long by 20 inches wide. Unfortunately, some of these beds are no longer present. The doors are centered on the cells and are 67 inches tall by only 21 inches wide. The cage is a combination of solid metal panels and those panels with the typical lattice design for light and ventilation, which are located on the doors and on the rear walls. The side panels and those behind the beds are solid. The only breeze would have been felt when the wind was blowing from the front or back of the cage. The most impressive feature of this cage is the massive locking system that opened and closed the cell doors. The levers are housed in a box on a side wall and are attached to the front of the cage. Very little is known about this cage, such as the firm that fabricated it, the time span it was used, and its original location in town.

Leakey

Real County

LOCATION: Real County Historical Museum in Leakey

OWNER: Real County Historical Museum

DATE BUILT: 1918

SIZE: 108 square feet

In 1884, Leakey was the county seat of Edwards County, taking over the duties and responsibilities of the town of Bullhead, which formerly held that distinction. During this period, law was enforced by placing prisoners in a metal cage housed in a small wooden building. Rocksprings became the final county seat of Edwards County in 1891, and the cage was moved

Leakey cage (photo courtesy of Darryl Pearson).

there and installed in the new two-story limestone jail in 1895; the jail stands today. In 1913, Real County was carved out of Edwards County and Leakey became its only county seat. The first courthouse was built that year, and a two-story stone version appeared in 1918. The cage discussed here was placed on the lower floor of the new courthouse between the County Records Vault and the office of the sheriff.

Unlike the strap iron cages, this one was constructed using sheets of steel for the walls. The openings for light and airflow were punched out by machine. Variations of this method were used to fabricate the cages in Athens and Dessau. The floor plan is two cells positioned side by side with separate doors for each cell. The cell to the left is 70 square feet while the smaller cell is only 32 square feet. Two rectangular openings at the bottom of each door could have been used to pass food to prisoners. The door on the right has an unusual curved metal feature (broken) that may have been used as a doorstop. Another unusual feature of this cage is the presence of two massive locks for each door. Brackets on the rear walls of the cells may indicate supports for a bed frame. All four walls have numerous square openings that were cut out of the sheets of metal, but the roof cannot be described because it is missing. When the courthouse was expanded in 1978, the cage was removed. In 1990, the Leakey Museum Board obtained it and moved it to the local museum, where it was placed on a concrete slab. The history of the town and cage was provided by personal interviews with Scott Kolb and Marjorie Kellner of Leakey.[17]

Lexington

Lee County

LOCATION: Lexington Log Cabins and Heritage Center, 524 Fourth Street in Lexington

OWNER: City of Lexington

DATE BUILT: 1875

SIZE: 88 square feet

The cage illustrated here was originally located in the first official lockup in the county seat of Giddings. It was in a two-story brick building constructed in 1875 at a cost of $5,500 and located on city block 146.[18]

Lexington cage (photo courtesy of Rhonda K. Holley).

The following information was taken from interviews with residents[19] and *A History of Lee County, Texas.*[20] When the town built its next jail in 1915, this metal cage was moved to Lexington, where it was placed inside a wooden structure on the east side of Belton Street between Second and Third Streets. Today, this area is a vacant lot. The building that housed the cage was covered in tin and boasted a concrete floor. It faced west and only had two windows: one on the north side and one on the south side. The size of the building is not known, but locals remember that it was just a "little" larger than the cage, and there was just enough extra space to have a narrow walkway all around the cage with a little extra width at the entrance. It was torn down sometime during the early 1960s. The cage on exhibit today is missing two walls and the ceiling. The construction is impressive and resulted in a very strong structure. The sides consist of four steel plates riveted to other parts of the building, and the plates are tied together with steel bars. The windows are made of strap iron, and the bars were cold riveted to a frame in a crosshatch pattern that allowed light and ventilation for the prisoners. The front consists of three metal plates with one serving as the door. According to different accounts, the missing roof and walls were hauled off by ranchers who used them in constructing cattle chutes and bridges over wet areas. Adolf Herter salvaged the pieces of the old jail that are on display, and Terrell Hester, Alph Perry, and Dennis Boetcher placed them at the site. The notorious outlaw William "Bill" Preston Longley was arrested in 1877 for murder and placed in this cell in Giddings while awaiting trial. On October 11, 1878, he was executed; his grave and a state historical marker are in the Giddings City Cemetery. The following is written on the front of the cell: "A portion of the cell was built for custodial security of Bill Longley while awaiting trial in Giddings. Born October 6, 1851; Died October 11, 1878."[21] Ruby Vance researched this structure and authored a short monograph that describes it in detail, and her work has been added to the site files at the Texas Archeological Research Laboratory in Austin, Texas. This cage was moved to the Lexington Log Cabins and Heritage Center circa 1979.

Lockhart

Caldwell County

LOCATION: Private Property

OWNER: Privately Owned

DATE BUILT: Unknown

SIZE: 33 square feet

This one-of-a-kind metal cage was discovered when the owners observed an unusual large piece of metal lying on the surface; it was obscured with roots and other forms of vegetation. It was extremely heavy, but they were able to stand it up and examine it. They had found two panels made of very old strap iron, virtually identical to those associated with metal cages. The pattern was flat bars of iron arranged in a crisscross pattern and held together by rivets. Later, metal plate was seen sticking above the ground. Only a few inches were visible; they started digging to see what it was. The owners were surprised when the bottom had not been reached after several feet of digging. This second find was the rest of a metal cell that had been used to house offenders below ground level.[22] Finding a jail buried like this is most unusual, and it is the only one in the current sample. Several theories were advanced as to why it was there and who had used it. The amount of labor involved to move this very heavy object and bury it deep in the ground presents a strong argument against it having been moved to

Lockhart cage (photo courtesy of Rhonda K. Holley).

that location from another part of town, where it may have been housed inside a building.

Lockhart is in a part of Texas where hostilities between the settlers and Comanche were a frequent occurrence. The presence of military artifacts such as a US Army collar insignia and several bullet casings suggests that there could have been a small detachment of soldiers there at one time. Perhaps the cage was fabricated and used by the military for captive Indians or disobedient soldiers. Another possibility is that it was part of a local plantation and used to punish slaves. Mary Douglas is a local historian who learned that there had been a plantation in the general area. The presence of an underground lockup on a plantation is supported by a former slave named Gus Johnson, who was part of a plantation near Houston: "De jail builded undergroun' like de storm cave and it have a drop door with de weight on it, so dey couldn't git up from de bottom. It sho' was dark in dat place."[23] The time during which this cage was used is not known, but similar specimens were constructed during the latter part of the nineteenth century and through the early part of the twentieth.

Montgomery

Montgomery County

LOCATION: Corner of State Highway 149 (Liberty Street) and Clepper Street in front of the Community Building in Montgomery

OWNER: City of Montgomery

DATE BUILT: Nineteenth century

SIZE: 60 square feet

The city of Montgomery is to be commended for its preservation of this historic metal cage, which now rests on a concrete slab beneath a wooden roof for protection from the elements. The Pauly Jail Building Company of Saint Louis, Missouri, was the manufacturer; their identification plate is affixed to the front of the cage. This symmetrical structure consists of two cells of equal size. The walls were constructed of flat pieces of metal attached by rivets in a crisscross pattern (a.k.a. lattice construction), which created open spaces for ventilation and natural light. The ceiling is a solid

Montgomery cage (photo courtesy of Ericka Morgan).

metal plate. There is no metal floor, and this means that it was probably ordered from the company without one or it is no longer present. The cells are partitioned by a solid metal wall on which two bunk bed frames are attached on each side. The beds are hinged, allowing them to be raised upright for more room in the cell when not in use. The doors were secured with a hasp and lock. Behind each of these areas is a solid sheet of metal that may have been added as a means of preventing prisoners from attempting to escape by cutting the lock. These doors are virtually identical to those on the cage in Valley Mills, which was also made by the Pauly Company. Sonya Clover and Billy Ray Duncan, citizens of Montgomery, provided the following information:[24] This cage was originally housed in a wooden one-room structure that has been described as made by local labor and very primitive. It is believed to have been the second jail in the county. The exact date of construction is not known but it was prior to 1889 when it was moved from Conroe to Montgomery next to the railroad depot where it was the only jail in town. There were no Sanborn maps at the agencies visited for Montgomery, Texas.

Palo Pinto

Palo Pinto County

LOCATION: Old Jail Museum Complex in Palo Pinto at Fifth and Elm in Palo Pinto

OWNER: City of Palo Pinto

DATE BUILT: Unknown

SIZE: 100 square feet

The historical information below was provided by Sherry Whitaker and Richard Buciner, docents at the Old Jail Museum in Palo Pinto, and Cindy Lewis of the Palo Pinto Historical Society.[25] This cage was brought to the museum from Albany in Shackelford County, where it was housed in a small structure. It was used as a lockup from 1880 to 1941. The single exterior door opens into a small room where prisoners were allowed to wait until they were locked up or released. The rest of the cage consists of one large cell that was opened and closed by a massive locking system operated from the outside. This is one of the few remaining locking

Palo Pinto cage (photo courtesy of Rolland C. Reynolds Jr.).

Portable cage in Palo Pinto (photo courtesy of Rolland C. Reynolds Jr.).

systems in extant cages that is still operational. In the cage is a metal bench that may have served for sleeping as well as sitting. At this time, I am not aware of other jail furniture and there are no brackets on the walls to suggest attached bunks. The only other floor plan similar to this one that I am aware of is in the county jail in Claremont, the former county seat of Kent County. There is a smaller cage on display also. It measures 32 inches across the front, 33 inches across the back, 47 inches on the sides, and 76 inches tall. Supposedly it was placed on a wagon and used to transport prisoners to the state prison in Huntsville. There is a small metal plate welded to the back that was used as a seat during transport. Its origin is not certain but one story is that it was constructed from iron that came from the old jail and assembled to represent the cage that was actually used.

Richland

Navarro County

COUNTY: Navarro

LOCATION: Pioneer Village Museum in Corsicana

OWNER: Navarro County Historical Society

DATE BUILT: Unknown

SIZE: 79 square feet

This cage was originally housed in the old Richland City Jail. Les Cotten is a former sheriff of Navarro County, and he believes that the structure that enclosed it was brick and that the overall size of the old jail was less than 200 square feet.[26] This cage has two cells of equal size and was designed to sleep eight with two folding metal bunks on each wall. The panels that compose the cage were made from flat strips of metal arranged in a criss-cross pattern held together with rivets. No windows were necessary because of the perforated walls, which provided excellent light and ventilation. However, these benefits may have been compromised by its placement in a building with few windows. The roof and floor are solid sheets of metal. In contrast to other similar cages, the two doors are 2 feet wide and 6 feet 4 inches tall. Behind the lock of each door is a solid sheet of metal that was probably added as an extra measure of security. Even though the

Richland cage (photo courtesy of Darryl Pearson).

Bunk beds in Richland cage (photo courtesy of Rolland C. Reynolds Jr.).

manufacturer of this cage has not been identified, it is strikingly similar to the cages in Crawford, Montgomery, and Valley Mills that were fabricated by the J. Pauly Company in Saint Louis. There are stories that it was put on a flatbed truck driven by Deputy Harmon Chandler from Eureka, who transported prisoners from holding cells to the county jail. The combination of cage and truck was referred to locally as "Harmon's Hoodlum Wagon." Bobbie Young is the curator at the Pioneer Village Museum in Corsicana and she said that this story is not true.[27]

Tyler

Smith County

LOCATION: Next to the Smith County Courthouse at 100 North Broadway Street in Tyler

OWNER: County of Smith

DATE BUILT: Unknown

SIZE: 59 square feet

Tyler cage (photo courtesy of Rolland C. Reynolds Jr.).

This small cage occupies a footprint of only 59 square feet. At about 6 1/2 feet tall, it was a very confined space, especially considering there were two cells and two bunks in each one. The metal bed platforms measure 24 by 72 inches and are attached to a solid metal wall separating the cells. This metal cage was built by the Pauly Jail Building Company in Saint Louis, Missouri. The age of its manufacture is not known, but the strap-iron construction with cold rivets suggests sometime in the latter part of the nineteenth century. The construction is similar to the Pauly cages that are in Crawford, Montgomery, and Valley Mills. The absence of a metal floor is an indication that it was probably ordered from the factory without one. Towns did this when they planned to attach the cage to an existing floor. Graffiti adorns the walls that support the beds.

Valley Mills

Bosque County

LOCATION: Private Property

OWNER: Privately Owned

DATE BUILT: Early 1900s

SIZE: 64 square feet

This is another two-cell cage that was manufactured by the Pauly Jail Building Company in Saint Louis, Missouri. The company's plaque is attached to the front of the cage. This cage was originally housed in a brick structure secured to a concrete slab that measured approximately 72 square feet. Mark Greer, the current owner, purchased the structure and cage at a public sale. The brick walls were not stable, and it had to be demolished before the cage could be removed and transported to his property.[28] Only two Sanborn maps for Valley Mills were available at the time of this study, 1909 and 1932. It is not depicted on the former, but in 1932 it was located next to a Farm Implement Warehouse on Avenue B and across from an auto repair shop and garage; it was referred to as the city jail.[29] At the time the map was copyrighted in 1933, the population of Valley Mills was 1,936. The length of service of this calaboose is not known, but it is generally believed by the owner and other residents of Valley Mills that it was used occasionally as a jail until sometime in

Valley Mills cage (photo by the author).

the 1950s. At 64 square feet, the cage dominated the interior space. The construction is like other Pauly cages in Crawford and Montgomery. It has two folding bunks on each wall and lacks amenities such as sanitary facilities or electricity. The walls and ceiling are of the lattice design, and the floor is solid metal. The two cells are of equal size and are separated by a wall of solid metal. The hooks that held the bunks when in the folding position are still present.

Epilogue

Only a handful of these early calabooses and jails remain, but those that do are a reminder of the way prisoners were treated in the not so distant past. It is my hope that this book will have educated its readers in what it was like to be locked up in a tiny Texas jail during the so-called lawless days of Texas. It is virtually impossible to describe the charm of these buildings, and those that are available for viewing are in my opinion well worth a visit.

Appendix A
General Information, Calabooses

Town	County	Material	Square Feet	Date Built	Floor Plan	Site Number
Arp	Smith	Concrete	128	1930s	2i	41SM473
Bartlett	Williamson	Concrete	361	Post-1912	3a	41WM1275
Bedias	Grimes	Wood	80	1920s	1a	41GM459
Best	Reagan	Concrete	180	1920s	1a	41RG76
Boling	Wharton	Concrete	256	Unknown	2c	41WH128
Brownfield	Terry	Wood	280	Early 1900s	1d	41TY116
Burlington	Milam	Wood	72	Circa 1910	1a	41MM389
Caldwell	Burleson	Concrete	187	1935	2b	41BU111
Cameron	Milam	Wood	200	1892	2e	41MM387
Camp Wood	Real	Concrete	162	1928	2c	41RE154
Carbon	Eastland	Concrete	79	1919–21	1a	41EA37
Castroville	Medina	Concrete Blocks	152	1920s	2a	41ME256
Chillicothe	Hardeman	Concrete	194	Post-1921	1b	41HX127
Clifton	Bosque	Concrete	363	Unknown	2d	41BQ328
Comfort	Kendall	Brick	99	Unknown	2a	41KE276
Crandall	Kaufman	Brick	69	Unknown	1a	41KF170
Crawford	McLennan	Wood	171	Unknown	2h	41ML305
D'Hanis[1]	Medina	Brick	200	Circa 1907	2a	41ME248
Deport	Lamar	Wood	100	Unknown	1a	41LR321

Town	County	Material	Square Feet	Date Built	Floor Plan	Site Number
Desdemona	Eastland	Brick	111	Unknown	1a	41EA36
East Bernard	Wharton	Brick	175	Unknown	2a	41WH129
Eden	Concho	Concrete	225	Unknown	3c	41CC354
Fayetteville	Fayette	Wood	96	1887	2a	Not Recorded
Flatonia	Fayette	Wood	236	1890	2a	41FY581
Florence	Williamson	Concrete	85	Unknown	1a	41WM1274
Fort Griffin	Shackelford	Rock	118.5	1878	1a	41SF6
Frisco[2]	Collin	Concrete	180	1912	2f	41COL250
Gause	Milam	Concrete	88	1920s	1a	41MM384
Glazier	Hemphill	Concrete	168	1912	1b	41HH34
Goldsmith	Ector	Concrete	236	1938	2a	41EC30
Goree	Knox	Brick	170	Unknown	2a	41KX114
Granger	Williamson	Concrete	432	Unknown	3b	41WM1273
Grapeland	Houston	Wood	116	1906	2e	41HO285
Grapevine	Tarrant	Concrete	80	1909	1a	41TR264
Hermleigh	Scurry	Wood	80	Circa 1913	1a	41SC65
Holland	Bell	Blocks	150	Unknown	2a	41BL1369
Holliday	Archer	Concrete	200	1925	2a	41AR10
Hubbard City	Hill	Concrete	178	Unknown	2a	41HI327
Jewett	Leon	Brick	144	Unknown	1a	41LN486
Kemp	Kaufman	Brick	131	1912	1a	41FK164
La Coste	Medina	Concrete	129	1915	2f	41ME250
La Grange	Fayette	Concrete	164	Post-1921	1a	41FY582
Lakeview	Hall	Concrete	109	Unknown	1c	41HL84
Leonard	Fannin	Concrete	117	1919	1c	41FN146
Linden	Cass	Brick	102	Unknown	1a	41CS355
Mcgregor	McLennan	Concrete	140	1922–38	2a	41ML304
Marble Falls	Burnet	Concrete	238	Unknown	2f	41BT516
Marion	Guadalupe	Tin	282	Unknown	2e	41GU189
Marquez	Leon	Wood	196	Unknown	1a	41LN495
Mason	Mason	Rock	255	1857	1a	41MS104
Miles	Runnels	Concrete	135	Post-1921	2a	41RN278
Monahans	Ward	Wood	192	1928–29	1a	41WR86
Moore	Frio	Concrete	170	Unknown	1a	41FR115

Town	County	Material	Square Feet	Date Built	Floor Plan	Site Number
Moran	Shackelford	Wood	85	Unknown	1a	41SF160
Odell	Wilbarger	Concrete	100	Post-1908	1a	41WG38
Pilot Point	Denton	Concrete	117	1920s	1b	41DN585
Plaska	Hall	Concrete	142	Unknown	1c	41HL85
Port O'Connor	Calhoun	Concrete	120	1909	1a	41CL98
Powell[3]	Navarro	Wood	83	Circa 1923	2a	Not Recorded
Presidio	Presidio	Concrete	264	Late 1920s	2a	41PS1221
Quemado	Maverick	Concrete	124	1937	2a	41MV399
Riesel[4]	McLennan	Wood	77	1910	2a	41ML306
Ringgold	Montague	Concrete and Stone	83	Unknown	1a	41MU78
Rochester	Haskell	Brick	120	Unknown	1a	41HK42
Rosebud	Falls	Concrete	177	Post-1914	2a	41FA89
Rosser	Kaufman	Concrete	76	Unknown	2a	41KF166
Rowena	Runnels	Wood	110	Circa 1910	1a	41RN279
Royse City	Rockwall	Concrete	129	1911–21	2a	41RW28
San Marcos[5]	Hays	Wood	138	1884	2a	Not Recorded
Santa Anna	Coleman	Concrete	192	Post-1921	1a	41CN305
Seadrift	Calhoun	Concrete	163	Circa 1914	1a	41CL99
Sealy	Austin	Wood	140	1887	1b	41AU100
Skidmore	Bee	Wood	147	1898	1a	41BE27
Somerville	Burleson	Concrete	163	1940s	2a	41BU110
Spofford	Kinney	Wood	73	Unknown	2h	41KY186
Stiles	Reagan	Wood	90	Circa 1903	1a	41RG38
Stockdale	Wilson	Concrete	72	Unknown	1a	41WN122
Thorndale	Milam	Concrete	140	1930	2g	41MM385
Tioga	Grayson	Brick	228	Circa 1906	1a	41GS242
Tivoli	Refugio	Wood	192	Unknown	2f	Not Recorded
Trenton	Fannin	Tin	120	1930s	1a	41FN145
Turkey	Hall	Concrete	170	1924	2f	41HL86
Wallis	Austin	Tin	170	1908	1b	41AU102
Weesatche[6]	Goliad	Wood	Unknown	Unknown	1a	Not Recorded

Town	County	Material	Square Feet	Date Built	Floor Plan	Site Number
Wellborn	Brazos	Concrete	144	Unknown	1a	41BZ177
White Deer	Carson	Concrete	216	Unknown	1a	Not Recorded
Wortham	Freestone	Concrete	180	1915	2a	41FT643

Appendix B
General Information, Jails

Town	County	Material	Square Feet	Date Built	Site Number
Beeville	Bee	Wood	448	1874	41BE31
Comanche	Comanche	Stone	775	1940s	41CJ112
Gail	Borden	Stone	768	1896	41BD36
Hearne	Robertson	Brick	483	1911-25	41RT576
Henrietta	Clay	Wood	304	Unknown	41CY20
Jayton	Kent	Stone	880	Unknown	41KT173
Marathon	Brewster	Stone	648	Nineteenth Century	41BS2689
Memphis	Hall	Concrete	350	1920–31	41HL83
Port Neches	Jefferson	Concrete	351	1917	Not Recorded
Post	Garza	Brick	418	Circa 1925	41GR936
Sabinal-1	Uvalde	Concrete Blocks	324	Unknown	41UV504
Sabinal-2	Uvalde	Tin over Wood	324	Unknown	Not Recorded
Trinity	Trinity	Brick	610	1895	41TN183
Van Horn	Culberson	Brick	397	1912	41CU840

Appendix C
General Information, Cages and Cells

Town	County	Material	Square Feet	Date Built	Floor Plan	Site Number
Athens	Henderson	Metal	76	Unknown	2a	Not Recorded
Blooming Grove	Navarro	Metal	64	Unknown	1a	Not Recorded
Crawford[1]	McLennan	Metal	171	Unknown	2a	41ML305
Crystal City	Zavala	Metal	42	Unknown	1a	Not Recorded
Dessau	Travis	Metal	68	Unknown	1a	Not Recorded
Emory	Rains	Metal	130	Unknown	2d	Not Recorded
Falls City	Karnes	Metal	49	Unknown	1a	Not Recorded
Helena	Karnes	Metal	42	Unknown	1a	Not Recorded
Hico	Hamilton	Metal	100	Unknown	1a	Not Recorded
Knox City	Knox	Metal	73	Unknown	2a	Not Recorded
Lampasas	Lampasas	Metal	177	Unknown	2d	Not Recorded

La Pryor	Zavala	Metal	107	Unknown	2a	Not Recorded
Leakey	Real	Metal	108	1918	2b	Not Recorded
Lexington	Lee	Metal	88	1875	1a	41LE329
Lockhart	Caldwell	Metal	33	Unknown	1a	Not Recorded
Montgomery	Montgomery	Metal	60	Nineteenth Century	2a	41MQ314
Palo Pinto	Palo Pinto	Metal	100	Unknown	2c	Not Recorded
Richland	Navarro	Metal	79	Unknown	2a	Not Recorded
Spofford[2]	Kinney	Metal	73	Unknown	2a	41KY186
Tyler	Smith	Metal	59	Unknown	2a	Not Recorded
Valley Mills	Bosque	Metal	64	Early 1900s	2a	Not Recorded

Appendix D
Floor Plans of Calabooses

Introduction

The sample consists of calabooses that vary in size from one room or cell to those with three cells. The largest group comprises those with only one cell, followed by calabooses with two cells. Only three calabooses have three cells. Although a photograph of each calaboose is included in this book, these images do not always clearly portray the arrangement of the interior rooms. Therefore, examples of the various floor plans are illustrated below. Not every calaboose was available for the interior to be examined. Only those with known floor plans are included in this appendix. The location and size of windows and doors vary, and a metal cage with one or more cells is present in some examples.

Calabooses with One Cell

Floor Plan 1a consists of calabooses with one door in the front of the building. It is usually in the center, but in a few cases it may be slightly offset to the right or left. The cell consists of an open room that sometimes had furniture, plumbing, and/or electricity. This floor plan does not include those with a metal cage inside. Known examples of this floor plan are in Bedias, Best, Burlington, Carbon, Crandall, Deport, Desdemona, Florence, Fort

Griffin, Gause, Grapevine, Hermleigh, Jewett, Kemp, La Grange, Linden, Lorenzo, Marquez, Monahans, Moore, Moran, Odell, Port O'Connor, Ringgold, Rochester, Rowena, Santa Anna, Seadrift, Skidmore, Stiles, Stockdale, Tioga, Trenton, Wellborn, and White Deer.

1a. Bedias floor plan

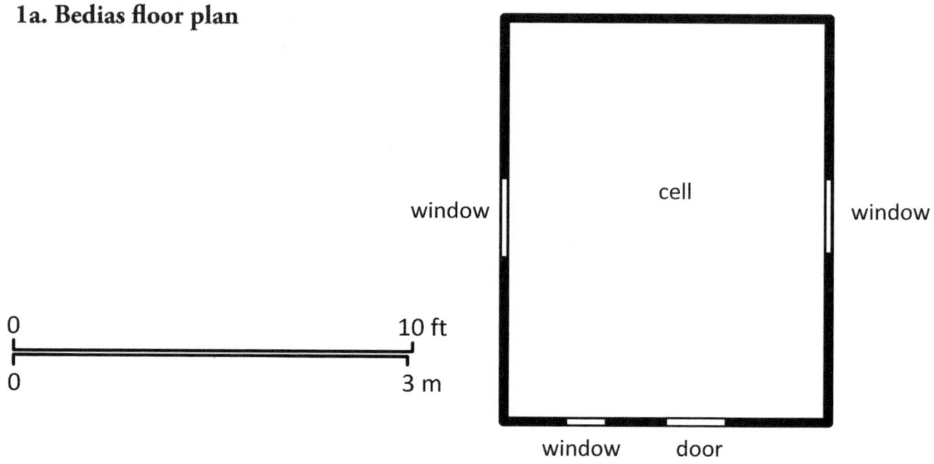

Floor Plan 1b consists of calabooses with one door to a building with two rooms. The front room or entry area was typically used by law enforcement personnel. These areas sometimes had furniture and electricity. The single cell is in the rear of the building. The entry areas may have been used as a cell when the calaboose was overcrowded. Known examples of this floor plan are in Chillicothe, Glazier, Pilot Point, Sealy, and Wallis.

Floor Plan 1c consists of calabooses with one door in the front of the building that allows entry to a small room that provided space for law enforcement officers to engage the prisoners out of the weather. The door may be to the right or left of center. The single cell is opposite the entry room. Known examples of this floor plan are in Lakeview, Leonard, and Plaska.

1b. Chillicothe floor plan

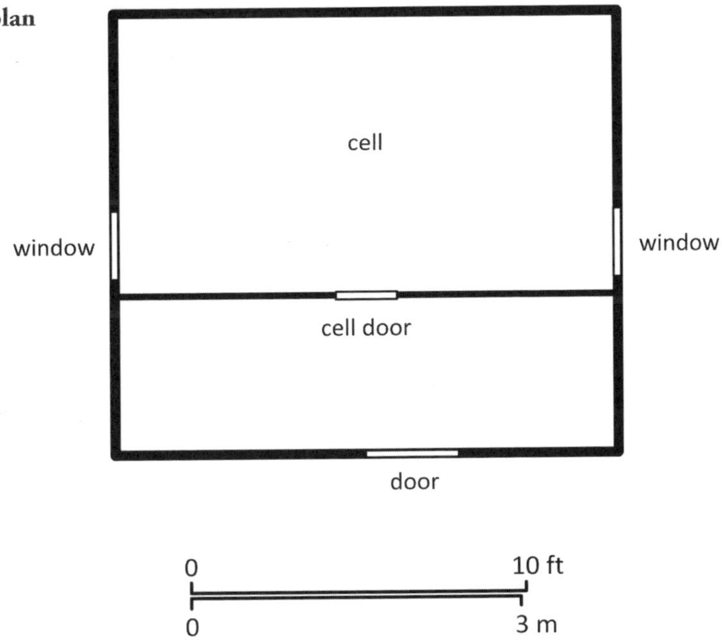

1c. Lakeview floor plan

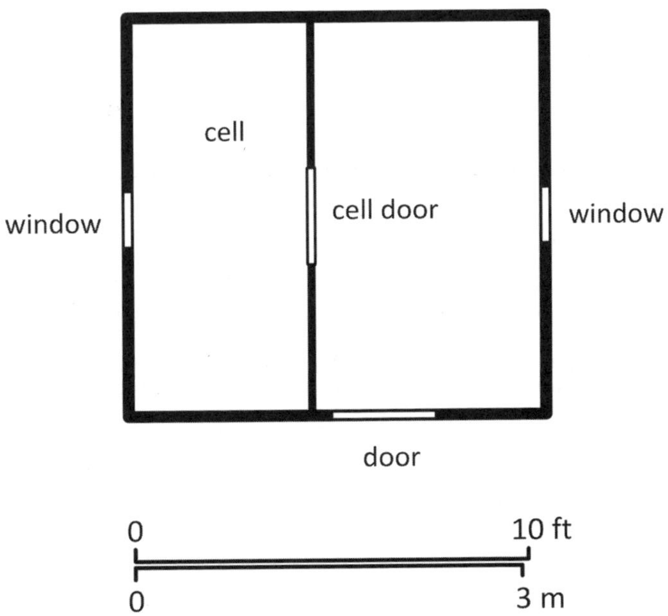

Floor Plan 1d consists of calabooses with one door that opens to a room with a free standing cage inside that was made of iron or steel. The cage may be in the corner as in this example or in the center. The door may be to the right or left of center. Although this floor plan may be identical to some of those mentioned above, it is described separately because of the presence of a metal cage. Known examples of this floor plan with a cell still in place are in Brownfield and Weimar.

1d. Weimar floor plan

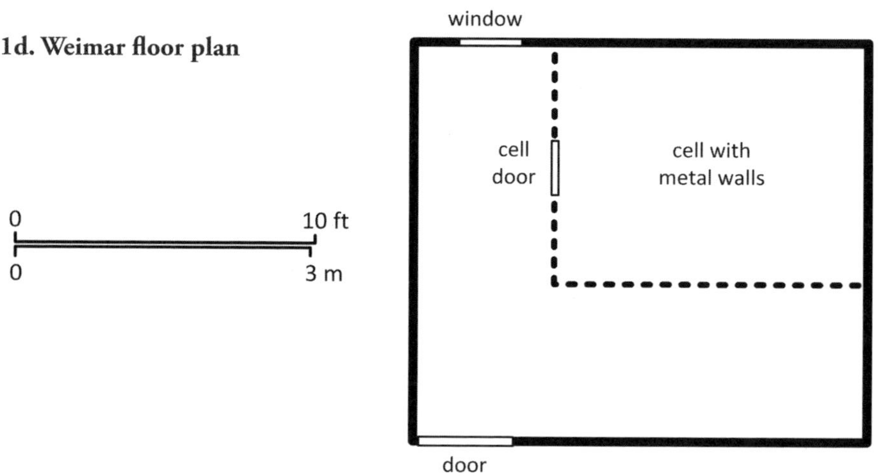

Calabooses with Two Cells

Floor Plan 2a consists of calabooses with two cells side by side. There is a separate door for each cell and they open to the outside. In most cases, the doors are centered on the cells. The calabooses in Riesel and Rosser are different in that their doors are directly adjacent to each other. Known examples of this floor plan are in Castroville, Comfort, Corsicana (formerly in Powell), D'Hanis, East Bernard, Fayetteville, Flatonia, Goldsmith, Goree, Holland, Holliday, Hubbard City, Kyle (now in San Marcos), McGregor, Miles, Presidio, Quemado, Riesel (formerly in Mart), Rosebud, Rosser, Royse City, Somerville, and Wortham.

2a. Somerville floor plan

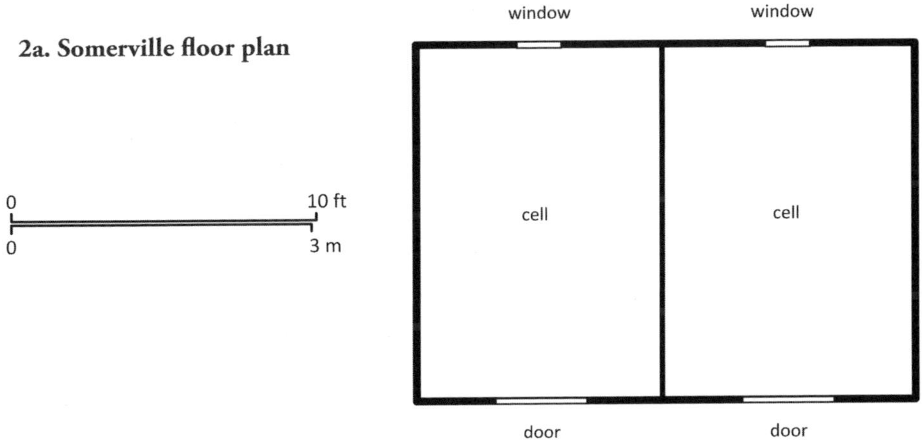

Floor Plan 2b consists of calabooses with two cells side by side. This floor plan differs from 2a because there is a middle room that was used by law enforcement officers and possibly as a cell when the regular cells were overcrowded. The only door opens to the outside and is centered on the middle room. The calaboose in Caldwell is the only known example of this floor plan.

2b. Caldwell floor plan

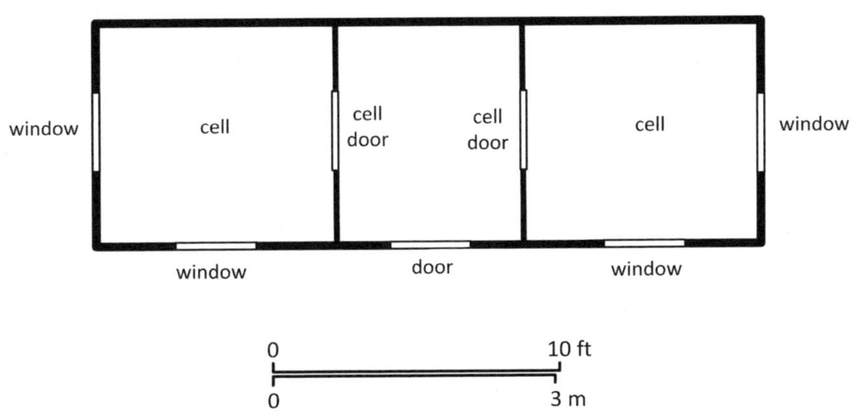

Floor Plan 2c consists of calabooses with two cells side by side. There is a room in front that was used by law enforcement and possibly as a cell when the regular cells were overcrowded. There is only one door that opens to the outside. Known examples of this floor plan are in Boling, Camp Wood, Sabinal, and Van Alstyne.

2c. Boling floor plan

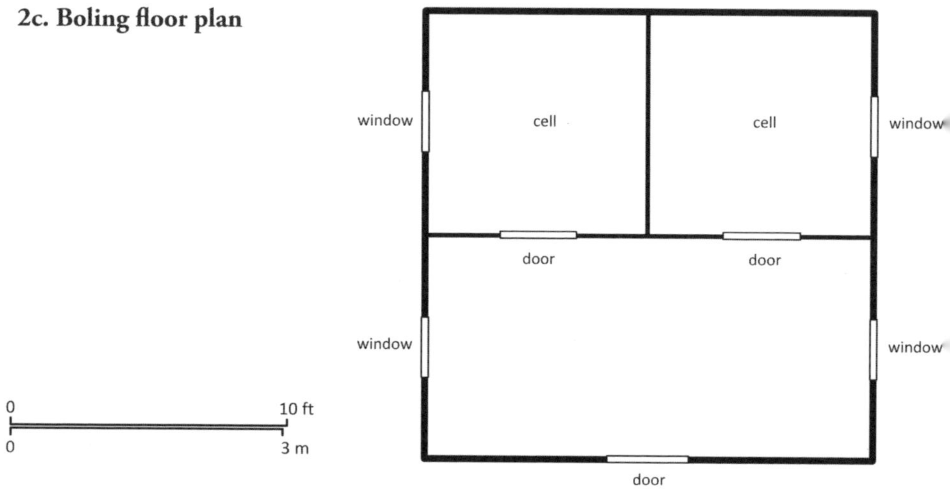

Floor Plan 2d consists of calabooses with two cells side by side and a large room to the left that was used by law enforcement and possibly as a cell when the regular cells were overcrowded. The only outside door opens to the large room to the left of the cells. The calaboose in Clifton is the only known example of this floor plan.

Floor Plan 2e consists of calabooses with two cells in a straight line divided by a wall in the center. The cells are usually equal in size and the doors are at the ends of the building. Known examples of this floor plan are in Cameron, Crapeland, and Marion.

2d. Clifton floor plan

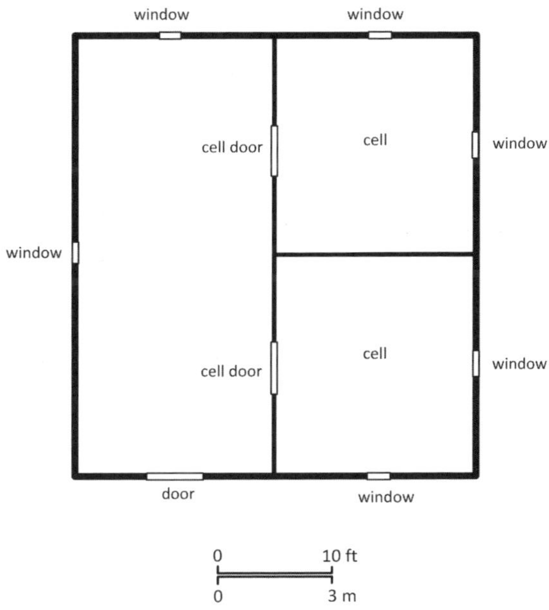

2e. Grapeland floor plan

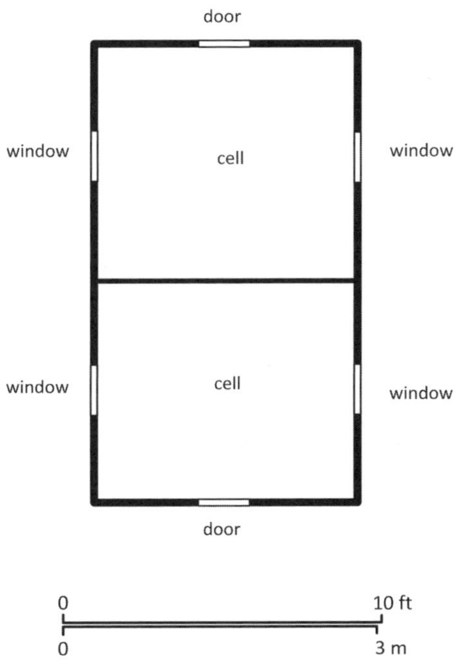

Floor Plan 2f consists of calabooses with two cells in a straight line. The only door to the outside is at the front of the building. A door in the middle of the building leads to the second cell. The middle door may be offset to the right or left. Known examples of this floor plan are in Frisco, LaCoste, Marble Falls, Tivoli, and Turkey.

2f. Turkey floor plan

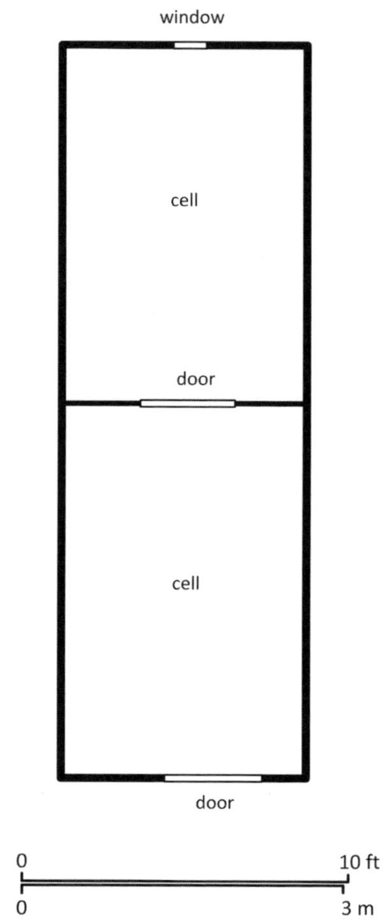

Floor Plan 2g consists of calabooses with two cells of equal size in a straight line. There is only one door to the outside, but there are two interior doors. The first connects the two cells and the second leads to a formal bathroom. The calaboose in Thorndale is the only known example of this floor plan.

2g. Thorndale floor plan

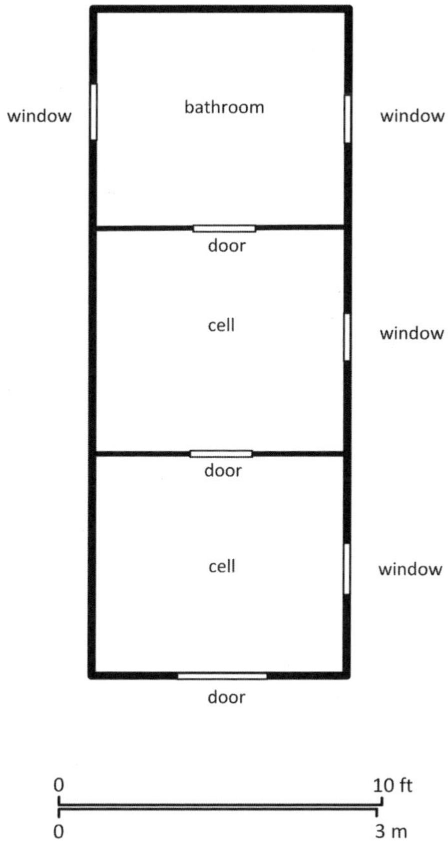

Floor Plan 2h consists of calabooses with only one door in the front of the building that opens to a room with two metal cells inside. The location of the door may vary but it is usually to the right or left of center. Although this floor plan may be identical to some of those mentioned above, it is described separately because of the presence of a metal cage. Known examples of this floor plan are in Crawford, Spofford, and Valley Mills.

2h. Crawford floor plan

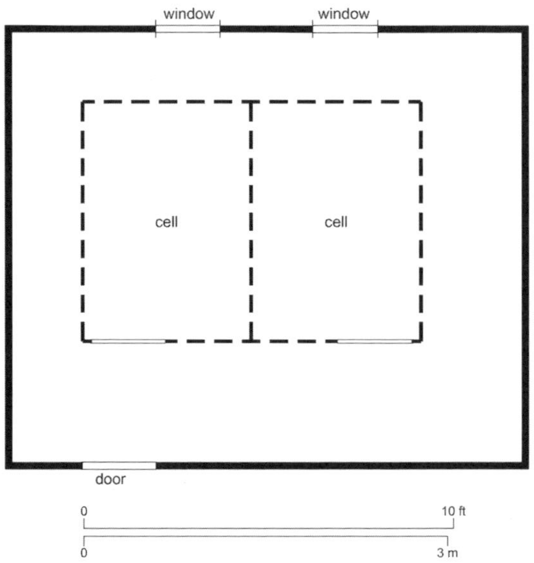

Floor Plan 2i consists of calabooses with only one door in the front of the building that opens to a small vestibule. The doors to the two cells are to the right and left of the vestibule. The calaboose in Arp is the only example of this floor plan.

2i. Arp floor plan

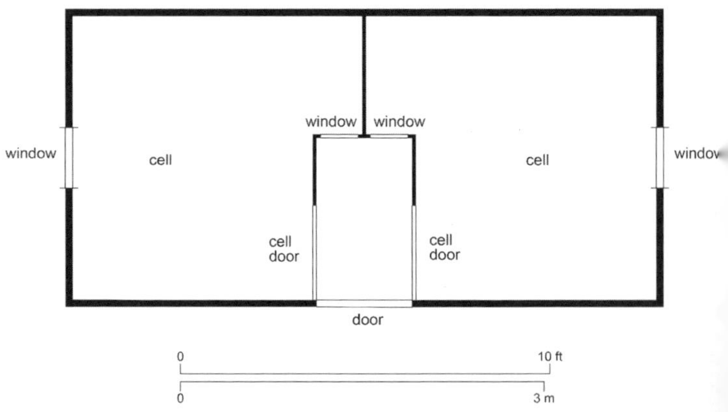

Calabooses with Three Cells

Floor Plan 3a consists of calabooses with one large cell in the front and a single door to the outside. The other two cells are on the back side by side and have separate doors. The calaboose in Bartlett is the only known example of this floor plan.

3a. Bartlett floor plan

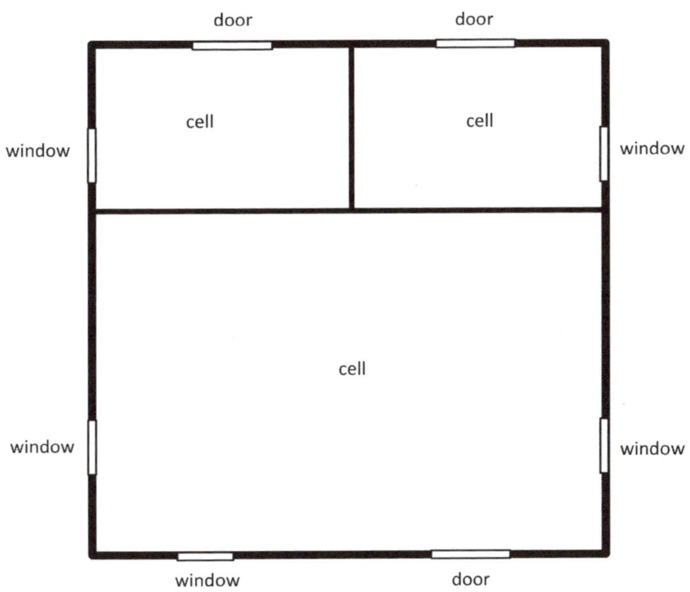

Floor Plan 3b consists of calabooses with three cells side by side with doors that open from each cell to the outside. Known examples are in Granger and Comanche. However, the structure in Comanche is considered to be a jail because of its larger size.

3b. Granger floor plan

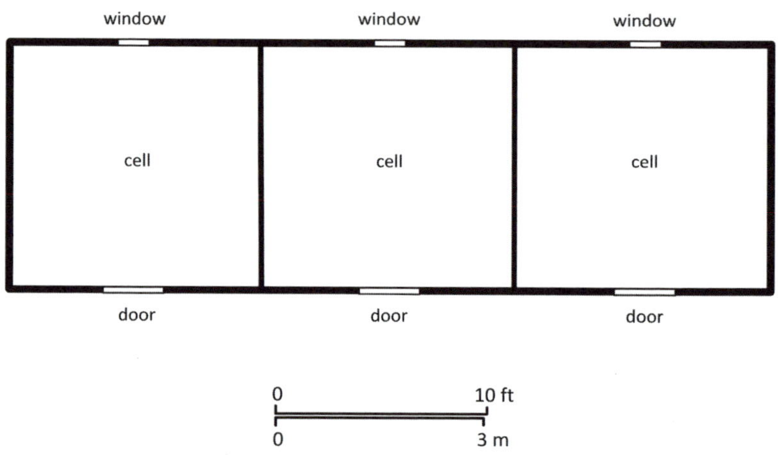

Floor Plan 3c is arranged by entry through two doors side by side into separate cells. On the right side, there is one large cell that occupies the entire footprint of approximately 7 by 15 feet. The door on the left side provides access to a smaller cell that is half the size of the larger one. Behind it is a second cell of equal size, and they are divided by a wall of poured concrete. Entry to the cell at the back is through a door on the dividing wall of the large cell. Eden is the only known example of this floor plan.

3c. Eden floor plan

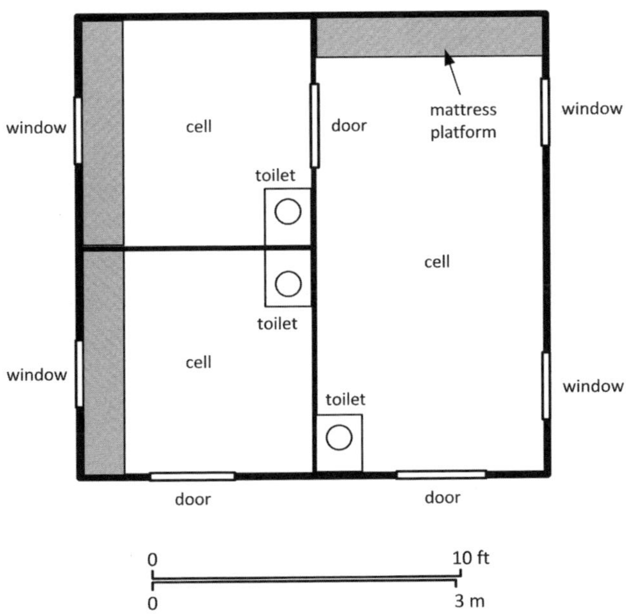

Appendix E

Floor Plans of Cages and Cells

Introduction

The sample consists of metal cages that vary in size from one to two cells. The largest group comprises those with two cells. These cells do not have windows. Light and ventilation was achieved through the walls and doors with bars. Most were fabricated by companies that specialized in jail and prison hardware, and some have plaques that provide the name of the builder.

Cages with One Cell

Floor Plan 1a consists of cages with only one cell and a single door in the front. Sleeping accommodations would have been a freestanding bed or one or more metal bunks attached to one of the walls. Known examples are in Blooming Grove, Crystal City, Dessau, Falls City, Helena, Hico, and Lexington. The cage in Lockhart is placed in this group because it has one door and one open room. However, the cage was buried and the door opened from the top.

1a. Blooming Grove floor plan

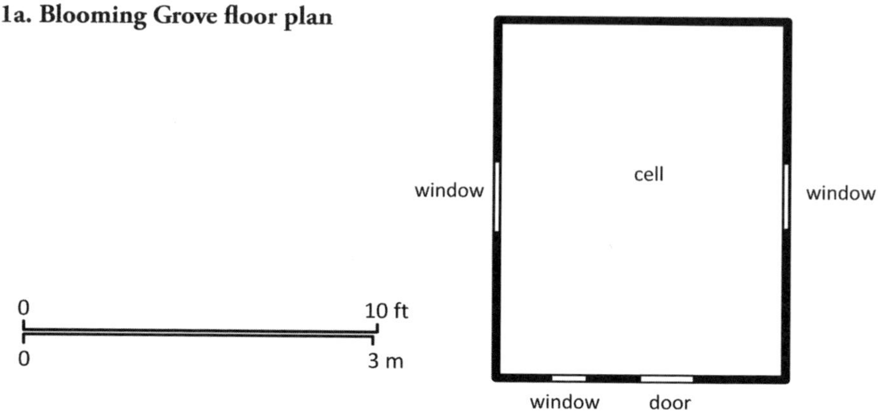

Cages with Two Cells

Floor Plan 2a onsists of cages with two cells of equal size arranged side by side. Some doors are offset to the left and some are centered on the cells. Known examples are in Athens, Corsicana, Crawford, Knox City, La Pryor, Montgomery, Spofford, Tyler, and Valley Mills. The cage in Crawford conforms to this floor plan, but it is discussed in chapter 5 because it is in the original structure. The cage in Spofford conforms to this floor plan, but it is discussed in chapter 5 because it is in a partially intact structure in its original location.

2a. Knox City floor plan

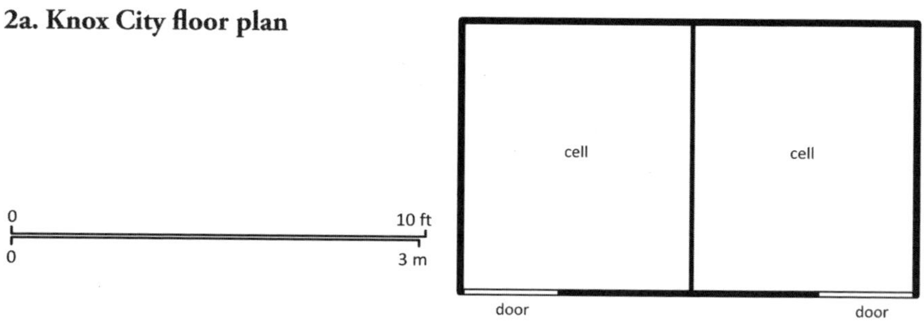

Floor Plan 2b consists of cages with two cells side by side that are unequal in size. Leakey is the only known example of this floor plan.

2b. Leakey floor plan

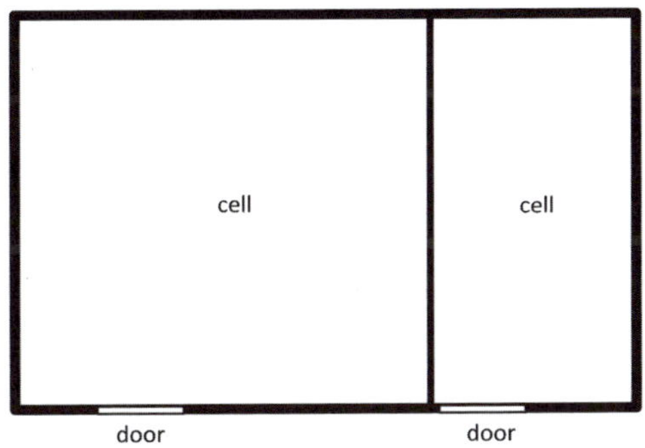

Floor Plan 2c is characterized by cages with a single door to the outside that is offset to the left. Entry through this door is into a long narrow room with a metal bench across the back. This may have been used as a holding cell. Once inside this area, there is a door to the right that opens into a large cell with a metal bench across the full length of the long side. Palo Pinto is the only known example of this floor plan.

2c. Palo Pinto floor plan

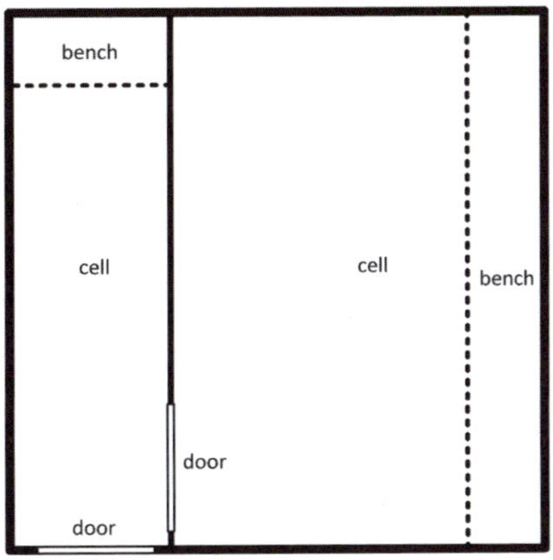

Floor Plan 2d is characterized by cages that have a single door to the outside that is offset to the right. It opens into a large empty area that could have been used as a place for inmates to be able to move around away from their cramped cells. When the outside door was closed, this room could also have served as a separate cell. Once inside, there are two cells of equal size with doors to the larger area and metal bunks across the back. Known examples are in Emory and Lampasas.

2d. Emory floor plan

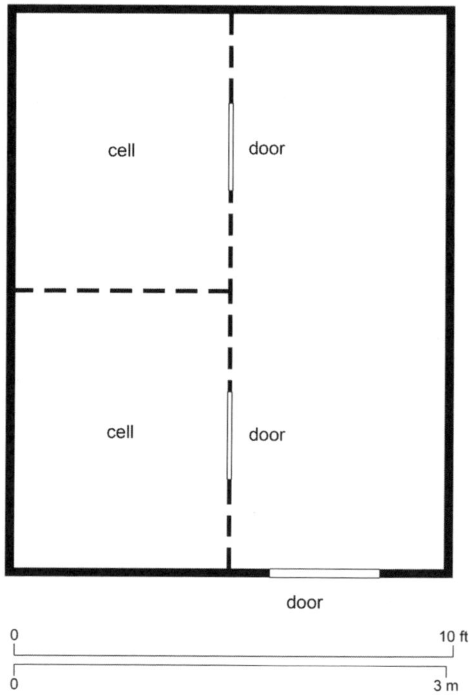

Notes

Introduction

1. *Cameron Herald*, December 24, 1914.
2. Willard B. Robinson and Todd Webb, *Texas Public Buildings of the Nineteenth Century* (Austin: University of Texas Press, 1974).
3. Edward Blackburn Jr., *Wanted: Historic County Jails of Texas* (College Station: Texas A&M University Press, 2006).
4. Thad Sitton and James H. Conrad, *Nameless Towns: Texas Sawmill Communities, 1880–1942* (Austin: University of Texas Press, 2010).
5. Blackburn, *Wanted: Historic County Jails of Texas.*
6. *Kaufman, Texas, April 1885*. Sanborn Map and Publishing Company, 117 and 119 Broadway, New York City, sheet 1.
7. *Forney, Kaufman County, Texas, Oct. 1901*. Sanborn-Perris Map Company, 11 Broadway, New York City, sheet 2.
8. *Forney, Kaufman County, Texas, March 1919*. Sanborn Map Company, 11 Broadway, New York City, sheet 2.

Chapter 1

1. Edward Blackburn Jr., *Wanted: Historic County Jails of Texas* (College Station: Texas A&M University Press, 2006), 47–48.
2. Joan Upton Hall, *Just Visitin': Old Texas Jails* (Abilene, TX: State House Press, McMurry University, 2007), 92.
3. *Muskogee Times-Democrat*, March 12, 1907.
4. *Daily Banner*, June 22, 1879.
5. Thad Sitton and James H. Conrad, *Nameless Towns: Texas Sawmill Communities, 1880–1942* (Austin: University of Texas Press, 2010), 94.
6. *Orange Daily Leader*, September 9, 1921.
7. *Hubbard City News*, September 21, 1907.
8. *Galveston Daily News*, May 12, 1876.
9. American Heritage Dictionary of the English Language, 5th ed., copyright 2016 by Houghton Mifflin Harcourt Publishing, published by Houghton Mifflin Harcourt Publishing. All rights reserved.

10. *Democrat* (McKinney, Texas), April 3, 1884.
11. *Sherman Daily Register*, January 25, 1887.
12. *Evening Telegraph*, July 14, 1870.
13. http://www.thefreedictionary.com/wight.
14. *Honey Grove Signal*, December 6, 1895.
15. Interview with Christopher S. Till of Comanche, Texas, in 2016.
16. Interview with Lyle Stubbs, mayor of Trinity, Texas, in 2013.
17. Interview with Fred Maier of Holliday, Texas, in 2013.
18. Ross Estes, *I Remember Things: An Informal History of Tioga, Texas*, comp. and ed. Robert J. Duncan (Quanah, TX: Nortex Press, 1977), 75.
19. *Daily Bulletin*, July 21, 1911.
20. *Orange Daily Tribune*, August 23, 1902.
21. *Honey Grove Signal*, February 17, 1905.
22. *Orange Daily Tribune*, May 28, 1904.
23. *Southern Mercury United with the Farmers Union Password*, October 5, 1905.
24. *Denton County News*, August 18, 1892.
25. *Brenham Daily Banner*, September 15, 1892.
26. *Caldwell News and the Burleson County Ledger*, June 6, 1935.
27. Interview with Charles Sebesta of Snook, Texas, in 2013.
28. Blackburn, *Wanted: Historic County Jails of Texas*, 84–85.
29. *Orange Daily Tribune*, July 9, 1902.
30. Interview with Evelyn Stowers of Eagle Lake, Texas, in 2013.
31. *Palestine Daily Herald*, December 4, 1903.
32. Interview with Evelyn Stowers of Eagle Lake, Texas, in 2013.
33. Interview with Cathy Touvell of Petrolia, Texas, in 2013.
34. Interview with Jayne Stuart of Grapeland, Texas, in 2013.
35. *Bartlett Tribune and News*, March 31, 1922.
36. R. K. DeArment, "The Sheriff Who Took On the Apache Kid," *Wild West: The American Frontier* 25, no. 4 (2012): 48.
37. Interview with Donald Hash of Van Alstyne, Texas, in 2013.
38. Plaque on wall of cage at the Lexington Log Cabins and Historical Society property.
39. O. Henry, "The Fourth in Salvador," *McClure's Magazine*, July 1903, 328–34.
40. Horace P. Flatt, *The Early Years of Kemp, Texas*, no date, 18.
41. John Neal Phillips, *Running with Bonnie and Clyde* (Norman: University of Oklahoma Press, 2002), 88–101.
42. Interview with Tom Mac Holmes, editor of the *Trenton Tribune*, in 2017.
43. Interview with James Hilliard of Tioga, Texas, in 2017.

Chapter 2

1. E. T. Barnum Iron and Wire Works in Detroit, Michigan, p. 48.
2. E. T. Barnum Iron and Wire Works in Detroit, Michigan, p. 49.
3. E. T. Barnum Iron and Wire Works in Detroit, Michigan, p. 50.
4. E. T. Barnum Iron and Wire Works in Detroit, Michigan, p. 49.
5. E. T. Barnum Iron and Wire Works in Detroit, Michigan, p. 51.
6. E. T. Barnum Iron and Wire Works in Detroit, Michigan, p. 49.
7. E. T. Barnum Iron and Wire Works in Detroit, Michigan, p. 52.
8. E. T. Barnum Iron and Wire Works in Detroit, Michigan, p. 50.
9. Edward Blackburn Jr., *Wanted: Historic County Jails of Texas* (College Station: Texas A&M University Press, 2006), 12–13.

10. Interview with Mark Greer of Valley Mills, Texas, in 2016.

11. Blackburn, *Wanted: Historic County Jails of Texas*, 133.

12. *Denison Press*, September 2, 1938.

13. *Hubbard City News*, September 21, 1907.

14. Interview with Dolores Herrington of Athens, Texas, in 2016.

15. Interview with Shari Watson, head docent for the Old Jail Museum in Palo Pinto, Texas, on April 12, 2017.

16. Grayson County Frontier Village, *The History of Grayson County, Texas*, vol. 2, *Family Histories* (Tulsa, OK: Heritage Publishing, 1981).

17. Federal Writers' Project, *Born in Slavery: Slave Narratives from the Federal Writers' Project, 1936 to 1938* (Washington, DC: Library of Congress, 2001). https://www.loc.gov/collections/slave-narratives-from-the-federal-writers-project-1936-to-1938/about-this-collection/.

Chapter 3

1. Edward Blackburn Jr., *Wanted: Historic County Jails of Texas* (College Station: Texas A&M University Press, 2006), 47–48.

2. Joan Upton Hall, *Just Visitin': Old Texas Jails* (Abilene, TX: State House Press, McMurry University, 2007).

3. T. Lindsay Baker, *More Ghost Towns of Texas* (Norman: University of Oklahoma Press, 2003).

4. Willa Christopher Muller, *The Roads of Texas* (College Station: Texas A&M University Press, 1989).

Chapter 4

1. Personal communication with James Malanaphy, architectural historian, at the Texas Historical Commission in Austin, Texas, on March 22, 2017.

2. Emma Watts-Plumpkin, "History of Corrugated Iron," *World Archaeology*, no. 28 (March 7, 2008), https://www.world-archaeology.com/features/history-of-corrugated-iron/.

3. Austin County Courthouse Records Book M, p. 90, on file at the county clerk's office in the Austin County Courthouse in Bellville, Texas.

Chapter 5

1. Interview with Paul Arnold of Arp, Texas, on January 17, 2015.

2. Interview with Paul Arnold of Arp, Texas, on January 17, 2015.

3. *Arp, Smith County, Texas, Oct. 1939*. Sanborn Map Company, New York City, sheet 2.

4. Interview with Paul Arnold of Arp, Texas, on January 17, 2015.

5. *Bartlett, Williamson & Bell Counties, Texas November 1921*. Sanborn Map Company, 11 Broadway, New York City, sheet 3.

6. Interview with Barbara Sandobal of Bartlett in 2014.

7. Interview with Joyce Jackson White of Bartlett in 2014.

8. Interview with Mackie Bobo-White of Bedias in 2015.

9. J. L. "Mike" Werst Jr., "The Story of Best," in *The Reagan County Story: A History of Reagan County, Texas*, ed. Gussie Edens and J. L. "Mike" Werst Jr. (Seagraves, TX: Pioneer Book Publishers, 1974), 214–15.

10. Merle R. Hudgins, "Boling, TX," Handbook of Texas Online, accessed March 3, 2017, http://www.tshaonline.org/handbook/online/articles/hlb43.

11. Interview with Jane Blay of the Terry County Heritage Museum in 2016.

12. Lelia M. Batte, comp., *History of Milam County, Texas* (San Antonio, TX: Naylor, 1956), various pages.

13. Interview with Leo Helpert of Burlington in 2013.

14. Interview with Gene Klein of Burlington in 2016.

15. Interview with Jack Brooks of Rockdale on April 6, 2017.

16. *Caldwell News and the Burleson County Ledger*, June 6, 1935.

17. Interview with Louis Hudson of College Station, Texas, in 2017.

18. Mavis P. Kelsley Sr. and Donald H. Dyal, *The Courthouses of Texas*, 2nd ed. (College Station: Texas A&M University Press, 2007), 56.

19. Joan Upton Hall, *Just Visitin': Old Texas Jails* (Abilene, TX: State House Press, McMurry University, 2007), 60.

20. Edward Blackburn Jr., *Wanted: Historic County Jails of Texas* (College Station: Texas A&M University Press, 2006), 238–40.

21. *Cameron Tex.* Sanborn Map and Publishing Company, 117 and 119 Broadway, New York City, September 1885, sheet 1.

22. Inscription on a plaque at the calaboose in Cameron.

23. Joseph A. Hill, "Prisoners and Juvenile Delinquents," in *Prisoners and Juvenile Delinquents in the United States, 1910* (Washington, DC: Department of Commerce, Bureau of the Census, Government Printing Office, 1918), 294.

24. Kelsley and Dyal, *Courthouses of Texas*, 196.

25. Real County Centennial 2013 marker.

26. Real County Centennial 2013 marker.

27. Real County Centennial 2013 marker.

28. Interview with Madge Burgess of Carbon in 2013.

29. Interview with Don May of Carbon in 2013.

30. Interview with employees at the Castroville City Hall who did not identify themselves.

31. *Chillicothe, Hardeman County, Texas, May 1921.* Sanborn Map Company, 11 Broadway, New York City, sheet 3.

32. Interview with Mary Orbeck of Clifton on March 2, 2017.

33. Interview with Jerry Hill, former constable of Clifton, on March 2, 2017.

34. Interview with Kaye Callaway, owner of the Cell Block, in 2013.

35. Carmen M. Hernandez posted a comment on my website on May 29, 2015.

36. David Minor, "Crandall, TX," Handbook of Texas Online, accessed March 3, 2017, http://www.tshaonline.org/handbook/online/articles/hlc56.

37. Vivian Elizabeth Smyrl, "Crawford, TX," Handbook of Texas Online, accessed March 3, 2017, http://www.tshaonline.org/handbook/online/articles/hlc58.

38. Interviews with Raydean Damon and Margie Thomas of Crawford in 2013.

39. Interview with Earl Booker of Crawford in 2013.

40. T. Lindsay Baker, *Building the Lone Star* (College Station: Texas A&M University Press, 1986).

41. *Hondo Anvil Herald*, August 10, 1907.

42. Interview with Dottie and Ray Wolff of D'Hanis in 2014.

43. Interview with Pat McGraw of D'Hanis in 2014.

44. Volume 5 of the "Record of Election Returns" for Medina County dated November 3, 1942, on file at Medina County Elections Office.

45. Interview with Pat McGraw of D'Hanis in 2014.

46. Interview with Thomas and Nanalee Nichols of Deport in 2013.

47. Noel Wiggins, "Desdemona, TX," Handbook of Texas Online, accessed February 21, 2017, http://www.tshaonline.org/handbook/online/articles/hld18.

48. Joe Grimshaw of Fort Worth, Texas, "Muddy Streets and Dirty Deeds: Crime and Punishment in Desdemona, a West Texas Oil Field Town," annual meeting of West Texas Historical Association, Lubbock, Texas, April 3, 2009.

49. Mary Jane Gentry, "Thurber, The Life and Death of a Texas Town" (master's thesis, University of Texas–Austin, 1946), http://catalog.lib.utexas.edu/record=b3724619.

50. Ray Spitzenberger, "East Bernard, TX," Handbook of Texas Online, accessed February 20, 2017, http://www.tshaonline.org/handbook/online/articles/hje03.

51. Interview with Linda Bubela at the Wharton County Historical Museum in 2013.

52. Interview with Liz Cubage of Fayetteville on February 16, 2017.

53. Wayne Stewart, "Fayetteville: Home of the Only Precinct Courthouse in State," *Texas Farm and Home*, July 2014, 16–19.

54. Interview with Judy Pate, director of the E. A. Arnim Museum, on February 25, 2017.

55. "Flatonia Happenings," *LaGrange Journal*, February 13, 1890.

56. "Flatonia Happenings," *La Grange Journal*, February 27, 1890.

57. "Flatonia Flashes," *La Grange Journal*, April 22, 1886.

58. *Flatonia, Fayette Co., Tex*. Sanborn-Perris Map Company, 117 and 119 Broadway, New York City, September 1891, sheet 2.

59. *Flatonia, Fayette County, Texas*. Sanborn Map Company, 11 Broadway, New York City, August 1912, sheet 5.

60. Minutes of the Flatonia City Council dated May 9, 1950, p. 91. On file at city hall in Flatonia.

61. Minutes of the Flatonia City Council dated June 13, 1950, p. 91. On file at city hall in Flatonia.

62. Clara Stearns Scarbrough, "Florence, TX," Handbook of Texas Online, accessed March 3, 2017, http://www.tshaonline.org/handbook/online/articles/hlf16.

63. *Fort Griffin*, chamber of commerce booklet by Miss Ollie Clarke, 1935.

64. "The Fort Griffin Civil Jail," unpublished manuscript researched and written by Shirley W. Caldwell of Albany, Texas, p. 1. On file at the Old Jail Art Center in Albany, Texas.

65. Shackelford County Court Minutes, August 12, 1878.

66. "Fort Griffin Civil Jail," 3.

67. "Fort Griffin Civil Jail," 2.

68. "Fort Griffin Civil Jail," 3.

69. "Fort Griffin Civil Jail," 3.

70. "Fort Griffin Civil Jail," 1.

71. Shackelford County Court Minutes, August 12, 1878.

72. Interview with Jane Lenoir of Fort Griffin State Park on April 17, 2014.

73. Frisco City Minute Book Number 1, p. 26. This is a handwritten document located on the fifth floor of the Frisco City Hall in the office of the City Secretary Records Department.

74. *Frisco, Collin County Texas*. Sanborn Map Company, May 1949, New York, sheet 1.

75. Interview with Susanne Kerley of the Frisco Heritage Center in 2014.

76. Interview with Sonny McSpedden on February 20, 2017.

77. Interview with Susanne Kerley of the Frisco Heritage Center in 2014.

78. Edrie Wilson Browder, *Gause, Texas: A Legacy in Pieces* (Privately published, 1997), 25.

79. Interview with Darlene Anglen of Gause in 2014.
80. Interview with the owner of the Gause calaboose in 2014.
81. Interview with Wallace Forrest of Canadian on March 3, 2017.
82. Minutes of the commissioners' court, vol. 3, p. 540, on file at the county clerk's office of the Hemphill County Courthouse in Canadian, Texas.
83. Marker placed at the calaboose by the city of Goldsmith.
84. Edloe A. Jenkins, "Goree, TX," Handbook of Texas Online, accessed March 3, 2017, http://www.tshaonline.org/handbook/online/articles/hlg30.
85. Barbara McCandless, "Granger, TX," Handbook of Texas Online, accessed March 3, 2017, http://www.tshaonline.org/handbook/online/articles/hjg08.
86. *Granger, Williamson County, Texas.* Sanborn Map Company, 11 Broadway, New York City, April 1910, sheet 3.
87. *Granger, Williamson County, Texas.* Sanborn Map Company, 11 Broadway, New York City, November 1921, sheet 2.
88. *Temple Daily Telegram*, March 15, 1910.
89. Calvin S. Story, "Grapeland, TX," *Handbook of Texas Online*, accessed July 30, 2017, http://www.tshaonline.org/handbook/online/articles/HJG09.
90. Interview with Jayne Stuart of Grapeland in February 2013.
91. *Crossroads to Progress: Grapeland, the Queen City of the Sand Flats* (Houston: Houston County Historical Commission, 1972).
92. Charles H. Young, "Grapevine, TX (Tarrant County)," Handbook of Texas Online, accessed March 3, 2017, http://www.tshaonline.org/handbook/online/articles/heg02.
93. Minutes of the Grapevine City Council dated 1909, p. 5. On file at the city secretary's office in Grapevine, Texas.
94. Grapevine Historical Society and Ross Bannister, "An Historical Moment in Time: The Grapevine Nightwatchman," *Northeast Newsletter*, vol. 3, p. 8. No date.
95. Interviews with area residents Gerald Corkran, Paula Hatfield, and Elyndabeth Toland in 2013.
96. Text on Texas Historical Commission marker number 1946 awarded to the former Hermleigh calaboose in 1972.
97. Interview with architectural historian Adam Alsobrook of the Texas Historical Commission in Austin in 2013.
98. Interview with Wayne Deaver of Holland in 2013.
99. Interview with deputy sheriff of West, Texas, in 2013.
100. Jeannine Goble Hodge, *History of Holliday, Texas* (Privately published 1972), 48.
101. Hodge, *History of Holliday, Texas*, 48.
102. Hodge, *History of Holliday, Texas*, 48.
103. Interview with Fred Maier of Holliday in 2014.
104. Hodge, *History of Holliday, Texas*, 51.
105. Jack Loftin, *Trails through Archer: A Centennial History, 1880–1980* (Austin, TX: Nortex Press, 1979), 232.
106. *Hubbard City, Hill County, Texas.* Sanborn Map Company, 11 Broadway, New York City, October 1904, sheet 3.
107. *Hubbard City, Hill County, Texas.* Sanborn Map Company, 11 Broadway New York City, January 1916, sheet 4.
108. *Hubbard City, Hill County, Texas.* Sanborn Map Company, 11 Broadway New York City, February 1935, sheet 2.
109. Interview with a worker at city hall in Jewett who asked to remain anonymous.
110. Dr. Horace P. Flatt, *The Early Years of Kemp, Texas.* Unpublished and undated

manuscript on file at the Kaufman County Library and Kaufman County Historical Commission, p. 18.

111. John Neal Phillips, *Running with Bonnie and Clyde* (Norman: University of Oklahoma Press, 1996), 88–101, at 93–94.

112. Ron Franscell, *Crime Buff's Guide to Outlaw Texas* (Guilford, CT: Globe Pequot Press, 2011), 95.

113. Hays County Police Court, May term 1873. Commissioners' Court Minutes, p. 162; and July 14, 1873, p. 167, on file at the county courthouse in San Marcos.

114. Interview with Kate Johnson, chair of the Hays County Historical Commission, on April 8, 2017.

115. Interview with Kate Johnson, chair of the Hays County Historical Commission, on April 10, 2017.

116. Mavis P. Kelsley Sr. and Donald H. Dyal, *The Courthouses of Texas*, 2nd ed. (College Station: Texas A&M University Press, 2007), 135.

117. Edward Blackburn Jr., *Wanted: Historic County Jails of Texas* (College Station: Texas A&M University Press, 2006), 159–60.

118. Interview with Yvonne Chandler Ludwig on November 15, 2014.

119. Plaque attached to the front of the calaboose in La Coste.

120. Interview with Yvonne Chandler Ludwig on November 15, 2014.

121. Blackburn, *Wanted: Historic County Jails of Texas*, 118.

122. Blackburn, 118.

123. Blackburn, 118.

124. Blackburn, 118.

125. Blackburn, 118.

126. *LaGrange, Tx*. Sanborn Map Company, 117 and 119 Broadway, New York City, August 1885, sheet 3.

127. *LaGrange, Tx*. Sanborn Map Company, 117 and 119 Broadway, New York City, November 1890, sheet 2.

128. *LaGrange, Tx*. Sanborn Map Company, 11 Broadway, New York, October 1921, sheet 3.

129. Interview with Catherine Poppe of LaGrange in 2014.

130. Kelsley and Dyal, *Courthouses of Texas*, 105.

131. Blackburn, *Wanted: Historic County Jails of Texas*, 117–19.

132. Interview with Terry Watson of Memphis in 2015.

133. Interview with Joe Sudderth of Leonard on February 16, 2017.

134. Minutes of the city council meeting on May 20, 1919, in the City Council Minute Book, 1917–38, on file at city hall in Leonard, Texas, p. 50.

135. Minutes of the city council meeting on June 20, 1920, in the City Council Minute Book, 1917–38, on file at city hall in Leonard, Texas, p. 66.

136. "Jail House Renovated." Unpublished article in the possession of Joe and Brian Sudderth. Some of the men who helped build it were Lacy Conway, R. M. Gober, J. M. Dunn, J. J. Lorance, Dee Davis, Fred Clifton, and A. J. Ford.

137. Interview with Joe Sudderth of Leonard on February 16, 2017.

138. Interview with Emily Henderson, executive director of the Linden Economic Development Corporation, on April 29, 2016.

139. Margaret Hanover Smith, "McGregor, TX," *Handbook of Texas Online*, accessed May 22, 2018, http://www.tshaonline.org/handbook/online/articles/hgm04.

140. Interview with Pet Fehler of McGregor in 2013.

141. Interview with Ronnie Moe of McGregor in 2013.

142. Interview with Ronnie Moe of McGregor in 2013.

143. Vivian Elizabeth Smyrl, "Marble Falls, TX," *Handbook of Texas Online*, accessed August 19, 2017, http://www.tshaonline.org/handbook/online/articles/HGM03.

144. *Velasco Times*, August 25, 1892.

145. Interview with Sarah Cummings of the Marble Falls Chamber of Commerce on August 24, 2017.

146. Vivian Elizabeth Smyrl, "Marion, TX (Guadalupe County)," Handbook of Texas Online, accessed March 2, 2017, http://www.tshaonline.org/handbook/online/articles/hlm28.

147. Mark Odintz, "Marquez, TX," Handbook of Texas Online, accessed March 2, 2017, http://www.tshaonline.org/handbook/online/articles/hlm30.

148. *Bryan Morning Eagle*, December 28, 1907.

149. Interview with Darryl Pearson on April 4, 2017.

150. Blackburn, *Wanted: Historic County Jails of Texas*, 84–85.

151. Kelsley and Dyal, *Courthouses of Texas*, 190.

152. Blackburn, *Wanted: Historic County Jails of Texas*, 225–26.

153. William R. Hunt, "Miles, TX," Handbook of Texas Online, accessed February 23, 2017, http://www.tshaonline.org/handbook/online/articles/HLM67.

154. "First Monahans Jail," an undated memorandum by Edd E. Cox. On file at the chamber of commerce in Monahans, Texas.

155. Joan Upton Hall, *Just Visitin': Old Texas Jails* (Abilene, TX: State House Press, McMurry University, 2007), 140.

156. Ruben E. Ochoa, "Moore, TX (Frio County)," Handbook of Texas Online, accessed February 25, 2017, http://www.tshaonline.org/handbook/online/articles/hlm83.

157. "Moran, TX," Handbook of Texas Online, accessed February 25, 2017, http://www.tshaonline.org/handbook/online/articles/hlm85.

158. Interview in 2013 with local resident in Moran who did not give his name.

159. Charles G. Davis, "Odell, TX," Handbook of Texas Online, accessed February 26, 2017, http://www.tshaonline.org/handbook/online/articles/hl006.

160. Lisa C. Maxwell, "Pilot Point, TX," Handbook of Texas Online, accessed February 27, 2017, http://www.tshaonline.org/handbook/online/articles/hgp04.

161. H. Allen Anderson, "Plaska, TX," Handbook of Texas Online, accessed February 27, 2017, http://www.tshaonline.org/handbook/online/articles/hnp44.

162. Interview with Jess Reed of Port O'Conner in 2016.

163. Interview with Nancy Pomykal of Port O'Conner in 2016.

164. Interview with Bobbie Young of the Pioneer Village and Museum in Corsicana on April 17, 2017.

165. Interview with Bobbie Young of the Pioneer Village and Museum in Corsicana on April 17, 2017.

166. Kelsley and Dyal, *Courthouses of Texas*, 205.

167. Interview by Brad L. Newton, executive director of the Presidio Municipal Development District of Presidio, with Edmund Nieto on February 4, 2017.

168. Ruben E. Ochoa, "Quemado, TX," Handbook of Texas Online, accessed February 27, 2017, http://www.tshaonline.org/handbook/online/articles/hlq01.

169. Mark Odintz, "Riesel, TX," Handbook of Texas Online, accessed February 27, 2017, http://www.tshaonline.org/handbook/online/articles/hlr20.

170. Dorothy Kuehl, comp., *Where in the World Is Riesel? A Centennial History of Riesel, Texas, 1881–1981* (Riesel, TX: Riesel Centennial Committee, 1981), 122.

171. Interview with Ruth Foster of Riesel on August 1, 2017.

172. David Minor, "Ringgold, TX," Handbook of Texas Online, accessed February 27, 2017, http://www.tshaonline.org/handbook/online/articles/hlr21.

173. Interview with Max Brown of Ringgold on March 28, 2017.

174. William R. Hunt, "Rochester, TX," Handbook of Texas Online, accessed February 27, 2017, http://www.tshanline.org/handbook/online/articles/hlr30.

175. Evelyn Clark Longwell, "Rosebud, TX," Handbook of Texas Online, accessed February 27, 2017, http://www.tshaonline.org/handbook/online/articles/hjr14.

176. Interview with Molly Trezsie Wilson, Rosebud City secretary, in 2013.

177. Brian Hart, "Rosser, TX," Handbook of Texas Online, accessed February 27, 2017, http://www.tshaonline.org/handbook/online/articles/hlr45.

178. A. E. Skinner, "Rowena, TX," Handbook of Texas Online, accessed February 27, 2017, http://www.tshaonline.org/handbook/online/articles/hlr47.

179. Interview with Beverly Teplicek, a member of the Runnels County Historical Commission and resident of Rowena, in 2014.

180. Brian Hart, "Royse City, TX," Handbook of Texas Online, accessed February 27, 2017, http://www.tshaonline.org/handbook/online/articles/HJR15.

181. *Royse City, Rockwall County, Texas.* Sanborn Map Company, 11 Broadway, New York City, March 1911, sheet 5.

182. *Royse City, Rockwall County, Texas.* Sanborn Map Company, 11 Broadway, New York City, June 1921, sheet 3.

183. Millie Jean Coppedge, "Reminiscing Royse City," *Royse City Herald Banner*, May 7, 2009.

184. Interview with Julia Bryant, director of the Royse City Chamber of Commerce, in 2015, Santa Anna, TX.

185. Mark Odintz, "Santa Anna, TX (Coleman County)," Handbook of Texas Online, accessed February 28, 2017, http://www.tshaonline.org/handbook/online/articles/HJS08.

186. Gladys Nevins Hunter, *Historically Speaking: Coleman County, Texas* (San Angelo, TX: Anchor Press, 1077), 56–57.

187. *Santa Anna, Coleman County.* Sanborn Map Company, New York, May 1930, sheet 2.

188. Interview with Montie Guthrie of San Angelo in 2014.

189. Interview with Mickey Dodson of San Angelo in 2014.

190. Interview with Gary Patterson of San Angelo in 2014.

191. Gladys Nevins Hunter, *Historically Speaking: Coleman County, Texas*, 56–57.

192. Interview with Ralph Terry of Coleman on July 26, 2017.

193. Rebecca Rubert, "Seadrift, TX," Handbook of Texas Online, accessed February 28, 2017, http://www.tshaonline.org/handbook/online/articles/hjs12.

194. Interview with Elmer DeForest, mayor of Seadrift, on February 7, 2017.

195. Charles Christopher Jackson, "Sealy, TX," Handbook of Texas Online, accessed February 28, 2017, http://www.tshaonline.org/handbook/online/articles/hgs06.

196. Interview with Nancy Narron, a member of the Sealy Area Historical Society, in 2016.

197. Laura Caldwell, "Skidmore, TX," Handbook of Texas Online, accessed February 28, 2017, http://www.tshaonline.org/handbook/online/articles/hls55.

198. Interview with Kay Mix, chairperson of the Skidmore Historical Society, on September 11, 2016.

199. Chapter II of the Civil Code, Article 6; Section B for Somerville, Texas. These records were recently destroyed in a flood. Therefore, the rest of this reference is not available.

200. Chapter VI of the Mayor's Court, Article 24 and Article 27. These records were recently destroyed in a flood. Therefore, the rest of this reference is not available.

201. Interview with Walker J. "Bubba" Scott of Somerville on February 7, 2017.

202. Interview with Walker J. "Bubba" Scott of Somerville on February 7, 2017.

203. Interview with Walker J. "Bubba" Scott of Somerville on February 7, 2017.

204. Interview with Lonnie Ray of Somerville in 2015.

205. Interview with Ann Guadango of Somerville on February 7, 2017.

206. Ruben E. Ochoa, "Spofford, TX," Handbook of Texas Online, accessed February 28, 2017, http://www.tshaonline.org/handbook/online/articles/HNS68.

207. Blackburn, *Wanted: Historic County Jails of Texas*, 274–75.

208. Claudia Hazlewood, "Stockdale, TX," Handbook of Texas Online, accessed February 28, 2017, http://www.tshaonline.org/handbook/online/articles/hjs27.

209. Interview with Banks Akin, Stockdale city manager, on February 7, 2017.

210. Vivian Elizabeth Smyrl, "Thorndale, TX," Handbook of Texas Online, accessed March 1, 2017, http://www.tshaonline.org/handbook/online/articles/hjt04.

211. Proceedings of the Thorndale City Council meeting dated July 14, 1930, 17–18. Minutes on file at Thorndale City Hall.

212. Proceedings of the Thorndale City Council meeting dated July 19, 1930, 18. Minutes on file at Thorndale City Hall.

213. Proceedings of the Thorndale City Council meeting dated August 11, 1930, 19. Minutes on file at Thorndale City Hall.

214. Interview with Fred Keefer Jr., former chief of police in Thorndale, in 2013.

215. Janet Mace Valenza, "Tioga, TX," Handbook of Texas Online, accessed March 1, 2017, http://www.tshaonline.org/handbook/online/articles/hlt19.

216. *Tioga, Grayson County Texas*. Sanborn Map Company, 11 Broadway, New York City, January 1914, sheet 2.

217. *Tioga, Grayson County Texas*. Sanborn Map Company, 11 Broadway, New York City, October 1922, sheet 3.

218. Interview with local historian James Hilliard of Tioga in 2013.

219. Ross Estes, *I Remember Things: An Informal History of Tioga, Texas*, comp. and ed. Robert J. Duncan (Quanah, TX: Nortex Press, 1977), 75.

220. Christopher Long, "Tivoli, TX," Handbook of Texas Online, accessed March 1, 2017, http://www.tshaonline.org/handbook/online/articles/HLT21.

221. Interview with Bart Wales, director of the Refugio County Museum, on February 8, 2017.

222. Brian Hart, "Trenton, TX," Handbook of Texas Online, accessed September 29, 2016, http://www.tshaonline.org/handbook/online/articles/hlt31.

223. Interview with Tom Mac Holmes in 2013.

224. "Gateway to Fannin County," document written by Janice Golden Smith and submitted to the Texas Historical Commission with the application for a historical marker that was dedicated on April 29, 2000. On file at the Fannin County Historical Commission.

225. John Leffler, "Turkey, TX," Handbook of Texas Online, accessed March 1, 2017, http://www.tshaonline.org/handbook/online/articles/hlt36.

226. Charles Christopher Jackson, "Wallis, TX," Handbook of Texas Online, accessed March 1, 2017, http://www.tshaonline.org/handbook/online/articles/hjw02.

227. Austin County Courthouse Records Book M, p. 90, on file at the county clerk's office in the Austin County Courthouse in Bellville, Texas.

228. Interview with Donnie Marek of Wallis in 2016.

229. Craig H. Roell, "Weesatche, TX," Handbook of Texas Online, accessed March 2, 2017, http://www.tshaonline.org/handbook/online/articles/hlw11.

230. Interview with Larry Riemenschneider of Veribest, Texas, in 2016.

231. Interview with Hal Joyce of San Angelo on April 11, 2016.

232. Christina L. Gray, "Wellborn, TX," Handbook of Texas Online, accessed March 2, 2017, http://www.tshaonline.org/handbook/online/articles/hlw17.

233. *Wortham, Texas*. Sanborn Map Company, New York, January 1926, sheet 3.

234. A. C. Black, "Old Wortham Calaboose," *Mexia Daily News*, July 27, 2002.

235. Black, "Old Wortham Calaboose."

236. Interview with Diana Echartea, former city secretary of Wortham, on June 2, 2014.

237. Interview with Kasi Wright, city secretary of Wortham, on June 2, 2014.

Chapter 6

1. Edward Blackburn Jr., *Wanted: Historic County Jails of Texas* (College Station: Texas A&M University Press, 2006), 34.

2. Blackburn, *Wanted: Historic County Jails of Texas*, 34.

3. Blackburn, *Wanted: Historic County Jails of Texas*, 34.

4. *Beeville, Bee Co. Texas*. Sanborn-Perris Map Company, New York, August 1898, sheet 1.

5. *Beeville, Bee Co. Texas*. Sanborn-Perris Map Company, New York, June 1904, sheet 2.

6. Telephone conversation with Kay Mix of Beeville in 2015.

7. Mavis P. Kelsley Sr. and Donald H. Dyal, *The Courthouses of Texas*, 2nd ed. (College Station: Texas A&M University Press, 2007), 43.

8. Interview with Christopher S. Till of Comanche in 2016.

9. Interview with Tommy Harvey in 2016.

10. Blackburn, *Wanted: Historic County Jails of Texas*, 34–41.

11. Borden County Historical Survey Committee, "Borden County Jail," *Borden Citizen*, June 1967.

12. Historical Marker number 457 awarded to the Borden County jail in Gail, Texas, in 1967.

13. Interview with city of Hearne employee, Robert Nelson, of Hearne, in 2013.

14. Interview with architectural historian Adam Alsobrook of the Texas Historical Commission in Austin in 2013.

15. Blackburn, *Wanted: Historic County Jails of Texas*, 70–71.

16. Blackburn, *Wanted: Historic County Jails of Texas*, 70–71.

17. *Henrietta, Clay County, Texas*. Sanborn-Perris Map Company, March 1885, sheet 1.

18. Blackburn, *Wanted: Historic County Jails of Texas*, 70–71.

19. *Henrietta, Clay County, Texas*. Sanborn-Perris Map Company, February 1891, sheet 1.

20. *Henrietta, Clay County, Texas*. Sanborn-Perris Map Company, July 1896, sheet 2.

21. *Henrietta, Clay County, Texas*. Sanborn-Perris Map Company, January 1902, sheet 5.

22. *Henrietta, Clay County, Texas*. Sanborn-Perris Map Company, January 1907, sheet 5.

23. *Henrietta, Clay County, Texas*. Sanborn-Perris Map Company, March 1912, sheet 10.

24. *Henrietta, Clay County, Texas*. Sanborn-Perris Map Company, March 1922, sheet 2.

25 *Henrietta, Clay County, Texas*. Sanborn-Perris Map Company, March 1934, sheet 2.

26. Charles G. Davis, "Jayton, TX," Handbook of Texas Online, accessed March 27, 2017, http://www.tshaonline.org/handbook/online/articles/hlj02.

27. Interview with county judge Jim White of Jayton in 2017.

28. Martin Donell Kohout, "Marathon, TX," Handbook of Texas Online, accessed September 28, 2016, http://www.tshaonline.org/handbook/online/articles/hlm26.

29. Blackburn, *Wanted: Historic County Jails of Texas*, 47–48.

30. H. Allen Anderson, "Memphis, TX," Handbook of Texas Online, accessed April 16, 2017, http://www.tshaonline.org/handbook/online/articles/HGM05.

31. Interviews with the owner and Shari Watson, former employee, at the *Hall County Herald* in 2015.

32. Jerry Winkler, "Port Neches Jail Holds Many Memories," *Port Arthur News*, November 29, 1979.

33. Winkler, "Port Neches Jail Holds Many Memories."

34. W. T. Block, "Little History Exists on Port Neches Jail House," *Beaumont Enterprise*, January 17, 2007.

35. Winkler, "Port Neches Jail Holds Many Memories."

36. Christine Rappleye, "More Like Mayberry Than Alcatraz," *Beaumont Enterprise*, April 28, 2003.

37. *Port Arthur News*, February 18, 1935.

38. *Port Arthur News*, April 22, 1935.

39. *Port Arthur News*, December 23, 1935.

40. *Port Arthur News*, June 10, 1940.

41. Interview with Chelsea Moore, a librarian at the Hebert Public Library in Port Neches, on September 29, 2016.

42. Ralph Ramos, "Old Jail Could Tell Many Tells," *Port Arthur News*, no date.

43. Interview with Chelsea Moore, a librarian at the Hebert Public Library in Port Neches, on September 29, 2016.

44. Blackburn, *Wanted: Historic County Jails of Texas*, 133.

45. Interview with city employee Walter Perez in 2016.

46. Ruben E. Ochoa, "Sabinal, TX," Handbook of Texas Online, accessed February 28, 2017, http://www.tshaonline.org/handbook/online/articles/hjs01.

47. Interview with Rose del Bosque in Sabinal on November 16, 2014.

48. Interview with Rose del Bosque in Sabinal on November 16, 2014.

49. Interview with Rose del Bosque in Sabinal on November 16, 2014.

50. Interview with Rose del Bosque in Sabinal on November 16, 2014.

51. Interview with Rose del Bosque in Sabinal on November 16, 2014.

52. Interview with Lyle Stubbs, mayor of Trinity, Texas, and owner of the jail, in 2013.

53. Historic photo in the possession of Lyle Stubbs, mayor of Trinity, Texas, viewed in 2013.

54. *Trinity, Trinity County Texas*. Sanborn Map Company, New York, May 25 1925, sheet 6.

55. Martin Donell Kohout, "Van Horn, TX," Handbook of Texas Online, accessed August 28, 2017, http://www.tshaonline.org/handbook/online/articles/hgv01.

56. Blackburn, *Wanted: Historic County Jails of Texas*, 91.

57. Interview with county judge Carlos G. Urias of Van Horn in 2016.

58. Interview with county judge Carlos G. Urias of Van Horn in 2016.

59. *Van Horn, Culberson County, Texas*. Sanborn Map Company, New York, March 1950, sheet 1.

Chapter 7

1. Interview with Dolores Herrington of Athens on August 1, 2017.

2. E. T. Barnum Iron and Wire Works, No. 650 General Catalog, Detroit, Michigan, copyrighted 1924.

3. Interview with Beth Nemeth of at the Blooming Grove City Hall in 2017.

4. Interview with Roger G. Moore, archaeologist with Moore Archeological Consulting, in Houston, Texas, on April 12, 2017.

5. Interview with the owner of the Dessau cage in 2016.

6. Interview with Jeanine Hays, secretary to the county judge, in 2015.

7. Interview with Ramona Noone of the Karnes County Museum on April 8, 2017.

8. Robert H. Thonhoff, "Helena, TX," Handbook of Texas Online, accessed April 07, 2017, http://www.tshaonline.org/handbook/online/articles/hnh18.

9. Joan Upton Hall, *Just Visitin': Old Texas Jails* (Abilene, TX: State House Press, McMurry University, 2007), 108–11.

10. Interview with Ramona Noone of Helena on April 10, 2017.

11. Interview with Ramona Noone of Helena on April 10, 2017.

12. Hall, *Just Visitin': Old Texas Jails*, 117–19.

13. E. T. Barnum Iron and Wire Works, No. 650 General Catalog, Detroit, Michigan, copyrighted 1924.

14. Interview with Jane Klein of the Billy the Kid Museum in Hico in 2016.

15. *Knox County News*, December 3, 1909.

16. *Knox County News*, December 17, 1909.

17. Interviews with Scott Kolb and Marjorie Kellner of Leakey on April 17 and 18, 2017.

18. Edward Blackburn Jr., *Wanted: Historic County Jails of Texas* (College Station: Texas A&M University Press, 2006), 208–9.

19. Interviews with Nancy Perry, Beverly McMurrey, and Annette Woodward of Lexington on August 1, 2017.

20. Nance Hamilton, ed., "A History of Lee County, Texas," vol. 2. Published by the Lee County Historical Commission, Giddings, TX, 2000.

21. Writing on front of the cell, author and date unknown.

22. Interview with Mary and Monty Douglas of Lockhart in 2015.

23. Federal Writers' Project, *Born in Slavery: Slave Narratives from the Federal Writers' Project, 1936 to 1938* (Washington, DC: Library of Congress, 2001), 138, 165. https://www.loc.gov/collections/slave-narratives-from-the-federal-writers-project-1936-to-1938/about-this-collection/.

24. Interviews with Sonya Clover and Billy Ray Duncan of Montgomery in 2013.

25. Interviews with Sherry Whitaker and Richard Buckner, docents at the Old Jail Museum in Palo Pinto, and Cindy Lewis, of the Palo Pinto Historical Society, on April 9, 2017.

26. Interview with Les Cotton, former sheriff of Navarro County, on April 17, 2017.

27. Interview with Bobbie Young of the Pioneer Village Museum in Corsicana on April 17, 2017.

28. Interview with the Mark Greer of Valley Mills on August 1, 2017.

29. *Valley Mills, Bosque County, Texas Oct. 1932*. Sanborn Map Company, New York, sheet 1.

Appendix A

1. No longer standing.
2. No longer standing.
3. Now in Corsicana.
4. Originally in Mart, Texas.

5. Originally in San Marcos but once sold to city of Kyle.

6. This calaboose was photographed by a resident of the town who did not take measurements.

Appendix C

1. This cage is listed in both calabooses and cages. The measurements include the structure.

2. This cage is listed in both calabooses and cages. The measurements exclude the structure.

Bibliography

Books

Baker, T. Lindsay. *Building the Lone Star: An Illustrated Guide to Historic Sites*. College Station: Texas A&M University Press, 2000.

———. *More Ghost Towns of Texas*. Norman: University of Oklahoma Press, 2003.

Batte, Lelia M. *History of Milam County, Texas*. San Antonio: Naylor, 1956.

Blackburn, Edward Jr. *Wanted: Historic County Jails of Texas*. College Station: Texas A&M University Press, 2006.

Browder, Edrie Wilson. *Gause, Texas: A Legacy in Pieces*. Privately published by the author, 1997.

Estes, Ross. *I Remember Things: An Informal History of Tioga, Texas*. Compiled and edited by Robert J. Dmcan. Quanah, TX: Nortex Press, 1977.

Franscell, Ron. *The Crime Buff's Guide to Outlaw Texas*. Guilford, CT: Globe Pequot Press, 2011.

Grapeland Community Council. *Crossroads to Progress II: "Grapeland"—Queen City of the Sand Flats 1872–1987*. Privately published by the Houston County Historical Commission, 1969.

Grayson County Frontier Village. *The History of Grayson County, Texas*. Vol. 2: *Family Histories*. Tulsa: Heritage Publishing, 1981.

Hall, Joan Upton. *Just Visitin': Old Texas Jails*. Abilene, TX: State House Press, McMurry University, 2006.

Hamilton, Nance, ed. *A History of Lee County, Texas*. Vol. 2. Published by the Lee County Historical Commission, Giddings, TX, 2000.

Hodge, Jeanine Goble. *History of Holliday, Texas*. Privately published, 1972.

Hunter, Glady Nevins. *Historically Speaking: Coleman County, Texas*. San Angelo, TX: Anchor Press, 1977.

Kelsley, Mavis P., Sr., and Donald H. Dyal. *The Courthouses of Texas*. 2nd ed. College Station: Texas A&M University Press, 2007.

Kenney, Robert J., and Margaret Kenney. *The Reagan County Story: A History of Regan County, Texas*. Edited by J. L. Werst, Jr. Seagraves, TX: Pioneer Book Publishers, 1974.

Kuehl, Dorothy. *Where in the World Is Riesel? A Centennial History of Riesel, Texas, 1881–1981*. Compiled by Dorothy Kuehl. Published by the Riesel Centennial Committee and printed by the Jones Printing Company, 1981.

Loftin, Jack. *Trails through Archer: A Centennial History, 1880–1980*. Austin, TX: Nortex Press, 1979.

Muller Willa, Christopher. *The Roads of Texas*. College Station: Texas A&M University Press, 1989.

Phillips, John Neal. *Running with Bonnie and Clyde*. Norman: University of Oklahoma Press, 1996.

Sitton, Thad, and James H. Conrad. *Nameless Towns: Texas Sawmill Communities, 1880–1942*. Austin: University of Texas Press, 2010.

Webb, Todd, and Williard B. Robinson. *Texas Public Buildings of the Nineteenth Century*. Austin: University of Texas Press, 1974.

Thesis

Austin, Mary Jane. "Thurber: The Life and Death of a Texas Town." Master's thesis, University of Texas at Austin, 1946. (Online Computer Library Center Number: 9468855 and Library of Congress Number F394.T59.)

Journals and Magazine Articles

DeArment, R. K. "The Sheriff Who Took On the Apache Kid." *Wild West: The American Frontier* 25, no. 4 (2012): 48.

O. Henry. "The Fourth in Salvador." *McClure's Magazine*, July 1903, 328–34.

Stewart, Wayne. "Fayetteville: Home of the Only Precinct Courthouse in State." *Texas Farm and Home*, July 2014, 16–19.

Watts-Plumpkin, Emma. "History of Corrugated Iron." *World Archaeology*, no. 28 (March 7, 2008), https://www.world-archaeology.com/features/history-of-corrugated-iron/.

No Author Cited

"Flatonia Flashes." *La Grange Journal*, April 22, 1886.

"Flatonia Happenings," *LaGrange Journal*, February 13, 1890.

"Flatonia Happenings," *La Grange Journal*, February 27, 1890.

Southern Mercury United with the Farmers Union Password, October 5, 1905.

Pamphlets, Booklets, and Newsletters

Dickson, J. N. "Portable Jail for Road Gangs: Pioneer Relic." Pamphlet published by the Grayson County Frontier Village, Dennison, n.d.

"Fort Griffin." Chamber of Commerce booklet by Miss Ollie Clarke, 1935.

"An Historical Moment in Time: The Grapevine Nightwatchman." *Northeast Newsletter*, vol. 3, p. 8. Grapevine Historical Society and Ross Bannister, n.d.

Sanborn Maps

Arp, Smith County, Texas, Oct. 1939. Sanborn Map Company, New York, sheet 2.

Bartlett, Williamson & Bell Counties, Texas, November 1921. Sanborn Map Company, 11 Broadway, New York City, sheet 3.

Beeville, Bee Co. Texas, June 1904. Sanborn-Perris Map Company, New York, sheet 2.

Cameron, Tex. Sept. 1885. Sanborn Map and Publishing Company, 117 and 119 Broadway, New York City, sheet 1.

Chillicothe, Hardeman County, Texas, May 1921. Sanborn Map Company, 11 Broadway, New York City, sheet 3.

Flatonia, Fayette Co., Tex. September 1891. Sanborn-Perris Map Company, 117 and 119 Broadway, New York City, sheet 2.

Flatonia, Fayette Co., Tex. August 1912. Sanborn-Perris Map Company, 117 and 119 Broadway. New York City, sheet 5.

Forney, Kaufman County, Texas, Oct. 1901. Sanborn-Perris Map Company, New York, sheet 2.

Forney, Kaufman County, Texas, March 1919. Sanborn Map Company. New York, sheet 2.

Frisco, Collin County Texas, May 1949. Sanborn Map Company, New York, sheet 1.

Granger, Williamson County, Texas, April 1910. Sanborn Map Company, 11 Broadway, New York City, sheet 3.

Granger, Williamson County, Texas, November 1921. Sanborn Map Company, 11 Broadway, New York City, sheet 2.

Henrietta, Clay County, Texas, Mar. 1885. Sanborn-Perris Map Company, New York, sheet 1.

Henrietta, Clay County, Texas, Feb, 1891. Sanborn-Perris Map Company, New York, sheet 1.

Henrietta, Clay County, Texas, July 1896. Sanborn-Perris Map Company, New York, sheet 2.

Henrietta, Clay County, Texas, Jan. 1902. Sanborn-Perris Map Company, New York, sheet 5.

Henrietta, Clay County, Texas, Jan. 1907. Sanborn-Perris Map Company, New York, sheet 5.

Henrietta, Clay County, Texas, March 1912. Sanborn-Perris Map Company, New York, sheet 10.

Henrietta, Clay County, Texas, March 1922. Sanborn-Perris Map Company, sheet 2.

Henrietta, Clay County, Texas, March 1934. Sanborn-Perris Map Company, New York, sheet 2.

Hubbard City, Hill County, Texas, October 1904. Sanborn Map Company, 11 Broadway, New York City, sheet 3.

Hubbard City, Hill County, Texas, January 1916. Sanborn Map Company, 11 Broadway New York City, sheet 4.

Hubbard City, Hill County, Texas, Feb. 1935. Sanborn Map Company, 11 Broadway New York City, sheet 2.

Kaufman, Texas, April 1885. Sanborn Map and Publishing Company, New York, sheet 2.

LaGrange, Tx. Sanborn Map Company, 117 and 119 Broadway, New York, August 1885, sheet 3.

LaGrange, Tx. Sanborn Map Company, 117 and 119 Broadway, New York, November 1890, sheet 2.

LaGrange, Tx. Sanborn Map Company, 11 Broadway, New York City, October 1921, sheet 3.

Royse City, Rockwall County, Texas. Sanborn Map Company, 11 Broadway, New York, March 1911, sheet 5.

Royse City, Rockwall County, Texas. Sanborn Map Company, 11 Broadway, New York City, June 1921, sheet 3.

Santa Anna, Coleman County. Sanborn Map Company, New York, May 1930, sheet 2.

Tioga, Grayson County Texas. Sanborn Map Company, 11 Broadway, New York City, January 1914, sheet 2.

Tioga, Grayson County Texas. Sanborn Map Company, 11 Broadway, New York City, October 1922, sheet 3.

Trinity, Trinity County Texas. Sanborn Map Company, New York, May 25 1925, sheet 6.

Valley Mills, Bosque County, Texas Oct. 1932. Sanborn Map Company, New York, sheet 1.

Van Horn, Culberson County, Texas. Sanborn Map Company, New York, March 1950, sheet 1.

Wortham, Texas. Sanborn Map Company, New York, January 1926, sheet 3.

Local Government Documents

Austin County Courthouse Records Book M, Page 90, on file at the county clerk's office in the Austin County Courthouse in Bellville, Texas.

Chapter II of the Civil Code, Article 6; Section B. These records were recently destroyed in a flood in Somerville. Therefore, the rest of this reference is not available.

Chapter VI of the Mayor's Court, Article 24 and Article 27. These records were recently destroyed in a flood in Somerville. Therefore, the rest of this reference is not available.

Frisco City Minute Book Number 1, p. 26. This is a handwritten document located on the fifth floor of the Frisco City Hall in the office of the City Secretary Records Department.

Hays County Police Court, May term 1873. Commissioner Court Minutes, Volume Book, p. 162, and July 14, 1873, Volume, p. 167. On file at the county courthouse in San Marcos.

Minutes of the City Council meeting on May 20, 1919, in the City Council Minute Book 1917–38, p. 50. On file at City Hall in Leonard, Texas.

Minutes of the City Council meeting on June 20, 1920, in the City Council Minute Book 1917–38, p. 66. On file at City Hall in Leonard, Texas.

Minutes of the Flatonia City Council dated May 9, 1950, p. 91. On file at City Hall in Flatonia.

Minutes of the Flatonia City Council dated June 13, 1950, p. 91. On file at City Hall in Flatonia.

Minutes of the Grapevine City Council, 1909, p. 5. On file at the city secretary's office in Grapevine, Texas.

Proceedings of the Thorndale City Council Meeting dated July 14, 1930, pp. 17–18. Minutes on file at Thorndale City Hall.

Proceedings of the Thorndale City Council Meeting dated July 19, 1930, p. 18. Minutes on file at Thorndale City Hall.

Proceedings of the Thorndale City Council Meeting dated August 11, 1930, p. 19. Minutes on file at Thorndale City Hall.

"Record of Election Returns" for Medina County dated November 3, 1942, vol. 5. On file at Medina County Elections Office.

Shackelford County Court Minutes. August 12, 1878, vol. 3, p. 540, of the Minutes of the Commissioner's Court on file at the county clerk's office of the Hemphill County Courthouse in Canadian, Texas.

Unpublished Works

Caldwell, Shirley. *The Fort Griffin Civil Jail.* Unpublished manuscript on file at the Old Jail Art Center in Albany, Texas.

Cox, Edd E. "First Monahans Jail." A memorandum . On file at the chamber of commerce in Monahans, Texas, n.d.

Flatt, Dr. Horace P. *The Early Years of Kemp, Texas.* Unpublished and undated manuscript on file at the Kaufman County Library and Kaufman County Historical Commission.

Sudderth, Joe, and Brian Sudderth. "Jail House Renovated." Unpublished article in the possession of Joe and Brian Sudderth.

Websites

Handbook of Texas Online

"Boling, TX," Merle R. Hudgins, accessed March 3, 2017, http://www.tshaonline.org/handbook/online/articles/hlb43.

"Crandall, TX," David Minor, accessed March 3, 2017, http://www.tshaonline.org/handbook/online/articles/hlc56.

"Crawford, TX," Vivian Elizabeth Smyrl, accessed March 3, 2017, http://www.tshaonline.org/handbook/online/articles/hlc58.

"Desdemona, TX," Noel Wiggins, accessed February 21, 2017, http://www.tshaonline.org/handbook/online/articles/hld18.

"East Bernard, TX," Ray Spitzenberger, accessed February 20, 2017, http://www.tshaonline.org/handbook/online/articles/hje03.

"Florence, TX," Clara Stearns Scarbrough, accessed March 3, 2017, http://www.tshaonline.org/handbook/online/articles/hlf16.

"Goree, TX," Edloe A. Jenkins, accessed March 3, 2017, http://www.tshaonline.org/handbook/online/articles/hlg30.

"Granger, TX," Barbara McCandless, accessed March 3, 2017, http://www.tshaonline.org/handbook/online/articles/hjg08.

"Grapeland, TX," Calvin S. Story, accessed July 30, 2017, http://www.tshaonline.org/handbook/online/articles/HJG09.

"Helena, TX," Robert H. Thonhoff, accessed April 07, 2017, http://www.tshaonline.org/handbook/online/articles/hnh18.

"Jayton, TX," Charles G. Davis, accessed March 27, 2017, http://www.tshaonline.org/handbook/online/articles/hlj02.

"Lorenzo, TX," Edloe A. Jenkins, accessed February 22, 2017, http://www.tshaonline.org/handbook/online/articles/hj114.

"Marathon, TX," Martin Donell Kohout, accessed September 28, 2016, http://www.tshaonline.org/handbook/online/articles/hlm26.

"Marble Falls, TX," Vivian Elizabeth Smyrl, accessed August 19, 2017, http://www.tshaonline.org/handbook/online/articles/HGM03.

"Marion, TX (Guadalupe County)," Vivian Elizabeth Smyrl, accessed March 2, 2017, http://www.tshaonline.org/handbook/online/articles/hlm28.

"Marquez, TX," Mark Odintz, accessed March 2, 2017, http://www.tshaonline.org/handbook/online/articles/hlm30.

"Memphis, TX," H. Allen Anderson, accessed April 16, 2017, http://www.tshaonline.org/handbook/online/articles/HGM05.

"Miles, TX," William R. Hunt, accessed February 23, 2017, http://www.tshaonline.org/handbook/online/articles/HLM67.

"Moore, TX (Frio County)," Ruben E. Ochoa, accessed February 25, 2017, http://www.tshaonline.org/handbook/online/articles/hlm83.

"Moran, TX," accessed February 25, 2017, http://www.tshaonline.org/handbook/online/articles/hlm85.

"Odell, TX," Charles G. Davis, accessed February 26, 2017, http://www.tshaonline.org/handbook/online/articles/hl006.

"Pilot Point, TX," Lisa C. Maxwell, accessed February 27, 2017, http://www.tshaonline.org/handbook/online/articles/hgp04.

"Plaska, TX," H. Allen Anderson, accessed February 27, 2017, http://www.tshaonline.org/handbook/online/articles/hnp44.

"Quemado, TX," Ruben E. Ochoa, accessed February 27, 2017, http://www.tshaonline.org/handbook/online/articles/hlq01.

"Riesel, TX," Mark Odintz, accessed February 27, 2017, http://www.tshaonline.org/handbook/online/articles/hlr20.

"Ringgold, TX," David Minor, accessed February 27, 2017, http://www.tshaonline.org/handbook/online/articles/hlr21.

"Rochester, TX," William R. Hunt, accessed February 27, 2017, http://www.tshaonline.org/handbook/online/articles/hlr30.

"Rosebud, TX," Evelyn Clark Longwell, accessed February 27, 2017, http://www.tshaonline.org/handbook/online/articles/hjr14.

"Rosser, TX," Brian Hart, accessed February 27, 2017, http://www.tshaonline.org/handbook/online/articles/hlr45.

"Rowena, TX," A. E. Skinner, accessed February 27, 2017, http://www.tshaonline.org/handbook/online/articles/hlr47.

Brian Hart, "Royse City, TX," Brian Hart, accessed February 27, 2017, http://www.tshaonline.org/handbook/online/articles/HJR15.

"Santa Anna, TX (Coleman County)," Mark Odintz, accessed February 28, 2017, http://www.tshaonline.org/handbook/online/articles/HJS08.

"Seadrift, TX," Rebecca Rubert, accessed February 28, 2017, http://www.tshaonline.org/handbook/online/articles/hjs12.

"Sealy, TX," Charles Christopher Jackson, accessed February 28, 2017, http://www.tshaonline.org/handbook/online/articles/hgs06.

"Skidmore, TX," Laura Caldwell, accessed February 28, 2017, http://www.tshaonline.org/handbook/online/articles/hls55.

"Spofford, TX," Ruben E. Ochoa, accessed February 28, 2017, http://www.tshaonline.org/handbook/online/articles/HNS68.

"Stockdale, TX," Claudia Hazlewood, accessed February 28, 2017, http://www.tshaonline.org/handbook/online/articles/hjs27.

"Thorndale, TX," Vivian Elizabeth Smyrl, accessed March 1, 2017, http://www.tshaonline.org/handbook/online/articles/hjt04.

"Tioga, TX," Janet Mace Valenza, accessed March 1, 2017, http://www.tshaonline.org/handbook/online/articles/hlt19.

"Tivoli, TX," Christopher Long, accessed March 1, 2017, http://www.tshaonline.org/handbook/online/articles/HLT21.

"Trenton, TX," Brian Hart, accessed September 29, 2016, http://www.tshaonline.org/handbook/online/articles/hlt31.

"Turkey, TX," John Leffler, accessed March 1, 2017, http://www.tshaonline.org/handbook/online/articles/hlt36.

"Van Horn, TX," Martin Donell Kohout, accessed August 28, 2017, http://www.tshaonline.org/handbook/online/articles/hgv01.

"Wallis, TX," Charles Christopher Jackson, accessed March 1, 2017, http://www.tshaonline.org/handbook/online/articles/hjw02.

"Weesatche, TX," Craig H. Roell, accessed March 2, 2017, http://www.tshaonline.org/handbook/online/articles/hlw11.

"Wellborn, TX," Christina L. Gray, accessed March 2, 2017, http://www.tshaonline.org/handbook/online/articles/hlw17.

Other

http://www.thefreedictionary.com/wight.

Miscellaneous

Carmen M. Hernandez posted a comment on my website regarding the Comfort calaboose on May 29, 2015.

Federal Writers' Project. *Born in Slavery: Slave Narratives from the Federal Writers' Project, 1936 to 1938*. Washington, DC: Library of Congress, 200. https://www.loc.gov/collections/slave-narratives-from-the-federal-writers-project-1936-to-1938/about-this-collection/.

"Gateway to Fannin County." Document written by Janice Golden Smith and submitted to the Texas Historical Commission with the application for a historical marker that was dedicated on April 29, 2000. On file at the Fannin County Historical Commission.

Grimshaw, Joe, of Fort Worth, Texas. "Muddy Streets and Dirty Deeds: Crime and Punishment in Desdemona, a West Texas Oil Field Town." Annual meeting of West Texas Historical Association, Lubbock, Texas, April 3, 2009.

"Prisoners and Juvenile Delinquents." In *Prisoners and Juvenile Delinquents in the United States, 1910*, by Joseph A. Hill. Washington, DC: Department of Commerce, Bureau of the Census, Government Printing Office, 1918, p. 294.

Index

Page numbers in *italics* indicate photographs; those in **bold** indicate maps.

Other Books in the Tarleton State University Southwestern Studies in the Humanities Series

In the Deep Heart's Core: Reflections on Life, Letters, and Texas
Craig E. Clifford

Cannibals and Condos: Texans and Texas along the Gulf Coast
Robert L. Maril

Rough and Rowdy Ways: The Life and Hard Times of Edward Anderson
Patrick Bennett

Larry McMurtry and the Victorian Novel
Roger W. Jones

Nueva Granada: Paul Horgan and the Southwest
Robert F. Gish

Beautiful Swift Fox: Erna Fergusson and the Modern Southwest
Robert F. Gish

Texas Women Writers: A Tradition of Their Own
Sylvia A. Grider and Lou H. Rodenberger

Riding the Wind and Other Tales
James Hoggard

State of Mind: Texas Literature and Culture
Tom Pilkington

Culture in the American Southwest: The Earth, the Sky, the People
Keith L. Bryant

Donald Barthelme: The Genesis of a Cool Sound
Helen M. Barthelme

West of the American Dream: An Encounter with Texas
Paul Christensen

San Antonio on Parade: Six Historic Festivals
Judith B. Sobré

Let's Hear It: Stories by Texas Women Writers
Sylvia A. Grider and Lou H. Rodenberger

Lone Star Chapters: The Story of Texas Literary Clubs
Betty H. Wiesepape

Pastoral Vision of Cormac McCarthy
Georg Guillemin

Exploding the Western: Myths of Empire on the Postmodern Frontier
Sara L. Spurgeon

Undaunted: A Norwegian Woman in Frontier Texas
Charles H. Russell

Lost Years of William S. Burroughs: Beats in South Texas
Robert E. Johnson

Birth of a Texas Ghost Town Thurber, 1886–1933
Mary J. Gentry and Lindsay T. Baker

Alexandre Hogue: An American Visionary--Paintings and Works on Paper
Susie Kalil

Fritos® Pie: Stories, Recipes, and More
Kaleta Doolin

Faded Glory: A Century of Forgotten Texas Military Sites, Then and Now
Thomas E. Alexander and Dan K. Utley

Marfa Flights: Aerial Views of Big Bend Country
Paul V. Chaplo

Still Turning: A History of Aermotor Windmills
Christopher C. Gillis

From the Frio to Del Rio: Travel Guide to the Western Hill Country and the Lower Pecos Canyonlands
Mary S. Black